THE LONG CENTURY'S LONG SHADOW

GERMAN AND EUROPEAN STUDIES

General Editor: Jennifer L. Jenkins

The Long Century's Long Shadow

Weimar Cinema and the Romantic Modern

KENNETH S. CALHOON

UNIVERSITY OF TORONTO PRESS
Toronto Buffalo London

Toronto Buffalo London
utorontopress.com

ISBN 978-1-4875-0563-9 (cloth)
ISBN 978-1-4875-3245-1 (EPUB)
ISBN 978-1-4875-3244-4 (PDF)

German and European Studies

Library and Archives Canada Cataloguing in Publication

Title: The long century's long shadow : Weimar cinema and the romantic modern / Kenneth S. Calhoon.
Names: Calhoon, Kenneth Scott, 1956– author.
Series: German and European studies.
Description: Series statement: German and European studies | Includes bibliographical references and index.
Identifiers: Canadiana (print) 20210153318 | Canadiana (ebook) 20210153482 | ISBN 9781487526955 (hardcover) | ISBN 9781487526979 (EPUB) | ISBN 9781487526962 (PDF)
Subjects: LCSH: Motion pictures – Germany – History. | LCSH: Motion pictures, German – History – 20th century. | LCSH: Romanticism – Germany. | LCSH: Art and motion pictures – Germany. | LCSH: Motion pictures and literature – Germany.
Classification: LCC PN1993.5.G3 C35 2021 | DDC 791.430943–dc23

The German and European Studies series is funded by the DAAD with funds from the German Federal Foreign Office

Deutscher Akademischer Austauschdienst
German Academic Exchange Service

University of Toronto Press acknowledges the financial assistance to its publishing program of the Canada Council for the Arts and the Ontario Arts Council, an agency of the Government of Ontario.

Canada Council for the Arts
Conseil des Arts du Canada

Funded by the Government of Canada
Financé par le gouvernement du Canada
Canada

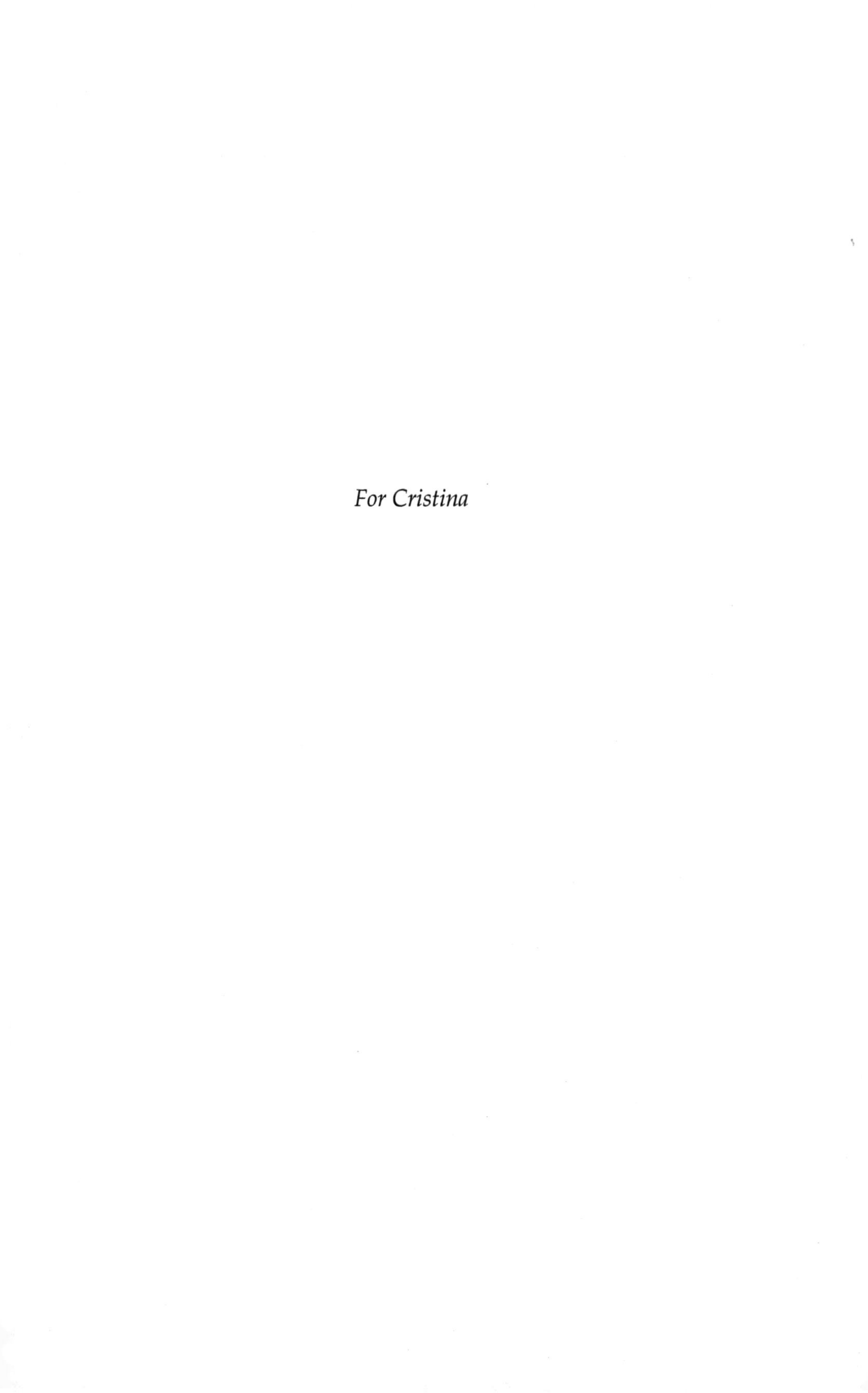

For Cristina

Contents

Illustrations

Acknowledgments

I gratefully acknowledge the following three entities, all of the University of Oregon, for providing essential and substantial material support toward the publication of this volume: the Oregon Humanities Center (Paul Peppis, Director), the College of Arts and Sciences (Harry Wonham, Divisional Dean for the Humanities), and the Department of German and Scandinavian (Ian McNeely, Head). Stephen Shapiro of the University of Toronto Press has my gratitude for shepherding the manuscript through the review and production process, as do my three anonymous readers for their generosity in both time and tone. I am indebted to Matthew Kudelka, my copy editor, whose sure touch has now graced two of my projects. I owe decades of thanks to Tony Kaes, with whom I took my first graduate seminar (Irvine, 1979), and who first excited my interest in German cinema of the Weimar period. Likewise Helmut Schneider, whose abiding friend- and mentorship dates from the same distant era. Bob Hullot-Kentor has been a constant inspiration and, in the case of this specific project, the source of a formulation that has sustained me throughout almost single-handedly. Also Thomas Schestag, for his probing and original engagement with my work, and John Lysaker, for offering encouragement when it was needed most. My erstwhile Bonn faction – Isolde Grabenmeyer, Rembert Hüser, Olaf Kriszio, and Nils Reschke – remain loyal reminders of one of the best years of my life. I have profited from the friendship of many colleagues at the University of Oregon, including Michael Allan (office neighbour and first kind face of the day), Leah Middlebrook, who shares in the struggle with unfailing aplomb, Tres Pyle, a true fellow traveller, and Sherwin Simmons, who is simply true blue. Jeffrey Librett comes in for some special appreciation for being reliably on the same wavelength. Other local colleagues whose support has been felt include Joyce Cheng, Mark Johnson, Nina Amstutz, Sonja Boos, Martin

Klebes, Sergio Rigoletto, Dawn Marlan, Corinne Bayerl, Sangita Gopal, Tze-Yin Teo, Katharina Loew, and Jenifer Presto. I have enjoyed steadfast intellectual guidance from, among others, Keya Ganguly, Martina Kolb, David Wellbery, Davide Stimilli, Rochelle Tobias, Rob Mottram, and Richard Block.

I wish to express my love for my daughter Martha and grandson Sean. All I do I do for you. Finally, I dedicate this book to my wife Cristina, with infinite and profound thanks.

THE LONG CENTURY'S LONG SHADOW

Introduction

"Thus the shadow of the object fell upon the ego." This formulation, from an influential essay of Freud's from 1917, summarizes the mechanism whereby a "mental constellation of revolt" passes over into the "crushed state of melancholia."[1] The ego, having found itself somehow spurned by an object with which it identifies, abandons the other person, withdraws into itself, and, because of that identification, becomes the object of its own grievous disappointment. The image Freud evokes – a subject beset by shadow – hints at the long tradition of portraying the melancholic as a figure whose head, its brow clouded, is propped up wearily by a single arm. The key elements of this convention have their counterparts in two German nouns, both of which approximate "melancholy," namely *Schwermut* and *Trübsinn*. The former connotes a heaviness of mood, the latter a "turbid" cast of mind or thought. These partner compounds have a Scholastic synonym in *tristitia,* the moroseness known to bedevil the woman or man who has taken holy orders. Traces of this condition are found in certain key works of German Romanticism, among them Caspar David Friedrich's painting *The Monk by the Sea* (1808/10), in which a solitary figure is shown standing at land's end, supporting his head with one hand while the storm that would darken his countenance gathers around him.[2] Though definitive of the Romantic period, Friedrich's paintings fell into neglect well before his death (in 1840) and were largely forgotten until, following a small exhibition in Berlin in 1906, they found new favour with the Expressionists. These works have a discernible afterlife in the likes of F.W. Murnau's *Nosferatu,* in which the brooding that fills the sea and sky is also personified by the vampire, who, drained of blood, is deprived of the sanguine disposition that is melancholy's opposite.[3] A study in lethargy, *Nosferatu* is a narrative extension of that metaphorical heaviness that anchors the experience of despondency in the sensation of corporeal gravity. Murnau's film even includes the warning not to utter the vampire's name "lest his shadow weigh upon you like an incubus with frightful dreams" (*dass euch nicht sein Schatten als wie ein Alp mit graussigen Träumen beschwere*).

This study investigates Weimar cinema and German Romanticism as kindred pathologies, the broad thesis being that Expressionist film (and Expressionism generally) was troubled by the same neoclassical ideal that, more than a century prior, had – in a manner consistent with a modern diagnosis of hysteria – stigmatized the surge of motion/emotion characteristic of Romantic art and literature. The aesthetic standard of placid and weightless poise was allied with the epistemological program that sought to separate the knowing subject from its force-context – a project that entailed the abstraction of sight from all bodily contingency. This was the platform from which a noted critic, writing in 1809, launched an assault on Friedrich, whose works not only furnished Weimar cinematography with a format and atmosphere but also, in their studied self-reflexivity, did what Jean-Louis Baudry (in 1975) challenged the student of the cinema to do: "examine the position of the subject facing the image."[4] Friedrich's neoclassical detractor faulted the painter's work for summoning in the viewer an excess of affect and thus betraying the true nature of the visual arts, which, by means of "forms that stand still," *touched* but did not *move*.[5] The decline of this essentially sculptural criterion coincided with the growing recognition of sight as integral to a body capable of moving (and of being moved).

This tension, central to the aesthetics that emerged toward the end of the eighteenth century, haunts the scenario from which, in the twentieth, Jacques Lacan drew his understanding of the "mirror stage," in which a strictly visual image of classical equilibrium is substituted for the internal self-experience of a subject animated by turbulence. The contortions of face and limb that characterize Expressionist screen performance resemble the symptoms of hysteria while also recalling the "spasmodic ecstasy" that Wilhelm Worringer (in 1907) attributed to both Gothic architecture and modernist art. Worringer held that the history of art was determined by the interplay of empathy and abstraction, the latter representing, in his view, a bulwark against the dynamic involvement of the subject with its surroundings. This very involvement is of a piece with the seeing body in transit, which is of consequence for the cinema and especially for the moment in the history of filmmaking when cinematography inhabited the realm dividing mobility from immobility – when motion was not yet the property of the camera but of objects before it. German cinema of the 1920s not only enjoys a unique status within this history but also isolates what is modern, even proto-cinematic, about Romantic art and literature, in terms of which Weimar filmmakers often projected their own ambitions, both technical and aesthetic.

To the extent that a rapport between these two moments has been entertained previously, the focus has generally fallen on citations – especially in the films of Murnau (*Nosferatu, Faust*) – of paintings by Friedrich, or on the obsession, in the same body of filmmaking, with doubles, mirrors, shadows, and twilight. Such formal and motivic affinities, which indicate the fascination that Romanticism engendered among modernists, and which helped lay the groundwork for modern art, offer trace evidence of a deeper genealogy linking the advent of the cinema, following Jacques Rancière, less to its own technological moment than to "the aesthetic regime of art" that arose a good century prior. This emergent aesthetic, which Rancière associates with a "defiguration of stories," entails the isolation of the "dramaturgy of the painterly gesture" against the backdrop of an art work's figural content.[6] The *mise en abyme* that became a hallmark of Weimar cinema (films within films, frames within frames, etc.) has its analogue in Romantic irony, which in turn reflects a general shift in emphasis onto enunciation, defined by Christian Metz as an act within a text that exposes the text as an act.[7]

This self-reflexivity also informs Friedrich's paintings, many of which feature a human subject, seen squarely from behind, standing before a land- or seascape much as the museumgoer stands before the canvas. The aforementioned criticism of Friedrich, specifically that one of his works consisted of moments and impressions that could not be synthesized from a single point in time or space, channelled an abiding neoclassicism, which faulted the Romantics for a *pathos* at odds with the ideal of motionless equipoise. A paragon of sculptural perfection thus hovers as the corrective to a subject whose physical movements translate emotional agitation. Even Lacan proposed "the statue in which man projects himself" as a foil for the energy erupting within the subject, while Freud hinted at the Baroque in his assessment of the often violent self-reproaches of the melancholic. In suggesting that these "complaints are really 'plaints' in the old sense of the word," he pursues a lexical modulation along the retrograde path by which an internal, psychic struggle is converted into the histrionics of lamentation.[8] As a pointedly theatrical style, the Baroque lends itself to Expressionist screen performance, in which passion is not just exteriorized but expressed through a body from which the subject appears alienated. Baroque painting, in which gestures are isolated, by light, for expressive emphasis, is a wellspring of the tenebrism that contributes to the visual and

1. *The Last Laugh* (1924), dir. F.W. Murnau.

dramatic character of Weimar film, which abounds with framings that incorporate or adapt the *pietà* and similar conventions inherited from the iconography of Early Modern art. When at the provisional close of Murnau's *The Last Laugh* (1924) a kindly nightwatchman stoops to console an aging comrade who has collapsed with fatigue and humiliation, both figures are enveloped by darkness but tightly encompassed by the "halo" cast by the nightwatchman's lamp (figure 1).

This shot, in which a natural tendency to empathize is legible as a physical inclination (leaning, bending, bowing toward), affords a visual summa of the "empathy aesthetics" that emerged in Germany during the later nineteenth century, wherein empathy was understood not merely as one subject's attunement to another's suffering but, more fundamentally, as the innate bodily awareness of every object as it struggled to maintain its integrity – to remain upright in the face of gravity.[9] Aesthetician Robert Vischer's belief that we find confirmation of our own uprightness in the vertical thrust of a tree may cast a new light on Friedrich's work, in which trees, which are often gnarled, broken, and bereft of their foliage, lean rather than stand (figure 2). Friedrich's paintings in fact play a game of hide-and-seek with the horizon,

2. Caspar David Friedrich (1774–1840), *Man and Woman Contemplating the Moon* (ca. 1818/24). Oil on canvas, 34 × 44 cm.

bpk Bildagentur/Alte Nationalgalerie, Staatliche Museen zu Berlin Photo: Jörg P. Anders /Art Resource, NY

the geometric landmark by which creatures that stand erect are assured of their stance. It is *revealed* in certain compositions, in which, for example, sea and sky are divided by a sharp line extending from one edge of the canvas to the other; in others, it *disappears* behind thickets, slopes, ravines, and gorges in which diagonals prevail.

Symmetrical with this division in Friedrich's catalogue is the dualism theorized by Worringer, who proposed *abstraction* as an artistic impulse contrary to empathy. Seen from this perspective, Friedrich's work may be thought to contain its own structural anodyne, as represented by cruciform patterns that instil in the viewer a sense of equilibrium. Similar patterns appear a century later in the mature work of Dutch artist Piet Mondrian, who explicitly banished the oblique from his compositions, insisting that only the balanced interrelation of line and plane could foster repose, which for him was the desired effect of art. Mondrian's alignment of what he called "neoplasticism" with inner quiet not only echoes Worringer's thesis but also indicates the degree to which that thesis maintains a key tension of the Age of Goethe, in which the serenity of classical form served as a countermeasure to the psycho-affective turmoil – the "storm and stress" – of Romantic emotion. Typically bent and twisted, the trees in Friedrich's paintings often gesture toward the paroxysm of human limbs characteristic of Expressionist art, as exemplified in the contorted and grimacing self-portrayals of Austrian painter Egon Schiele. The same agony determines the performance of the Expressionist screen actor, whose abrupt and broken gestures suggest the rapturous agitation that Worringer attributes at once to Gothic architecture and Expressionist painting, both of which arouse the sensation of being "convulsively swept up" (*krampfhaft emporgerissen*).[10]

The focus of this study, then, is the horizon within Weimar cinema that opens onto Romanticism. That the films of F.W. Murnau, Robert Wiene, Paul Wegener, Henrik Galeen, Fritz Lang, and many others exhibit a predilection for Romantic moods and motifs is a commonplace. In her monumental study *The Haunted Screen* (first published in France in 1952), Lotte Eisner anchored a critique of Expressionist film in this same affinity. With the trained eye of an art historian, and with frequent reference to writers and poets of what Heinrich Heine called the "art-epoch" (Goethe, Hölderlin, Novalis, Jean Paul, Hoffmann, Tieck, and Heine himself), Eisner stressed the pervasive ambiguity and foreboding fostered by spectral lighting and elusive boundaries, venturing that the technical capacities of the cinema had been "foreseen" by a literature that revelled in visual delirium and the volatility of fixed forms.[11] An "obsession with inanimate objects," likewise a Romantic idiosyncrasy, distinguished the films of Murnau, whom Eisner prized above all other German directors.[12] In his landscape she discerned an exceptional finesse, which she evokes with a simple lyricism of her own: "He films the fragile form of a white cloud scudding over the dunes, while the wind from the Baltic plays upon the scarce blades of grass. His camera lingers over a filigree of branches standing out against a spring sky at twilight."[13] A like sensibility is sounded by Werner Herzog, in whose early films Eisner noted a strong Romantic inclination. In his later *Grizzly Man* (2005), Herzog pauses over a length of leftover footage in which a stationary camera has inadvertently captured the fitful, wind-blown dance of a tall plume of grass. He remarks as to how such "seemingly empty moments [have] a strange, secret beauty," – how "images themselves develop their own life, their own mysterious stardom." *Nosferatu the Vampyre* (1979), Herzog's homage to Murnau's original *Nosferatu* of 1922, reinforces an aesthetic circuit from which, in Eisner's judgment, the "metaphysically-inclined" Germans could not break free. She recalls Tieck's observation that when dream and reality grow indistinct, only "forms born of darkness" seem genuine, adding that life "was a kind of concave mirror projecting inconsistent figures which vacillate like the images of a magic lantern."[14] The arc of Eisner's summation, reaching from Tieck to the likes of Paul Leni (*Waxworks*, 1924) and G.W. Pabst (*The Love of Jeanne Ney*, 1927), implicates cinematic Expressionism in a post-Enlightenment "reconciliation with darkness," as Jean Starobinski has characterized a new art that welcomed the "creative antagonism" of darkness and dream.[15]

Romanticism and Weimar cinema represent historically disparate moments, both of them modern, located at the opposite ends of the "long" century that extended from the French Revolution to the First World War. Both conflicts accelerated the decline of a world whose advancing decay released a flood of creativity in which exuberance and exhilaration intermingled with an often morbid attraction to the precipice at which the old order stood poised.[16] The guillotine, in fact, has the final say in Ernst Lubitsch's *Madame Dubarry* (1919). Straddling the *terreur* was a growing sensitivity, evident in literature and the arts, to the irresistible undercurrent of unconscious passions. The recognition of desire as death's accomplice would, over the course of that same long century, evolve into a formal field of inquiry that, as early as 1914, would take up the cinema as one of its objects.[17] Psychoanalysis is relevant here in part because of its incipience within older debates surrounding the integrity of artistic form. The point is not to "diagnose" Expressionist cinema but to consider Expressionism as the legacy of a centuries-old aesthetic that was already inherently diagnostic. Consider the merger of ecstasy and horror in Johann Heinrich Füssli's *The Nightmare* (1781). With its "mannerist" isolation of limbs and gestures, its heightened interplay of light and shadow, and its pointed staging of "the sleep of reason," Füssli's painting distils into a single composition the aesthetic and thematic elements that would eventually recombine in key exemplars of cinematic Expressionism.[18] The painting's riotous and instinctual sensualism posed a threat to the rational will, which, following Starobinski, neoclassical art of the late eighteenth century sought to counteract with a maximum of linear clarity and lucid wit. A "striving after abstraction" ensued, an emphasis on drawing and line, with a corresponding reduction in colour and shade.[19]

On the eve of Expressionism's advent a full century later, abstraction took its place in the vocabulary of art history as the formal guarantor of subjective self-definition, an Apollonian defence against an immense and vital nature that threatened the self with engulfment and oblivion. As an art-theoretical concept, abstraction arose in response to the growing espousal of empathy, which enabled the dissolution of the boundary dividing subject from object, as the true aesthetic faculty. Eisner herself appeals to empathy when, of Murnau, she observes that he "makes us feel the freshness of a meadow in which horses gallop around with a marvellous lightness."[20] British aesthetician Vernon Lee (Violet Paget), writing in 1912, held more fundamentally that we "attribute to lines not only balance, direction, velocity, but also thrust, resistance, strain, feeling, intention, and character."[21] The principle she describes is fully embodied in Ludwig Meidner, who, beginning that same year, produced powerful ink drawings of urban scenes in which lines do little other than convey thrust, resistance, strain, and so on.[22] This fortunate synchrony points to what is historically pivotal about Lee's formulation, which implicates, as the contrary of aesthetic response, the trend in philosophy that for centuries had sought to disable the body as an instrument of cognition, that is, to rid knowing of the corporeal self-experience from which the observer extrapolates resistance, strain, and other effects of physical force. To ascribe, as Eisner does, a "marvellous lightness" to the gamboling of horses is to violate the ban on the (essentially anthropomorphic) projection of internal sensations onto the external world.

Metaphor, as the device most suited to the imagined transference of internally felt states onto the perceived world, enjoyed an enhanced status among the Romantics, whose concern for the troubled boundary between inside and out (between dream and waking life) was defining.[23] French filmmaker and critic Eric Rohmer (who incorporated Füssli's *Nightmare* into his 1976 adaptation of Kleist's *Die Marquise von O*), praised Murnau and the Expressionists generally for a lyricism, born of metaphor, that achieved what modern poets had attempted: cinema had succeeded in "[shaking] the primitive inertia of the word."[24] Movement, which Rohmer names as "the essence of each thing," is released, paradoxically, through deceleration – a slowing "to the point of unexpected immobility."[25] A pure fascination was enabled by the Expressionist exaggeration of movement and gesture, which served to dissociate physical and facial expressions from the sentiments from which they might otherwise be thought to arise. The visual themes of *Nosferatu*, Rohmer writes, correspond to concepts that have "physiological and metaphysical equivalents *in us* (the concepts of suction and absorption, of being held or being crushed, and so forth)."[26]

The Romantics mined the expressive potential of metaphor by wresting it from the grip of rhetoric.[27] Herzog's assertion that "images themselves develop their own life" contains an echo of this release, much as an entire Romantic universe is condensed into that accidental shot of grasses suddenly buffeted by currents of air. Comparable images are found throughout the poetry and prose of Joseph von Eichendorff, who, in delivering the landscape of its materiality and language of its descriptive purpose, forged imagery composed largely of the intangible elements of space, light, and movement. The indirect effects of light, sound, and atmosphere arrive toward an immobile subject who is rarely more than a spatial counterposition to a distance known only by those same effects.[28] And to the extent that this subject is seldom the register or vessel of feeling, Eichendorff's practice accords with Rohmer's stated belief that filmmakers like Murnau regarded emotions and sentiments as obstacles to true fascination. Citing Rohmer on the "pictorial space" in Murnau's *Faust* (1926), Gilles Deleuze emphasizes the persistence of the fixed frame even after such fixity had ceased to be mechanically necessary. Once mobilized, the camera "acted out" motion already latent in the "pure movement-image" of the stationary shot. Deleuze's description of the set before the fixed camera as a depth-of-field, through which movement itself passes, and which is composed of parallel planes ("each having its independence or focus"), is compatible with Eichendorff's lyrical landscape, in which spatial intervals and zones are marked out along the axis of sight and sound.[29]

The Romantic landscape is a delimited space that envelops its subject. The images that fill it have no objective counterparts but are themselves the objects. As such, it exhibits a new mediality, in which the cinema is latent. The land- and seascapes painted by Friedrich between 1807 and 1839 are uniquely proto-cinematic. Sharp and transparent often to the point of surreality, these unique canvases anchor the fixed frame in a viewer who stands *transfixed* before a succession of distinct parallel planes, the spacing of which may appear to expand or contract, almost stereoscopically, along the centric ray of the composition. Certain of these paintings are provided with a human figure centred squarely within the frame and seen from behind – a positioning that accentuates (and renders abstract) the division of the image between a field "in front of" and another "in back of." George Lakoff and Mark Johnson have analysed how the "passage" of time is experienced as just that: movement through space projected as the continuum between *front* and *back*, by means of which the body orients itself in the world, and from which the temporal dimension of "before" and "after" is derived. These are themselves metaphors that map temporal flux onto the domain of spatial motion. Change is conceptualized in terms of relative movement in space, that is, either of objects moving toward a stationary subject, or of an observer moving from one spatial location to another.[30] This understanding of the felt correlation between time and physical movement may lend a particular status to poetical works in which a season or time of day arrives as if on foot (or wing).

A poem by Clemens Brentano (Eichendorff's exact contemporary) is an exemplary study in the relativity of motion. Written in the tradition of the folk ballad, the poem centres on a young fisherman, adrift at night on the Rhine, pining for his dead sweetheart. Suddenly she appears, hovering before him, a veritable hologram composed of celestial light reflected off the gentle waves. The youth wonders if she is cold and proffers his coat; a trembling in her knees, which merely projects the rippling of the water, makes her seem to be shivering. All of her silent movements – nodding, kneeling, reaching out and down toward the reflected starlight – mirror the motion of the tiny flatboat, itself a platform past which cities, swelling with the sound of bells, seem to float. Echoing the choir heard from within a "passing" convent, the boy mutely contemplates the vision, reciprocating the mournful sadness with which she appears to regard him. The apparition soon fades and disappears altogether as the river grows red with the rising sun. The youth is drawn farther downstream, where at one point he is touched materially by a sign from above: "A swallow streaked past overhead /And sprinkled [*netzte*] his breast." Finally, in the last two (of twenty-three) strophes, an "I" emerges, a new and discrete subjectivity imported by a different vessel, a ship arriving from distant regions. Pensive and filled with a pathos akin to that of the youth, this "I" takes stock of the latter, who *drifts* into consciousness, and who is now lying on his back as he floats out to sea. The final quatrain, which reprises the earlier intimation of divine grace, closes on a note of felt affinity: "A swallow passed overhead, / The boat swam along quietly, / The lad sang this song, / As if it were me [*Als ob ich's selber wär'*]."[31]

This newly emergent consciousness, subjunctively disjoined from the grieving youth and moving independently of him, is as a mobile shot. "It is always a great moment in the cinema," Deleuze writes, "when the camera leaves the character, and even *turns its back* on him, following its own movement at the end of which it will rediscover him."[32] These are not the same thing, to be sure. But they are sufficiently similar to prompt wonder at the medial prescience of this and other Romantic works, verbal and visual. Gazing upon the youth in his boat, the "I" that speaks at the end of Brentano's ballad does not stand "outside the mobility of duration," to borrow a phrase used by Norman Bryson with reference to the sovereign eye of the Renaissance painter. The poem is in fact punctuated by the kind of deictic markers that, as Bryson contends, monocular perspective disavows.[33] The boy is situated spatially

3. *Nosferatu – A Symphony of Terror* (1922), dir. F.W. Murnau.

with the help of adverbial prefixes that represent movement relative to the subject's location (*hinab, hinüber, heraus, einher*), and that can be extended figuratively to indicate the "passage" of time (*vorüber, vorbei*). Both eye and "I" are tethered to a body either moving or filled with a sense of its capacity to move. The boy's ghostly vision is an effect of movements that affect him; the empathy hinted at in the final line is already in force when the youth judges the maiden to be cold by the quaking of her knees, which merely projects the rocking of the boat. The "I" that emerges unexpectedly at the start of the penultimate stanza is itself mobile, conveyed by a sailing vessel roaming the seas: "I floated in by ship / From a world far away" (*Ich schwamm im Meeresschiffe / Aus fremder Welt einher*).[34]

This moment finds its complement in Murnau's *Nosferatu*, where the schooner commandeered by the vampire steers obliquely past a camera affixed to another craft, which, at an accelerated speed palpable to the viewer, glides into the field gradually vacated by the "death ship" (figure 3). The iris closes on the empty horizon only to reopen immediately on the infelicitous hero, his overland effort at odds with the fluidity of the prior shot.[35] After leading his horse down a treacherous embankment, he presses forward and out of frame before the iris contracts anew. Thus begins a long succession in which shots of strenuous and broken movement alternate with others whose character is determined by the sea, by turns agitated and calm. In one, the camera is placed beneath the foremast, pointing out over the heavily pitching bowsprit. In another, it looks directly down at the ship's roiling wash. In yet another, of necessity shot from a separate vessel, the sails and rigging of the swaying schooner fill the frame. Finally, under a breathless dawn, a camera placed upon *terra firma* records the ship as it steals silently into the port of an unsuspecting city on the Baltic coast.

In Brentano's ballad, the boat is an "apparatus" that encompasses the boy. It joins him physically to the motion of the water, fostering a correspondence between him, in his sheer vulnerability, and the frail apparition hovering before him. Repeatedly, he worries aloud about the instability of his tiny craft – that "she" might cause it to capsize – when she is but the effect of his own self-experience, which inhabits his perceptions of the external world. The "I" that suddenly concretizes at poem's end likewise moves within a space internal to the diegesis. Like the camera capable of *turning its back* on a character, it is an instance of embodied enunciation. It is contrary to the detached "eye" of linear perspective, which in its isolation beholds a strictly mental picture, an image underwritten by the geometry that, for the post-Cartesian world, was the true standard of incorporeality. If this "I," which may be read to arise from within the song sung by the grieving lad, also impersonates the consciousness of the poem overall, then Brentano's ballad puts itself forward as "a song sung from the Source of song." The phrasing is David Wellbery's, coined in regard to the specular phantasm with which an era of German poetry, beginning with Goethe's early lyric, sought to mask the loss of the self-identity from which "authentic utterances" would originate.[36] This "new species of unreality"[37] is exemplified in Brentano's poem, which stages the spectral recovery of the irrecuperable object – the pale wraith in whose mournful expression the boy beholds the mirror-image of his own grief. This tenuous reciprocity figures the identity the boy would reclaim, which is the unity of love, in which the experience of self is simultaneously that of vital forces within the subject and without. In the same poem, emotion seems inseparable from the current that jostles the boat and carries the disconsolate youth irresistibly out to sea. The boy and the eventual "I," both of them mobile, model the "*effort* of empathetic projection" through which, following Wellbery, the reader *grasps* the subjectivity around which the lyric utterances uniquely cohere.[38]

This desire for coherence where there is only division is a concern shared by film, a "species of unreality" in its own right. Cinematic texts, to quote Kaja Silverman, "confer subjectivity" on the viewer, and they achieve this through technical means that conceal those very means from the viewer's sight, effacing the apparatus, the corollary of which is a lack within the subject itself.[39] Those paintings by Friedrich that place a viewer, seen from behind, squarely within the frame in effect answer the question that the cinematic shot implicitly provokes the spectator to ask, namely, "Who is seeing this?," though canvases by the same painter in which no such figure is shown, these being the majority, suggest a tolerance for the absolute moment of fascination found also in Murnau's work, in which shots are seldom complemented by reverse-shots but function instead, in the words of Thomas Elsaesser, as "self-sufficient units."[40] The carefully structured pairing of shots with reverse-shots – characteristic of American cinema but largely absent in Murnau – is arguably a cognate of the empiricism that invalidates self-transitive intuition ("the force-experience of my own body in action") as a means of knowing.[41] This experience, of which empathy is a part, is the basis for apprehending internal connections between external events – of determining relations of cause and effect, of "before" and "after." Title cards indicating (in *Nosferatu*) that disparate actions are occurring "at the same hour" underscore the spatial gulf between actors, which the succession of shots can bridge only with the aid of a supernatural power. Witness the shot transitions that confirm the clairvoyance by means of which Count Orlok and Ellen, though separated by a continent, are joined; or the sequence of alternating shots of the two antagonists as they approach a common destination by different routes. If this "architecture of secret affinities," as Elsaesser describes it, serves to *lodge* within the viewer the same perilous allure that Orlok exercises over his prey,[42] then Orlok not only erodes the assurance afforded by a more conventional syntax but also personifies (with a vengeance) the subjectivity of which the aforementioned empiricism would empty the world – a world in which consciousness itself would have no part.[43]

Herzog's meditation on an unscripted shot of blowing grasses implicates, as the opposite of the "magic of cinema," the devitalized thinking that would separate objects from one another and from the matrix that envelops them.[44] Abstraction has a stake in this disenchantment, if its motive is indeed that of isolating the subject from the nexus of physical force. Such, roughly, is the function of the *imago* in the famous scenario proposed by Lacan, in which the young child finds in its mirror reflection a *Gestalt*, exterior to the self, which serves to foil "the turbulent movements that the subject feels are animating him." A provisional "mirage," this *imago* is "still pregnant with the correspondences that unite the *I* with … the phantoms that dominate him."[45] The metaphors to which Lacan takes recourse help trace a path along which Romantic figures find their way into Weimar cinema. The ghostly bride of Brentano's poem migrates easily into *Nosferatu* where, as Ellen, she is touched by the ominous breath that raises the surf and causes curtains to flutter as the fiend draws near. The same bride, a *fata morgana* enlivened by turbulence, projects the vulnerability of the youth, who anxiously implores her not to move (*O halte dich doch stille!*). His vulnerability, which makes him subject to the reader's grasp, is tantamount to the internal disequilibrium that is our common share. Its contrary is the state of repose that, from a viewpoint prevalent after the *fin de siècle*, was the benefit of abstraction. Brentano's "Auf dem Rhein" is only one of countless examples of the challenge that Romantic thought and practice pose to the dualism that, a century later, came to treat abstraction and empathy as antithetical impulses.

This polarity, whose formulation after 1900 provides the present study with its push-off point, is broadly continuous with the intellectual and cultural response, beginning just prior to 1800, to Kant's foundational claim that we cannot have knowledge of things or appearances independently of our intuitions of space and time. The critical-theoretical vocabulary that first emerged from within this post-Kantian ferment would – a century later and by multiple avenues – circle back on the cinema, exposing Weimar filmmaking as a *de facto* extension of the avant-garde that was German Romanticism.[46] The circle of German Romantic writings has here been expanded to include Goethe (his *Faust* in particular, but also his "Erlkönig" and other poems), traditionally thought too vast for Romanticism to encompass, and Johann Peter Hebel, an author unaffiliated with the Romantics but contemporary with them. Of central interest are the *Outpourings of an Art-Loving Friar* (1796, by Wilhelm Heinrich Wackenroder, with additions by Ludwig Tieck), *Heinrich von Ofterdingen* (1800, by Friedrich von Hardenberg, aka Novalis), and *The Nightwatches of Bonaventura* (published anonymously in 1804, now widely attributed to Ernst August Klingemann), as well as poetry and prose by the aforementioned Eichendorff. Several British Romantics are also included: Samuel Taylor Coleridge, Lord Byron, and both Percy Bysshe and Mary Wollstonecraft Shelley. Modernist art and literature constitute the third term in this project, which aims to underscore the "contemporaneity" of Weimar filmmakers and their Romantic forebears. Artists (Mondrian, Magritte, de Chirico, Schiele, Meidner, Marc, and Feininger) and writers (Conrad, Mann, Kafka, and Fitzgerald) help fill out a panorama that reaches from one moment to the other and, far from exhausting either, enlists instances of both in a dynamic of reciprocal illumination. The foregoing placement of

Nosferatu alongside Brentano's ballad is representative of an essentially notational approach that works to showcase what is emblematic about the examples it compares and combines. Consequently, the sampling of films discussed is limited to a short list of familiar titles: *Nosferatu*, *Tartuffe*, *The Last Laugh*, and *Faust* (Murnau), *The Student of Prague* (Stellan Rye), *The Cabinet of Dr Caligari* and *The Hands of Orlac* (Robert Wiene), *The Golem* (Paul Wegener), *The Street* (Karl Grune), *Siegfried*, *Metropolis*, and *M* (Fritz Lang), *Berlin, Symphony of a City* (Walther Ruttmann), and *The Blue Angel* (Josef von Sternberg). American films that feature prominently include *Frankenstein* (James Whale) and Disney's *Fantasia*.

Fantasia, to which the final chapter of this study is largely devoted, may be thought to rehearse the aesthetic genealogy whose diverse traces these chapters as a whole are at pains to expose. Released in 1940, this visual and musical extravaganza compresses into its two-hour span the arc that extends from Romanticism to modernism and beyond, giving body to the idea that abstraction, as practised by painters like Mondrian, Malevich, and Kandinsky, had its true origins in "absolute music." This concept, which Disney's master of ceremonies invokes, is coeval with the aesthetic paradigm that emerged in the German-speaking world around 1800.[47] *Fantasia* concentrates the Romantic notion of the absolute, transcendental subject in the figure of the conductor, who is repeatedly shown in a format introduced by Friedrich. Centred within the frame, his back to the audience, he faces into a blue void from which, along with the strains of Bach's *Toccata and Fugue in D minor*, he summons the abstract analogues of symphonic sound. Wave patterns, geometrical shapes, pulses, and fields or streaks of colour combine with natural-physical elements such as raindrops, ripples, rays of light, swirls of air, clouds and lightning, all of which proceed from the tableau that appears once Bach's composition settles into its theme: the forested slopes of mountains veiled in mist. This contraction of historical planes confirms, in its own way, a thesis set forth by Hans Belting, namely that abstraction in twentieth-century art realized a potential already latent in the Romantic landscape.[48] Mondrian's "dune paintings," which translate the motion and glint of the sea into an increasingly austere interplay of vertical and horizontal marks, reflect a contemporary understanding of the physical universe as comprised less of material bodies than of waves or fields of energy. At the same time, they reinterpret seascapes painted a century earlier by Friedrich, whose often severe horizons, bisected by standing figures or the masts of ships, establish a rectilinear scaffolding that, in Mondrian, finds its most programmatic reduction – a symmetry characterized by Robert Rosenblum as "an immaterial skeleton [transforming] matter into spirit."[49] In its opening gesture, *Fantasia* dissolves the boundary between material objects and the space from which they seem momentarily distilled. In explicitly associating this dissolution with the thrust of "absolute music," the film shares in the vision professed by the "author" of Coleridge's "Kubla Khan," who "with music loud and long" aspires to recover lost images that, in a dream, "rose up before him as things."[50]

Coleridge's poem stands as a crowning instance of the Romantic alignment of creativity with dreaming, wherein the hidden contents of the psyche are apprehended visually as objects outside of the self. A closely contemporaneous example of this turn is the account, in Wackenroder's *Outpourings*, of Raphael's struggle to realize his Sistine Madonna – of how the painter, after a period of frustration, dreamt one night of awakening suddenly to behold the completed canvas, which hung on the wall opposite his bed. Held within a bright beam of light, the painting now before him corroborated traits or features that, in waking life, had flashed momentarily before his soul but had eluded his more permanent grasp. The artist is thus cast as spectator to his own inspired vision – an apparition that, fixing him with a gaze described as deeply poignant, seemed at any moment to be on the verge of moving (*als wolle es sich bewegen*).[51]

The experience of waking not *from* a dream but *within* it is foundational to Novalis's novel fragment *Heinrich von Ofterdingen* (1800), in which the dreaming protagonist awakens and – still dreaming – is treated to a quasi-cinematic display of vaporous forms and effects of light. And more than a century later – at the close of the First World War – a famous patient of Freud's reported having dreamt of waking to behold a cluster of wolves looking back at him from a tree just beyond his bedroom window. The prolonged state of motionless looking with which the dreamer regarded the watchful animals is reminiscent of Freud's equally famous Dora, who stood for hours in motionless reverie before the same Sistine Madonna, in which she ostensibly found refuge from what Freud calls an "unconscious underpainting" (*unbewusste Untermalung*) of secret desire.[52] In turn, Dora has her Romantic precursor in the sorrowful Gretchen of Goethe's *Faust*, who appeals, before a devotional image of the *Mater dolorosa*, to the Holy Virgin's capacity for empathy while intoning the gestural disposition of shared pain: "Incline, / Thou rich in grief, oh shine / Thy grace upon my wretchedness"[53] (*Ach neige, / Du Schmerzensreiche, / Dein Antlitz gnädig meiner Not!*[54]).

Exhorted to bend forward in commiseration, the sacred object of Gretchen's entreaty stands in plain contrast to the plastic indifference of the neoclassical figure. The extraordinary pathos of this moment would seem to extend the reception of Raphael's painting, whose relocation to

Dresden in 1753 helped inaugurate a new aesthetic orientation, which Belting has characterized as a "farewell to Apollo."[55] This same epochal shift is reversed in the scene that plays out before Lacan's mirror, in which an ungainly and awkward subject – one always at risk of stumbling and falling – gives way to an image of balance and integrity.[56] This identification is symbolically undone in Mary Shelley's *Frankenstein* (1818), where the physical perfection of the De Lacey children ("their grace, beauty, and delicate complexions") is a foil for the creature's own "horrible deformity," which he glimpses in the reflective surface of a standing pool.[57]

The fragmented body-image personified, Shelley's creature affords a preview of the anxious contours, misshapen features, and disjointed limbs that compose much of the subject matter of Expressionism, which is the one style that Lacan explicitly exempts from the "Apollonian effect" of painting.[58] The creature's cinematic counterpart, from Whale's *Frankenstein* (1931), is literally a subject animated by turbulence, brought to life by energy harnessed from a violent electrical storm. An amalgam of figures culled from German cinema of the previous decade, the creature is the monstrous, suffering heir to Expressionism, bearer of the alienated self-image familiar, for example, from the surgically reconstituted protagonist of Wiene's *The Hands of Orlac* (1924) or Schiele's contorted self-portrayals. Lacan opposes an "orthopaedic totality" to such fragmentation, internally felt, which in phantasy may express itself as dismemberment or anatomical discontinuity, in life as the mechanical fitfulness of hysteria.[59] Eisner echoes Worringer's identification of the "spasmodic ecstasy" that both Gothic architecture and modernist art embody, and it is revealing that she should also favour the word "paroxysm" with respect to the Expressionist screen actor, whose gestures she assails as "brusquely galvanized and broken half-way." The faces of the rioting workers in Lang's *Metropolis* are thus "deformed by savage grimaces, gaping, crevice-like, unnatural," and Fritz Kortner's "frightful sneer" in *Warning Shadows* makes his "enormous" visage resemble "some African demon-mask." In Kortner she even observes the "habit of projecting his arms or trunk as if to rid himself of them."[60]

Eisner, for whom distortion and abstraction are synonyms, projects this synonymy across the range of Expressionist performance ("distortion of gestures") and visual design ("distortion of objects") – twin components that conform to the two principal types of hysteria, one in which psychical conflict is expressed somatically, indeed "theatrically," the other in which anxiety cleaves to external objects, both animate and inanimate.[61] She cites the Expressionist belief that "creative distortion" enabled the artist to "release an object's internal life," and she generalizes this attitude in terms of a "troubled mysticism" that has long plagued "the Germans," with their age-old predilection for "all that is obscure and undetermined."[62] She quotes Romantic and Expressionist writers in alternation, ascribing both movements to the same "primordial anguish" from which Worringer derived the German Gothic, an "intensity of expression" that left "Nordic man" captive to "a thundering orchestration of mechanical forces."[63] The imagery could well be Wackenroder's, and it must be stressed that Worringer, any "farewell to Apollo" notwithstanding, summons the neoclassical ideal of effortless composure as a foil for pathologizing the experience of being "convulsively swept up."[64]

Eisner's sensitivity to the Romantic dimension of Weimar cinema is acute, but her pointed censure of Romanticism, which entails an elevation of naturalism over style, draws support from Worringer, in whose work one of the defining polarities of the "art-epoch" is upheld. The same polarity, as suggested earlier, is alive within Lacan's take on the experience in which the child identifies with what appears as the plastic self-sufficiency of the figure in the mirror. For purposes of the present discussion, it is telling that this analytical framework, which has proved uniquely suited to the study of film and of cinematic spectatorship, (1) should be centred on a scenario that, in staging the formation of the ego, in effect rehearses an aesthetic shift consolidated in the wake of the French Revolution, and (2) should, as an aside, isolate Expressionism as an exception to the function of painting, namely that of pacifying the gaze. The vast Oedipal superstructure of *Metropolis* provides, for the moment, a parting example of a body whose spasmodic agony stands in direct antithesis to the harmony and self-possession of classical form. Deep within a subterranean region hidden from general view, a factory worker is shown straining unceasingly to reposition the arms of a circular dial that matches his physical dimensions. In a frame that implicitly negates the Vitruvian ideal of geometrical human proportion (figure 4), the overtaxed worker crumples, as if crucified, soon to be cradled and comforted by the film's empathetic hero.[65] A pointed *pietà*, this shot has various parallels within Weimar cinema. Given the role of the Maria-figure in *Metropolis*, however, Lang's film traces the most direct line back to Goethe's Gretchen, who, invoking the Virgin Mary's own shattering grief, wonders if anyone feels the pain burrowing into her every joint, which is the pain of remorse but also of an unabated desire that leaves her forever trembling.

The following chapters may at times give the impression of being in thrall to imagery that would seem to confirm Romanticism as a template for Weimar cinema. For this reason, it is important to acknowledge

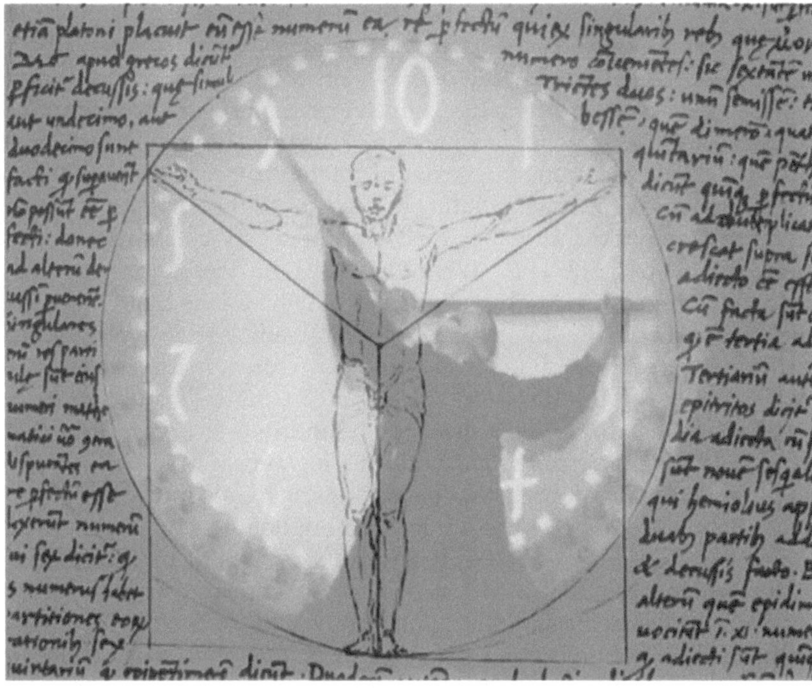

4. Giacomo Andrea, *Vitruvian Man* (ca. 1490). Biblioteca Ariostea, Ferrara. *Metropolis* (1926), dir. Fritz Lang.

clearly the medial differences between literature, the visual arts, and film. The intention here is not to diminish these differences but, on the contrary, to make them productive for an understanding of two very disparate moments. Neoclassicism had already belaboured the distinction between pictorial and poetic forms – a distinction that Lessing (in his *Laocoön* of 1766) redrew in terms of the spatial and consecutive character, respectively, of sculpture and verse. Lessing's "law of beauty," which rested on this boundary, worked to interdict the empathy that the visual portrayal of physical anguish was prone to arouse. The Romantics and their late eighteenth-century precursors were collective respondents to Lessing's insistence on the technical specificity of *poiesy* versus painting and sculpture. John Keats's "Ode on a Grecian Urn" (1819) is prominent in its isolation of a quintessentially classical object as a mediatic orphan ("foster-child of silence and slow time").[66] Friedrich's *Monk by the Sea*, which according to one contemporary review looked "as if it [the painting] were thinking Young's *Night Thoughts*," enacts a radical and potentially traumatic deframing that makes it impossible, in Albrecht Koschorke's words, to "abstract oneself [*sich hinauszuabstrahieren*] from the internal world of the image."[67]

This new aesthetic orientation, which Friedrich's work appears often to thematize, pertains just as much to Romantic lyric, in which metaphors, unmoored from the nexus of reference, become objects unto themselves. So described, painting and poetry of the "art-epoch" share in the rarefied indexicality that, for Metz, defines the cinema and grants it the "status of landscape." What Metz calls the "geography of enunciation" in film is a virtual space devoid of the markers that, in speech, affix interlocutors to stable locations. A low-angle shot is not (necessarily) identifiable with a subject-position within the diegesis, much as the "voice-off" in film is not anchored in a person standing *here* or *there* but rather "disperses itself across the entire surface of the image."[68] And much as the motifs in Eichendorff – a glancing reflection, a passing breeze, the decay of distant bells – are intangible indices of movement, so the geography of film is marked out not by people or material things but by vectors of direction, approach, recession, and so on. How is it possible, then, that a critical-conceptual language devised for the analysis of the cinema should so closely echo that used to describe what was novel about Friedrich's painting or Eichendorff's poetry? Does this similarity point to a common labour of subjectivity? It is around this possibility that these chapters gather.

Chapter One

The Turmoil of Forces

Images have an intelligence all their own. Albert Einstein, endowed with a remarkable ability to theorize visually, came to propose that the space between material objects was not a void but an electromagnetic field that undulated like hills or the surface of a lake.[1] Einstein published his General Theory of Relativity in 1915. In the same year, Dutch artist Piet Mondrian created his *Pier and Ocean*, in which a disciplined profusion of horizontal and vertical marks, contained within a cosmic oval, suggests the rhythm and movement of sunlit waves and, more generally, the "pulsating balance of forces that comprise the world" (figure 5).[2] Mondrian's extraordinary image advanced the cause of modernist abstraction, which, less than ten years earlier, Wilhelm Worringer had ascribed to a human need to isolate objects from one another and thus to extricate the viewing subject from a space that threatened to overwhelm the contours of the self – a space that bound objects together and granted them their "relativity in the world-picture" (*Relativität im Weltbilde*).[3] Worringer introduced abstraction as the counterpoint to empathy (*Einfühlung*), which his forerunner Theodor Lipps had determined to be the basis of aesthetic experience, understood as "objectified self-enjoyment."[4] The subject took pleasure in external objects that confirmed the subject's own internal sense of aliveness. Empathy was thus akin to the intuitive involvement that classical epistemology had long sought to banish from the realm of what could be known.[5] Philosopher Hans Jonas, himself an advocate for the "empathic study" of living organisms, cast the defining thrust of Humean empiricism, in its striving to rid "the picture of the world" of "images of force and causation," as a systematic attempt to invalidate "the self-experience of life."[6]

Self-experience factors into Jonas's discussion of sight, the traditional privilege of which is a function of its "effortlessness" – its independence

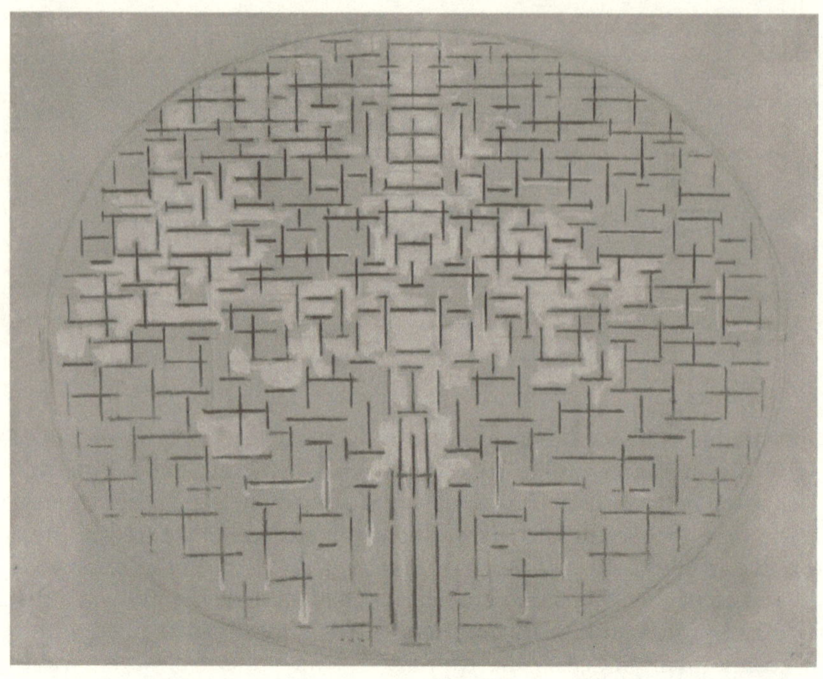

5. Piet Mondrian (1872–1944), *Pier and Ocean 5 (Sea and Starry Sky)* (1915)

Charcoal and watercolour on paper, 87.9 × 111.7 cm.
Museum of Modern Art, New York..
Art Resource/NY

of the proprioceptive motor sensations, such as those deriving from touch, that involve the percipient dynamically in the world perceived. The space separating the objects of sight from the subject they face is devoid of the force-context within which the mind integrates objects or events into a felt nexus of causality. This spatial distance, which distinguishes sight from the other senses, provides for an image that is at base *quiescent* – "a becalmed abstract of reality denuded of its raw power" (148). Jonas qualifies the "nobility" of sight – an ancient as well as neoclassical dogma – by asserting the dependency of seeing on hearing and, more particularly, touch. The hand, he argues, is a tactile organ that endows the human being with the unique capacity to "see" vicariously by means of touch (141). Jonas differentiates sight from both hearing and touch in terms that mirror Lessing's distinction between the simultaneity of presentation in the visual arts and the sequential

6. Caspar David Friedrich (1774–1840), *Monk by the Sea* (1808/10).

Oil on canvas, 110 × 171.5 cm.
bpk Bildagentur/Alte Nationalgalerie, Staatliche Museen zu Berlin
Photo: Andres Kilger/Art Resource, NY

character of poetry – a distinction eroded by the post-classical determination that the enjoyment of sculpture was as much an affair of the hand as of the eye. Whereas sight "discloses a world of co-present qualities spread out in space," the other senses synthesize a unity out of a sequence of impressions. This synthesis, Jonas writes, "must move along with the actual progress of the sensations, each of which fills the *now* of the sense from moment to moment with its own fugitive quality" (136).

Jonas could almost be describing Brentano's "Auf dem Rhein," itself a sequence of elusive sensations. The ballad, in which the pale phantasm's apparent trembling is an effect of the river jostling the boat, parses the difference between feeling and seeing as that between floating along and hovering aloft. His heart made "heavy" by grief, the young fisherman is carried downstream, past sites that are known to him by the sounds that reach his ears as he drifts by. Even visual cues – the dim glow of a candle or the glint of reflected sunlight – do not reveal material objects but instead approximate what Jonas refers to as the "immanent 'objectivity' of acoustic values" (137–8). This same "loose object-reference" is a defining feature of Eichendorff and is found in his exquisitely toned "Mondnacht" (1837), which culminates in the ecstatic sensation of imagined flight inspired by moonlit fields riffled by a gentle breeze.[7] In a vein familiar from Marx's "A spectre is afoot" (*Ein Gespenst geht um*), the breeze is described as passing, indeed "walking" (*Die Luft ging durch die Felder*).[8] This is not a personification, however, but a more fundamental anthropomorphism proper to perception that is at once self-perception – a knowledge of the world grounded in one's own experience of force and action.[9] Eichendorff's image of wheat fields undulating softly (*Die Ähren wogten sacht*) assimilates perceived phenomena to a body that has felt internally the effects of pressure, contact, resistance, and so on. Thus to the extent that Mondrian's *Pier and Ocean* captures the "pulsating balance of forces that comprise the world," it is the opposite of abstraction, which Jonas characterizes in terms of "the elimination of the causal connection from the visual account" (147).

Jonas's challenge notwithstanding, the Humean bias is all-pervasive. It can be discerned in the New Critical impatience with the "affective fallacy,"[10] as well as in the resistance, among some film theorists, to projecting human attributes onto the strictly mechanical procedures of cinematic enunciation.[11] Worringer's earliest and most important work paralleled the rise of the cinema, and his writings on Expressionism, which he championed for a time, were exactly contemporaneous with those German films commonly labelled "Expressionist," including Robert Wiene's *The Cabinet of Dr Caligari* (1920), Paul Wegener's *The Golem* (1920), and F.W. Murnau's *Nosferatu* (1922). Writing on *Caligari* in 1924, Bela Balázs contended that the "stylized ornamentality" of the sets acted as an aesthetic anodyne to the anxiety the film might otherwise induce.[12] This assessment echoes Worringer's more general thesis, which held that ornament, in whose anorganic linearity the origins of art were to be sought, served to insulate the subject from vital forces without.[13] Balázs in fact regarded *Nosferatu* as being more frightening for being more naturalistic and familiar. Alluding to a tale by the Brothers Grimm, he insists that "we learn the meaning of fear" when the nature closest to us alters its countenance and mien.[14] A "chill wind" circulated through Murnau's imagery, which Balázs carefully evokes: heavy mountain- and seascapes, nocturnal ruins, the moon half hidden by clouds, a strange silhouette in an empty courtyard, a deserted ship drifting silently into port, horses startled by something unseen, a door opening slowly of its own accord.[15]

The figures and motifs here summoned by Balázs are plainly Romantic. In this particular constellation, however, and against the backdrop of the early 1920s, they disaggregate into discrete pictorial components, such as those found in the paintings of Giorgio de Chirico, with their vacant piazzas, ominous shadows, distant vessels, and sense of the spatial extension that Worringer named as a source of agoraphobia (*Platzangst*) and the dread of space (*Raumscheu*)[16] – conditions to which those very paintings seem uniquely adapted. De Chirico's works, which at times *quote* Albertian perspective even as they push it to its limits, are thoroughly suffused with the very anxiety their formal austerity would presumably counteract.[17] The objects contained in his paintings – towers, smokestacks, marble statues, civic monuments, colonnades, sails, locomotives, wagons, clocks, banners, human figures (visible typically as a pair of tiny silhouettes, casting long shadows, in the far distance), and (up close) disconcertingly lifeless mannequins – seem isolated within an absolute Newtonian space consistent with the *pathos in distans* that Nietzsche invoked as the effective opposite of empathy.[18] The jointed "lay figures" found in many of de Chirico's prewar compositions – movable wooden models used by artists especially for the study of drapery – seem almost intended to demonstrate what for Worringer was the defining trait of the German Gothic: an asensual grammar that exposed the anatomical severity beneath every cascading fold and crease. Whereas the French Gothic had resounded with the "eternal music of all organic being," its belated German counterpart evolved a systematic play of mechanical principles, displacing nature, observed and felt, with its stylized distortion, its *grimace*.[19] Likewise German Expressionism, in which the Late Gothic enjoyed a certain stylistic revival. Both moments, following Worringer, were *intermezzi*, necessary preludes to the Renaissance (in the case of the Gothic) and, where Expressionism was concerned, to a new classicism that would take root not in Germany but in French or Italian soil.[20]

Accordingly, Worringer rejoiced at the unexpected discovery of Carlo Carrà's *Pine by the Sea* (1921), which embodied for him nothing less than "the lived experience of being." He recalls being "deeply affected" (*tiefbetroffen*), for the first time responding to "the breath … of a modern painting with *my* breath, with the breath of my entire being."[21] He claims not to have felt this way since encountering Cézanne, whose "silent music …, floating miraculously [*wunderbar schwebend*] above the line dividing immanence from evidence, clarity from mystery," resonated with the "inaudible chords of a new architectonics of the image."[22] Worringer's metaphorically rich account of Cézanne could be thought to hark back to the "unheard melodies" of Keats's "Grecian Urn,"[23] just as his reaction to a painting by an erstwhile Italian Futurist may recall a lyric poem by Goethe, in which a wanderer's growing sense of inner repose matches, with the onset of evening, the near breathlessness of the forest around him.[24] The assurance with which this famous poem closes ("soon / you too shall rest") approximates the aim of the impulse described by Worringer in terms of an urge to create points of rest (*Ruhepunkte*), to afford the mind, exhausted by the welter of sensations, a longed-for equilibrium.[25]

Abstraction, as the primary means by which this longing could be satisfied, conditioned a pleasure that was not intellectual but rather firmly rooted in the continuum of body and mind. Worringer even suggests, with a gesture to evolutionary psychology, that the morphological law of anorganic nature echoes quietly within the human organism like a faint memory (*wie eine leise Erinnerung nachklinge*).[26] Such instincts found intuitive corroboration in those early artistic expressions that, instead of imitating phenomena, laid bare the principles governing the phenomenal world. Gothic architecture was an advanced, hybrid development, in which strictly mechanical laws, grasped empathetically, "came alive."[27] The complexity of this somatic response is exemplified by Goethe's explicitly intuitive paean to the cathedral at Strasbourg, before whose imposing façade the young law student, weakened by a protracted illness, delights in the restoration of his own vigour.[28] Suddenly animated when the birds nesting in its many niches awake noisily to the first light of day, the massive structure complements the forest of the poem just mentioned, in which the birds, harbingers of inner quiet, *withhold* their song (*schweigen*).[29] This quiet is the blessing of dusk, and Goethe recalls how the dying light of evening often soothed his eyes, weary from examining the cathedral in its every detail, "with beneficent rest."

Goethe's rhapsodic account emphasizes the harmony and fluidity of the German Gothic; Worringer, almost 130 years later, stressed its mechanical, geometrical rigour. But the abstract and non-contingent was the very thing that, in Worringer's view, enabled the subject to achieve a state of calm amid nature's confusing tangle: "Rest and delight could only arise where one was confronted with something Absolute" (*Ruhe und Beglückung konnten nur da eintreten, wo man einem Absoluten gegenüberstand*).[30] This state of "standing opposite" (*Gegenüberstehen*), which implicates the "object" (*Gegenstand*) precisely as something relative to this stance, reveals in its lexical particularity what is structurally stringent about the mode of spectatorship that began to emerge toward the end of the eighteenth century. A shift, discernible in Goethe as he recalls (in 1770) his inner jubilation vis-à-vis the towering edifice at Strasbourg, is still in force in Worringer's description (from 1924) of his reaction to the small painting by Carrà ("deeply affected I remained standing before it"). Common to these historically disparate moments is the profound affinity between subject and object that dawns on the former in motionless (breathless) contemplation of the latter. The principle of "objectified self-enjoyment," of which both experiences may serve as examples, had conceptual precursors in German Romanticism.[31] Indeed, it finds literary expression in Novalis's novel-fragment *Heinrich von Ofterdingen* (1800), in which a chorus of travelling merchants claims that human beings were evolved of nature's desire to take pleasure in its own artistry.[32]

Parallels between Romanticism and Expressionism were affirmed by a number of Worringer's contemporaries, one of whom declared that Kandinsky, in liberating art from all mimetic convention, had realized Philipp Otto Runge's "dream of absolute musical color."[33] The synaesthetic metaphors that pervade Worringer's summary of Cézanne have a decidedly Romantic ring.[34] More fundamentally, they are true to the inherent metaphorizing of a being that cannot help but verbalize experience through corporeal self-intuition, which is also the basis for empathy.[35] Worringer observes in the Expressionists, as inheritors from the Gothic, twin strains of Scholasticism and mysticism, which in their opposition reflect the duality of *Geist* – a word that straddles the divide between pure logic on the one hand, and, on the other, a power of knowing that is "psycho-affective" (*seelisch-gefühlsmässig*). The Gothic cathedral thus combined rarified calculation with the "ardent mysticism of stained glass dissolving in flames of colour, or a tragic-phantasmatic pietà carved in wood glowing from within a twilit chapel" (*inbrünstige Mystik einer in Farbengluten vergehenden Glasmalerei oder einer aus Kapellendämmerung hervorleuchtenden tragisch-gespentischen Holzpietà*).[36]

The effect of this highly evocative formulation is to resituate medieval art and architecture, to which Worringer in turn traced the spiritual ancestry of Cézanne, Van Gogh, and their German successors, within a recognizably Romantic *mise en scène* – a setting steeped in spectral light and crepuscular mystery. Worringer's imagery seems culled from the so-called Romantic "religion of art," which, couched in the vocabulary of ecstasy and rapture, sought to aestheticize the sacred, to make art the object of a new secular fervour. The pre-eminent example is Wackenroder's *Outpourings of an Art-Loving Friar* (1796). Devoted almost exclusively to painters of the Renaissance, this collection of testimonial sketches culminates in a profile of the fictional composer Joseph Berglinger, bearer of a sadness similar to that of the monk himself, who at the outset recalls the melancholy that welled up within him at the mere thought of the lives and works of his "artistic saints." Joseph, as a tender and neglected youth, exhibited his own monastic bent, seeking refuge in churches, where the music insulated him against the discordant hum and murmur of the crowded marketplace.[37] There, in those lofty spaces, he exulted in the oratorios and peals of brass, which broke over him with the force of a thunderstorm:

> Expectantly, he would await the first sound of the instruments – and when it came bursting forth, mighty and sustained, shattering the dull silence like a storm from Heaven, and when the sounds swept over his head in all their grandeur, then it was as if his soul spread great wings, as if he were rising up from a desolate heath, as if the curtain of dark cloud were disappearing before his mortal gaze [*als wenn … der trübe Wolkenvorhang vor den sterblichen Augen verschwände*], and he were soaring up to the radiant Heavens. Then he would hold his whole body still and motionless, fixing his eyes unmoving [*unverrückt*] on the floor.[38]

This passage signals a remarkable turn. In a setting of the kind that would inspire the structure and decor of the metropolitan "film-palaces" of the later 1920s, a subject is interpellated, held in motionless thrall before the aesthetic proxy of divine or sovereign power.[39] Eyes downcast, he is rooted in place, triangulated perhaps by the oppositional arrangement of choirs as would befit the antiphonal style introduced by composers of the Venetian Baroque. It is, concomitantly, an instance of the Sublime, as Berglinger appears indifferent to survival in the face of overwhelming forces, be they real or metaphorical. Proper to the century of the "natural sign," the assimilation of music to the moods of weather is part of the "pastorale," the musical genre most inclined to attempt image-associations by simulating, say, spring, birdsong, rushing water, rising winds, thunder, or the return of tranquility once the storm subsides. Nietzsche, with respect to what he called the "discharge of music in pictures," observed the regularity with which a Beethoven symphony compelled individual listeners to speak metaphorically (*zu einer Bilderrede nötigt*).[40] Imagery of ascent reinforces the thrust of metaphor generally, that is, from ground to signified, where "ground" has its figural equivalent in the "desolate heath," or simply the dull floor beneath Joseph's feet, which is literally the last word of his experience. The dream of an aspiring soul taking wing reappears in Eichendorff's "Mondnacht," mentioned earlier, where in the iridescence of a moonlit evening "ears" of wheat (*Ähren*) offer the first hint of the aural in a landscape stirring to an almost imperceptible current of air.[41]

Framing its vision in terms of the same "as if" that proliferates in the above passage from Wackenroder, Eichendorff's poem opens with an image redolent of the Baroque: blossoms shimmering at the "kiss" of the moon's unearthly light.[42] Over their brief course, however, these stanzas level out. The "wide" spread of the wings that would carry the speaker's soul through the quiet night, like the breath passing through fields of grain, may reinforce a sense of horizontal movement and spatial expanse.[43] Wackenroder's Joseph, by contrast, an impassioned adherent of a sacred music that the Age of Reason had deemed passé, is oriented vertically, positioned low on a hierarchical axis that is also a conduit of desired ascent. The nostalgia shared by Joseph and the art-loving friar fuels the anachronistic collapse of distinct historical planes, a collapse that also serves a critical dialectic: artistic forms of old are "modernized" as foils against which the Enlightenment's formulaic rigidity and "machine sense" (*Maschinenverstand*), as Joseph calls it, are cast in sharp relief.[44]

A comparable (and not unrelated) conflation of historical styles is found in the synaesthetic pageant that is Disney's *Fantasia* (1940), whose first musical selection, an orchestral setting of J.S. Bach's *Toccata and Fugue in D minor*, is paired initially with imagery reminiscent of paintings by Friedrich – mountains seen from a lofty height, their forested slopes showing intermittently though brightly through breaks in the morning fog. As the piece progresses, natural forms are rendered abstract through formal analogy, as when diagonal streaks of rain merge with the back-and-forth strokes of violin bows, when ripples and waves of water or sound expose the "patterned integrities" of modern physics,[45] or when pedal tones generate associations of pure colour. One of the film's first reviewers, noting similarities to Kandinsky and Miró, credited the film with making modern art pleasing to those who otherwise "raise up their hands in horror at abstract paintings."[46] But *Fantasia*, which would also seem to realize Runge's "dream of absolute musical color," and which brims with motifs drawn from German Expressionist cinema as well as from both Romantic and modernist art, might best be understood as *overflow*.[47] And to the extent that its opening gesture is to assimilate Bach's composition for organ to the age of the symphony, it parallels Wackenroder's appropriation, for an emerging Romanticism, of music that is unmistakably Baroque. With a high degree of overdetermination, *Fantasia* abounds with evidence for the trio of ideas that inform the whole of the present study: that the German cinema of the Weimar era represents an intersection of Romanticism with modernism, that these films help reveal what was already modern, even cinematic, about Romantic literature and painting, and that these affinities ground the cinema less in the "machine sense" of technological modernity than in an aesthetic that emerged around 1800.[48]

For this modernist synchrony of distinct historical registers, Worringer may serve as a sounding board. Though he ultimately professes a Goethean aversion to "precipitous speculation" (*abgründige*

Spekulation),[49] he appears often to be under the spell of the Romantic image. This is apparent in his descriptions, cited earlier, of Gothic mysticism, of Cézanne, and of his own markedly empathic reaction to Carrà's *Pine by the Sea*. This last instance would exemplify the response that results when the formal processes at play in the work of art confirm vital tendencies within the viewer, who, thus freed of desire, is free to enjoy "the unclouded happiness of his purely organic existence" (*das ungetrübte Glück seines rein organischen Seins*).[50] Wackenroder's Joseph, who, upon hearing the first strains of music, felt "as if the curtain of dark cloud were disappearing before his mortal gaze" (*als wenn der trübe Wolkenvorhang vor den sterblichen Augen verschwände*), experiences a comparable pleasure, though his state of being transfixed before a spectacle that is not seen but envisioned, is more consistent with the feeling of rest that comes over one when "confronted with something Absolute" (*wo man einem Absoluten gegenüberstand*).

This absolute juxtaposition found its visual manifesto in Friedrich's *Monk by the Sea* (figure 6). The painting, which aroused controversy at its unveiling in 1810, is stripped of those trappings of the theatre that had defined the painted landscape since the seventeenth century, when nature had begun to emerge as an aesthetic object in its own right. Gone are the natural and architectural *repoussoirs* (large oaks and willows, the columns of ancient temples, etc.) which, placed at the vertical edges of the image, guided the eye toward the centre, eased the background farther into the distance, and established a proscenium for the staging of a biblical, mythological, or rustic scene.[51] To these conventions, *The Monk by the Sea* poses the starkest of contrasts. Friedrich's canvas pictures a solitary figure at water's edge, dwarfed by the immensity of sea and sky. Storm clouds are gathering; the waves appear agitated. A severe horizon extends from one edge of the unbounded image to the other. Friedrich described his monk as "deep in thought" (*tiefsinnig*) and encircled by gulls, their anxious cries imploring him not to venture into the looming tempest, just as the painting itself reproaches its impious viewer for attempting to fathom the unknown.[52] A caution against "precipitous speculation," *The Monk by the Sea* acquires an apotropaic quality, which is buttressed by an underlying geometry that can be read out of the shapeless expanse. The horizon line is sharpest just above the man's head, which draws the eye to the point of intersection between a horizontal and a vertical axis. The latter is anchored by the upright figure, whose placement conforms closely to the "golden ratio," a proportionality of composition thought to afford the viewer a feeling of equanimity and balance.[53] Mondrian, zealous in his adherence to this same formula, produced (especially after 1921) austerely schematic designs that not only embodied a supreme sense of composure but also had no precedent in their uncompromising two-dimensionality.[54] His somewhat earlier *Pier and Ocean* is a modern cousin of *The Monk by the Sea*, which achieves something that Mondrian, over the course of his career, pursued with increasing single-mindedness – the intimation of infinity through flatness and an articulation of endless space unrestricted by the material limits of the canvas.[55] Absent those internal framing devices mentioned above, Friedrich's painting, which enables the viewer to imagine "panning" beyond the edges at left and right, draws the background forward, reducing its depth, and thereby heightening the subject's confrontation with the Absolute – for Worringer the necessary condition of "psycho-affective" repose.

Film was scarcely a decade old when Worringer published *Abstraction and Empathy*. His theory of these two competing (and at times interdependent) impulses within the history of art is broadly relevant with respect to the ambiguity of the screen, which very early cinema tended to treat more as a decorated surface than as a window onto a three-dimensional panoply of people and places. The cinema had matured substantially by the time Wiene made *Caligari*, which vacillates self-consciously between "naturalism" and "style" – terms that Worringer aligns with empathy and abstraction respectively. While figures often traverse a palpable space between background and foreground, moving toward or away from the camera, the angular, "expressionist" sets themselves are distorted and patently flat (figure 7). Trees and shrubs are starkly artificial and are often simply painted onto exterior walls. The scrolling arabesques that appear on interior surfaces are the essence of "style" as Worringer understands it.[56] Irises, finally, which are used throughout Wiene's film, occasionally take the shape of a diamond, a format that Mondrian had begun experimenting with at this precise time.

At this same precise time, Mondrian published "an essay in dialogue form" titled *Natural Reality and Abstract Reality* (1919/20). The piece consists of seven "scenes," each of which begins with a haiku-like notation of the natural setting, for example, "Dusk. Flat countryside. Vast horizon. Far up: the moon"; or "Capricious forms; on the clear sky with moon, the trees stand out in black relief."[57] An art-lover, a naturalistic painter, and an "abstract-realist" painter, walking together from the country to the city and eventually to the studio of the abstract-realist, react in kind to the briefly described scene: "How beautiful!"; "What deep tones and colors!"; "What repose!" Mondrian (by way of his abstract-realist surrogate) advocates throughout for the rarified plasticism of purely abstract painting, which, through flatness and

7. *The Cabinet of Dr Caligari* (1920), dir. Robert Wiene.

rectilinearity, exposes the balance of relations present but "veiled" in the natural landscape. In the first of the two nocturnal scenes just cited, the horizon is the only line visible. However, an opposition to this line is expressed by the vast and luminous flatness of the sky, upon which "the moon places an exact point." This point, like the monk in Friedrich's painting, enables the viewer to "trace" a vertical line, which in its opposition to the horizon forms the right angle. The right angle determines the "balanced interrelation" of line and plane, which is the condition of repose. Mondrian's abstract-realist goes on to insist that an additional "accent" – a tree, for example – would cause the viewer to trace an oblique line between it and the moon, thereby upsetting the equilibrium of which the right angle was the true and "primordial" source.[58]

Mondrian's equation of the oblique with imbalance is confirmed with a vengeance by de Chirico, whose works communicate a feeling of generalized disquiet through the propagation of acute, often discordant diagonals. This is true of what is certainly his most famous painting, *Mystery and Melancholy of the Street* (1914), which abounds with the elements of which Mondrian sought to purify his own work (figure 8). De Chirico's painting shows a carefree young girl, who appears scissor-cut

8. Giorgio de Chirico (1888–1978), *Mystery and Melancholy of the Street* (1914).

Oil on canvas, 85 × 69 cm
Private Collection

from some Victorian children's reader, rolling a hoop in the direction of a low sun, the angle and intensity of which are indicated by the warm ground and the distended shadow of a figure, an apparent statue, which is otherwise hidden by the massive building at right. The sharp shadow cast by that same structure divides the foreground diagonally and reinforces the child's oblique path, which leads from left to right toward an unseen destination. Opposing that diagonal is a wood-paneled wagon, its doors thrown open, its enclosed interior dingy and barren. The atmosphere of menace, to which the lurking statue and gaping wagon contribute, is intensified by the disruptive incongruity of the perspective lines, which do not converge on a common vanishing point. The girl gives the impression of running downhill, but the angle of the rapidly receding arcade at left places her at the bottom of a steep incline.[59]

Two years before de Chirico painted *Mystery and Melancholy of the Street*, Franz Kafka published a slim volume of short prose pieces called *Betrachtung*, the title a singular noun that identifies "examination" or "inspection" as the common theme of these stories.[60] One of them, which consists of a mere four sentences, imagines a solitary city-dweller standing absent-mindedly at his window, surprised to behold a young girl strolling down the street below. Her face is bright in the setting sun until, suddenly, she is eclipsed by the shadow of a man overtaking her from behind. But the man simply continues on, leaving the child's face bright once again.[61] Her sunlit face contrasts with what one assumes to be the turbid brow of the melancholic observer. Unsure as to how to survive the onrush of spring, he has pressed his cheek against the window's latch, and this affords him – like the viewer of de Chirico's painting – an oblique perspective onto a child beset by shadow.

A comparable framing is used to disconcerting effect by Fritz Lang in *M* (1931), the director's first sound film, which opens with a high-angle shot of children playing a game of elimination (figure 9). Guided by a morbid rhyme warning of a murderous "man in black," the game provides the children with a means of processing their fear of a homicidal pedophile who has all of Berlin in the grip of terror. The angle and proximity of the camera make for an acute foreshortening of the standing figures, which is accentuated by the long shadows they cast. The camera, on a boom, veers searchingly upward to reveal the interior balcony of a block of working-class flats. When it stops, the floor and railing of the balcony, along with lines hung with laundry, create a pattern of parallel diagonals that dominate the frame. The shot exemplifies the vectoring employed throughout the film to foster a sense of emotional and corporeal imbalance. Telegraph wires, staircases, and streets are used to create sharply angular shapes. Other examples include a

9. *M* (1931), dir. Fritz Lang.

kitchen table, cropped by the frame to form a wide pentagon, which an anxious mother has set for her daughter (the sparest of *natures mortes*),[62] and a diamond-shaped display of knives, which frames and isolates the stalker as he turns to face a store window to avoid detection.[63]

The scene that introduces the killer, however, presents a different kind of cinematic hieroglyph. A young girl, on her way home from school, pauses to bounce a ball against a concrete advertising column. As the ball continues to bounce, the camera pans slowly up to the right, leaving the girl out of frame while closing in on a poster announcing a reward for the unknown predator. After enough time has elapsed for the viewer to read an account of the latest abduction, the placard is overshadowed by the silhouette of the culprit himself, who remains out of frame to the right (figure 10). The shadow bows toward the child (still off screen to the left), and with words heavy with innuendo, the killer is heard to exclaim "What a pretty ball you have!" "What's your name?" he then asks, counterbalancing the question that headlines the

10. *M* (1931), dir. Fritz Lang.

poster – a question to which his anonymous entrance comes in defiant response – "Who is the murderer?"[64]

These paired questions parallel the symmetry of the fields at left and right, which structure a shot that in turn prepares for the horrific crime later to transpire off screen. Much like de Chirico's *Mystery and Melancholy of the Street*, this signature scene from *M* exploits off-screen space as an "out-of-field," which, following Deleuze, "testifies to a more disturbing presence." Deleuze draws a distinction between two "qualitatively different" aspects of the out-of-field, one "relative," the other "absolute," which may be thought to correspond to the two phases of landscape painting discussed earlier. *The Monk by the Sea* would seem to enact the kind of absolute "deframing" that "opens on to a duration which is immanent to the whole universe, which is not a closed set and does not belong to the order of the visible."[65] Mondrian's lozenge paintings, in which triangles, hexagons, and trapezoids are "read" as rectangles because they "appear to extend beyond the edges of the canvas,"[66] demonstrate with some precision what Deleuze would later argue with regard to the "whole," which he likens to a "thread" that "traverses sets and gives each one the possibility … of communicating with another, to infinity."[67] Mondrian's own deep-seated concern with the relation of the finite to the infinite is expressed through his use of right angles to suggest planes that are not enclosed but expand *ad infinitum*.[68]

Mondrian's kinship to Friedrich has already been pointed out. Yet contemporary reactions to Friedrich's work bear witness to an experience quite contrary to the repose that was Mondrian's ideal. Writing in 1809, the influential art-critic F.W. Basil von Ramdohr faulted Friedrich's *Cross in the Mountains* (1807/8) for (among other things) spatial incongruities that required the viewer to occupy an empirically impossible standpoint. Ramdohr's observations have recently been repurposed by art-historian Joseph Leo Koerner, who holds that the critic, his conservatism notwithstanding, was alert to what was unprecedentedly modern about the painter's accomplishment: "With neither a firm ground on which to stand, nor a stable horizon on which to fix our gaze, we … encounter Friedrich's crucifix within an anxious state of visual disequilibrium."[69]

Ramdohr's criticism rests in part on the difference between "aesthetic" and "pathological" effect. The former was the true aim of painting, which reckoned with the association, in the mind of the viewer, of depicted objects with ideas. The latter, by contrast, consisted in the "arousal of an affect-laden condition" (*Erregung eines affektvollen Zustandes*). This darker pathos was proper to music, dance, and poetry, all of which played on emotions rooted in *motion*. One was irresistibly swept up in the rhythm and pace of these art forms, moving in consonance – in *sympathy* – with their movement.[70] Ramdohr does not pose this division as an absolute one, but to the extent that the "aesthetic," in his understanding, excludes corporeal intuition, it partakes of that same epistemological bias that, in cleaving subject from object, severs the connection that grounds *mimesis* in the deepest sense, conceived of as an inner attunement to the capacity of others to feel, indeed, to suffer. Much like Kant, Ramdohr associates the "aesthetic" with dispassion, whose antithesis is *compassion*, which Rousseau, already in 1755, had characterized as the natural, inborn abhorrence one feels on seeing a fellow creature in pain.[71]

Rousseau's thought helped spawn a generation of German poets and critics who trafficked in pathology. Goethe, who late in life explicitly diagnosed as "sick" everything "Romantic," produced in his earlier years the ballad "Erlkönig" (1782), which not only dramatizes affective contagion but also provides a template for the principle stated by Balázs with respect to Murnau's *Nosferatu*, namely that "we learn the meaning of fear" when the nature closest and most familiar to us changes its physiognomy and demeanour. Novalis proposed a kindred change as essential to his program of "romanticizing the world," which lent the commonplace a "mysterious aspect" (*geheimnisvolles Ansehn*).[72] Ramdohr, in complaining that the spruce trees in Friedrich's *Cross in the Mountains* were but silhouettes without depth or contour,[73] was witness to a general, abiding shift. (The trees in *Caligari* are just that – black silhouettes, flattened and sharply defined.) Matthias Claudius's "Abendlied" (1779), with its solemn forest standing black and silent (*Der Wald steht schwarz und schweiget*), is an earlier example of a poem concerned with the changed appearance of the ambient world in the ambiguous light of the moon.[74]

Claudius's Pietist lullaby is meant to offer solace; Goethe's ballad exposes the lullaby as a predatory masquerade. The basic scenario of "Erlkönig" is as follows: A young boy, racing through the night with his father on horseback, believes himself pursued by a supernatural fiend, whose appearance and blandishments the father (with diminishing confidence) attempts to rationalize as harmless natural phenomena – a wisp of fog, ancient willows, wind whistling through dry leaves.[75] Darkness outstrips reason, just as death overtakes the child, whose terror the father inherits. The sheer modernity of this moment is marked by its pronounced afterlife in Kafka's mini-tale, de Chirico's painting, and Lang's film. In each of these, a small child is "shadowed" while a spectator, made corporeally self-aware by the inability to move, looks on anxiously. This anxiety is of a piece with that of the dreamer who experiences the sensation of falling, or is unable to exercise force over persons and objects. Freud proposed that dreams of flying, floating, or falling paired the pleasures of raucous child's play with the fears activated by the recollection of those pleasures (a possible explanation of "Erlkönig," in which fear is conjoined with the excitement of tearing through the dark on a galloping horse).[76]

In a discussion broadly consonant with Freud's proposal, Jeannot Simmen has equated modernity with an ambiguous "pleasure in falling" (*Lust am Sturz*). When fear is no longer represented concretely, everything becomes vertigo-inducing (*schwindelerregend*), and the world "*falls* into a swoon" (*fällt in Ohnmacht*). Falling figures a delirious impotence symptomatic of a new-found freedom, which is tantamount to the loss of a stable ground to stand on. Koerner analyses Friedrich's *Cross in the Mountains* in almost identical terms, and much in the Romantic and pre-Romantic decades points to this modernity. Goethe, who struggled with a fear of heights, described his repeated climbs to the top of the towering spire at Strasbourg, where he would inch out onto the makeshift viewing platform until his peripheral vision was emptied of any part of the surrounding structure.[77] Friedrich's *Wanderer above the Sea of Mists* (1818), to be discussed later, places a solitary traveller at the brink of a precipice (figure 14). Simmen locates this epochal displacement of the horizontal by the vertical somewhat later. His pivotal reference is a painting by Gustave Courbet, *The Man Made Mad by Fear* (1843–5), whose subject, filling the frame and facing the viewer directly, is falling forward toward a precipice at his feet. The man, whose wide-eyed expression registers the first, startled awareness that the ground beneath him has given way, represents for Simmen a new kind of observer – one "who senses a change in the world's gravity" (*der die Schwere der Welt verändert spürt*).[78]

Weimar cinema can be seen to combine what for Simmen are two historically and culturally disparate ambitions: spiritual ascent, a prevailing theme of religious art during and after the Middle Ages, and the modern, mechanical conquest of the vertical, which culminated with the high-speed elevator (and the skyscrapers its invention made possible).[79] *Nosferatu* opens with a shot of a town square from high atop a Gothic church. In the first shot of *The Last Laugh* (1924), also by Murnau, the camera looks out from within a glass-fronted elevator descending through the atrium of a bustling metropolitan hotel. In Murnau's *Faust* (1926), the diabolical Mephisto bids the rejuvenated hero step onto his magic cloak, enticing him with the promise that "the spinning world will spread before you" (*und um dich dreht die Welt!*). Faust is thus borne upward along the studded spires of yet another Gothic church and past every thinkable accessory of the Romantic landscape: craggy peaks, oceans of mist, ice fields, rushing torrents, crashing waterfalls, old and broken trees that file by as silhouettes in the near foreground. Climbing, falling, and tilting past jagged pinnacles, the dizzying flight manifests the disequilibrium, known also to aviators, that equates with the absence of a visible horizon.[80] Mondrian's mature work, restricted to the intersection of vertical and horizontal lines, amounts to an elegant blueprint for an existence stabilized between these two axes. Friedrich's *Monk by the Sea*, which by one account "[prunes] earth, water and sky to their purest, transcendental core," laid the foundation for Mondrian's more thoroughly abstract rendering of the boundless horizon dividing sea and sky (figure 11).[81]

If the counterpoise this pattern synthesizes has its precursor in Friedrich's *Monk*, its contrary is to be found in Goethe's Faust, who is confident of never being lulled into complacency by the "beautiful moment." His spirit, which "unfettered ever forward presses" (*ungebändigt immer*

11. Piet Mondrian (1872–1944), *Lozenge Composition with Two Lines* (1931).

Oil on canvas, 80 × 80 cm
Stedelijk Museum, Amsterdam

vorwärts dringt),[82] personifies the *élan vital* – one of the two opposed drives that Mondrian's right angle maintains in balance. While Murnau's Faust is no more than a distant cousin of Goethe's, the former, cowering as he peers down over the edge of Mephisto's flying cloak, recalls Goethe himself, who compared the experience of gazing down from the soaring spire at Strasbourg with the vertiginous sensation of being suspended beneath a hot-air balloon.[83] Both experiences constitute secular variations on the ambition of heavenly ascent, which, following Norbert Schmitz, would eventually commend the elevator to the cinematic avant-garde and its dream of a perception relieved of the body's weight. Schmitz finds in the modern "lift" a particular expression of "a subtext of horizontals and verticals in which this motif evolves its aesthetic significance" – a formal structure uniquely compatible with an ambivalence toward the modern world, as revealed in the divide between avant-garde cinema and more conventional narrative film. While experimental filmmakers (René Clair, Dziga Vertov) were euphoric in their celebration of the conquest of height, narrative cinema "[exposed] the ancient fears behind the perfection of metropolitan life." Films that fall under this second category focus not on the liberation of ascent but on the risk of entrapment and the horrors of the plunging shaft.[84] Murnau's Faust is himself product of, and witness to, the magic that the cinema, from the moment of its advent, was intent on conjuring. Soaring and swerving above the earth, he is privy to the roller-coaster sensationalism of those fairground attractions that, in prompting a heightened awareness of the world's gravity, enabled participants to revel in the ambiguous pleasure of falling.[85]

Ramdohr's denunciation of Friedrich's *Cross in the Mountains* in effect isolates what is cinematic about a painting that undermines the viewer's psycho-affective integrity by refusing that viewer a firm and spatially consistent position from which to regard the natural prospect. The classicism to which Ramdohr was heir was anchored ultimately in the Greco-Roman ideal of the human physique – objective embodiment of the subjective coherence the painting would deny its viewer. Immortalized by the ancients in marble, this well-formed, graceful, and sensually unselfconscious body appears, in the twentieth century, to have provided one phase of psychoanalysis with a model for the emerging *I* – an image of completeness and physical self-possession, the assumption of which foils an internal sense of disunity and ungainliness.[86] This felt fragmentation is the product of a libidinal dynamism that has its cognate in the cinema, and it may be suggestive here to remember what Benjamin called the "dynamite of the tenth of a second," by means of which cinematography blasted the familiar world to pieces, enabling the viewer to travel "calmly and adventurously" amid its "far-flung ruins and debris." Techniques such as slow motion, the close-up, and frame enlargement revealed "entirely new structural formations of the subject." Slow motion in particular exposed the hidden mechanics behind familiar movement and created (here Benjamin is quoting Rudolf Arnheim) "the effect of singularly gliding, floating, supernatural motions."[87] At hand once again is the affinity to dreaming, as well as to the oneiric subjunctive already observed in Wackenroder and Eichendorff ("as if he were rising up from a desolate heath," etc.). To put it simply, the cinema satisfies a basic longing, theorized by Freud, for the sensory vividness of wish-fulfillment, following a regressive procedure whereby the mind figures the body to itself, translating desires into images, ideas into actions and affects.

Friedrich's paintings too may be thought at times to project a body with all its perceived faults. Filled with the twisted trunks of ancient and abused trees, the broken remnants of churches and abbeys, or vaguely anthropomorphic rock formations, these compositions summon within the viewer a sense of dynamic involvement, imagined effort, and hampered locomotion. This landscape reappears in a scene from Lang's *Siegfried* (1924), in which the hero, embodiment of a neoclassical standard, has to wrest himself from the snares thrown up by this terrain. Fresh from vanquishing the dragon of Wotan Wood, Siegfried arrives in the land of the Nibelungs, where the devious dwarf-king Alberich is lying in wait. Before pouncing, Alberich dons his mythic cloak of invisibility, leaving Siegfried, his face and limbs disfigured by strain, to resist an unseen force. (His contortions are reminiscent of Schiele's wrenched and grimacing subjects, who in like fashion seem constrained by invisible foes.) Siegfried soon prevails, and the hideous Alberich, divested of his magical cloak, offers treasure in exchange for his life.[88] In the subsequent shot, the hero's Olympian perfection stands out against the limping Alberich's stunted deformity, which he shares with the wreck of an old tree, eerily alive in death (figure 12). Framed by the vestibule of a dark cave, this shimmering tableau is an emblem of the cinema itself. After ushering Siegfried through narrow passages into the depths of the cave, Alberich calls forth a moving image – a film within the film – of the Nibelungs' underground toil. Dazzled by the spectacle, Siegfried is bewildered by its sudden disappearance, confirming the flatness of the cavern wall with the flat of his hand.

Siegfried is not the first to wonder at the "haptic" space that appears to open up momentarily behind a two-dimensional surface. At least since Stellan Rye's *The Student of Prague* (1913), which turns on a similar illusion, German cinema was accustomed to projecting its technical trickery as Mephistophelian magic, and to casting disillusionment in terms of the difference between possession and loss.[89] Time and time again, subjects are confronted with something that escapes their manual as well as mental grasp. Friedrich likewise places his beholder at the threshold of the unseen, and Novalis, in a small convoy of aphorisms on the arts, invokes Herder's discussion (from 1770) of the man born blind who, gaining the power of sight, makes sense of his visible surroundings only when he comes to associate shapes and colours, newly seen, with sensations internal to a body that first came to know the world

12. *Siegfried* (1924), dir. Fritz Lang.

through touch. In a manner consistent with Friedrich's later emphasis on the "inner eye," Novalis claims the imagination as a substitute for *all* the physical senses, and the first of these aphorisms, which corroborates the experience of the man once but no longer blind, hints at what is fundamentally haptic about recognition: "Everything visible clings [*haftet*] to the Invisible."[90]

The cavernous setting of Alberich's deceptive wizardry brings Plato's cave-analogy to mind. A richer correspondence is found, however, in Novalis's *Ofterdingen*, in which cave and fantasy are forged into a cinematic prototype. When the reader first encounters the youthful Heinrich, he is awake in bed, his mind racing in the aftermath of stories told that same evening by a visitor from afar. His agitation accords with the "pathological" as defined by Ramdohr, and Heinrich, noting a desire to dance and a penchant for thought verging on music, exhibits every hallmark of being carried away. Falling at last into a slumber, he dreams of every conceivable adventure until, at daybreak, he finds his way into a subterranean vault suffused with opalescence. The dream is one in which "objectified self-enjoyment," to revive Lipps's expression, is manifestly auto-erotic: Heinrich immerses himself in a shimmering bath, where tantalizing maidens body forth at his mere touch.[91] His experience, in which pictures arise and intermingle in his mind before surrounding him as visible entities, is a distant prelude to *Fantasia*, which (especially with respect to Bach's *Toccata and Fugue*) proposes explicitly to screen the geometrical shapes and colour patterns that presumably occur to the listener in the concert hall.

Fantasia could even be construed as a working commentary on Schopenhauer's conception of music as a means of giving form to the invisible – a medium that, while not reflective of phenomena, corresponds sensibly to the vast architecture of the cosmos. Something similar has already been affirmed regarding Mondrian, who sought, through the careful placement of vertical and horizontal marks, not to mention the progressive reduction of his colour palette, to convey the pulse and balance of the natural world. At the same time, Disney's film retreats from what is abstract and experimental about its opening gesture, indulging at times in the most cartoonish anthropomorphism, as when orange-capped mushrooms, made to resemble (someone's limited idea of) Chinese peasants, move to Tchaikovsky's "Dance of the Sugar Plum Fairy."[92] The puerile sweetness of this and other examples from *Fantasia* would ratify the self-evidence with which, following Jonas, empirical science has striven to rid the physical record of life's testimony. Goethe's "Erlkönig" enacts a dispute between objective science, for which "dead matter," to cite Jonas, afforded "the standard of intelligibility," and the projection of living human traits onto nature (74). The poem mounts a terrifying crescendo while descending the scale of the senses from visual, then aural sensation to outright bodily seizure – the ogre's lethal grip coupled with the father's tightening embrace. It thereby subverts the established privilege of sight, the power of which was that of distancing the object from the organ of perception and thus substituting image, with its "[inherent] element of abstraction," for effect (32).

Jonas's thought entails a fundamental challenge to the epistemology that would invalidate the very "self-transitive" experience that provides "the connective tissue between perceived natural events" (37). Einstein found the path to his General Theory of Relativity by means of a fortuitous hypothesis ("the happiest thought of my life") concerning an observer in a state of free-fall who, because all other bodies fall and accelerate at the same speed, is "justified in interpreting his state as being 'at rest.'"[93] The free-fall, which for Simmen is *the* metaphor of modernity, affords an experiential ground for the theorem that objects, which appear separated by empty space, are in truth joined by a common gravitational field.[94] Worringer, writing at the very time that Einstein was working out his "thought-experiment," held that abstraction in the arts served to affirm the distance between objects, placing them in absolute relation rather than positioning them spatially and relative to one another. Balázs, for whom the "dream-substance" of the cinema was not subject to empirical-physical laws, ascribed to film the unique "poetic" capacity to render unto sight the visceral, even "demonic" force with which one *gravitates* toward far-off horizons and succumbs to cries beckoning from abroad. And as if to anticipate a moment in Lacan, Balázs asserts that the landscape is not objective nature but a "face" that, at a given spot, is suddenly seen gazing upon us from the muddled lines of an anamorphic puzzle-picture (*Vexierbild*).[95]

Within four years of the release of *Caligari*, Balázs in effect testified on behalf of the boy in Goethe's ballad, who sees a demon amid the trees and hears its seductive whisper in the rustling of dry leaves. Addressing himself to the "latent physiognomy of things" known to "every child," Balázs ventured that film, with its particular power to reveal the *Mienenspiel* – the play of gestures upon the "face of things" – was the true home of Expressionism.[96] The same poem dramatizes what Balázs called the deep and mysterious "coquetry" by means of which the landscape exercises its attraction over the subject, "as when the silhouette of a passing ship on the darkening horizon entices, bewitches and beguiles the man watching from shore."[97] The image evokes Friedrich while seeming to paraphrase Heine's "Die Nacht am Strand," from his lyric cycle *Die Nordsee* (1825–6).[98]

Similarly suggestive of Friedrich is the final shot of Herzog's *Nosferatu the Vampyre*, in which the protagonist presses his horse headlong into the wind, almost disappearing at the horizon as the sky roils overhead.[99] Somber in its beauty, the scene frames a motif common to Romanticism and Expressionism while honouring the very filmmaker who, in Eisner's words, "makes us feel" the "marvellous lightness" of bounding horses. The long nineteenth century was not so protracted as to supersede, over its course, an everyday familiarity with horses, almost unique in their combination of grace and tactile appeal. Kandinsky's astonishing *Blue Rider* (1903), from which an entire collective took its name, vibrates with the energy of the urgent midnight ride staged in "Erlkönig," as well as in other of Goethe's poems.[100] Franz Marc (mortally wounded on horseback near Verdun in 1916) is best-known for his vivid renderings of horses, their heads turned toward hills that mirror the sensual contours of the animals themselves. His *Blue Horse II* (1911) places the animal much as Friedrich oriented his wanderer. Perfectly centred and facing away from the viewer, it stands muscular but motionless before an unframed vista of valleys, summits, clouds, and mist.[101] His *Horse in a Landscape*, from the previous year, places the creature's red haunches at the lower right flank, but its back and neck arch upward and to the left so as to insert the head squarely between viewer and vanishing point. This placement is in a sense undone in Kafka's single-sentence vignette, also from *Betrachtung*, which evokes a rider, leaning into the wind, gaining speed to the point of shedding spurs and reins until, as if rider and mount had become one, the horse's head and neck dissolve from the panorama of the quivering plain.[102] This disappearance matches the ambition, expressed in writing by Marc, of "submerging" oneself in the soul of an animal in order to "imagine its field of vision."[103]

Kafka's vignette of the speeding horse is followed by another on the deceptive lightness of trees in the snow: With a slight push (*mit kleinem Anstoss*), it seems, one could shove them aside (*wegschieben*); as it turns out, they are wedded firmly to the earth, though this also (as if the whole thing were not enigmatic enough) is only apparent.[104] In these two consecutive prose pieces, which treat of acceleration and inertia respectively, experience is processed in terms of what Jonas described as "the interpolation of the images of force and causation into the picture of the world" – the last vestige of the animism from which materialism had sought to liberate knowledge (36–7). A knowledge resulting from the gradual separation of essence from existence isolates objects, which become "aloof from the turmoil of forces." This detachment, which equates with the distance from the object that sight ensures, aligns closely with the goal of abstraction as Worringer understood it. The following explanation – by Jonas – makes this alignment especially clear: "From the onrush and impact of reality, out of the insistent clamor of its proximity, the distance of appearance (*phenomenon*) is won: image, in the place of effect, can be looked at and compared, in memory retained and recalled, in imagination varied and freely composed" (31).

Thus in the years immediately preceding the First World War, empathy (of which Jonas was a later and more philosophically schooled advocate) is recruited as part of an aesthetic that subverted the rationalist separation of sight from the body in motion. Kafka's piece on the horse and its rider is especially forceful in its merger of seeing and moving. But to the extent that all things physical seem to dissipate with the horse's acceleration, Kafka's sentence approximates what Deleuze believed to be an "emancipation" of movement, that is, "pure movement extracted from bodies or moving things." With reference to Murnau's *The Last Laugh*, Deleuze characterized the newly mobilized camera as a "*general equivalent* of all the means of locomotion that it shows or that it makes use of," which in this particular film include elevator, bicycle, and revolving door. Pure movement decomposes space, dividing it into fractions and segments in a manner comparable to Cubist or "simultaneist" painting.[105] Marc took his work in this direction, attempting, in Sherwin Simmons's analysis, to "intuit and image the abstract forces at work within the materiality of the organic and inorganic."[106] Abstraction was no longer the contrary of empathy but its crowning consequence. Marc's experiments with pictorial space, in which ground became indistinguishable from signified, were consistent with the discovery by modern physics that energy and matter were variants of the same thing. His canvases grew shallow but dynamic, with crystalline forms spaced out across a horizontal grid. This "frieze format" is analogous to the "relief in time" that, for Deleuze, characterizes film. This same shift in compositional approach parallels the advent of the unchained camera as Deleuze conceives it: once mobilized, the camera "acted out" a tendency already latent in the fixed shot of "primitive" cinema.[107] This latency can be gleaned from Friedrich's paintings, which, *in their mesmerizing fixity*, disclose a potential realized by the cinema, in which the shot acts like consciousness itself.

13. René Magritte (1898–1967), *Not to Be Reproduced* (*La reproduction interdite*) (1937).

Oil on canvas, 81.3 cm × 65 cm.
Museum Boijmans Van Beuningen, Rotterdam
Banque d'Images, ADAGP/Art Resource, NY

Chapter Two

Under the Sign of Insomnia

In 1937 the Belgian Surrealist René Magritte produced a canvas titled *La reproduction interdite* (figure 13). Featured is a young man, his back to the viewer, standing before a large mirror. The mirror's gilded frame rests upon a stone ledge, on which a French copy of Edgar Allen Poe's *Gordon Pym* is clearly displayed. True to the pictorial irony typical of Magritte's work, the figure does not behold his face but rather sees himself as the viewer sees him: from behind. The irony does not end there, however, for the reflection appears to be facing the wall presumably at the figure's back – and thus into a space emptied of himself and of any viewing subject.

Magritte's composition is provocative in its exposure of the means, inherited from the Renaissance, that painters used to create the illusion of spatial depth. Even as modern artists increasingly embraced a two-dimensional interpretation of visual experience, photography and eventually the cinema committed anew to monocular perspective, which, as Metz puts it, "inscribes an empty emplacement for the spectator-subject, an all-powerful position which is that of God himself." *La reproduction interdite* suggests itself to discussions of the cinematic screen, which Metz characterizes as a "strange mirror" – one that "returns [to] us everything but ourselves, because we are wholly outside of it." Indeed, Surrealist art shares in what Metz understands to be the dual character of film, which exhibits an "unaccustomed perceptual wealth" even while being "stamped with unreality to an unusual degree." The objects that appear on the screen do not exist in actual space, though they did so when the camera captured their image. They have become phantoms, "*replica[s]* in a new kind of mirror," their reflections "delegated," as it were, to the spectator. Identifying with the camera through the projector (its surrogate), the spectator is ubiquitous, all-present in the scene from which he is visually absent. As befits this ubiquity, the spectator is undeterred by sudden shifts in the position of the camera. And as with lucid dreams, the filmgoer is doubly aware – first, that he is perceiving something imaginary, and second, that it is *he* who is perceiving it. Magritte's painting, in probing the space behind the figure before the mirror and finding it vacant, does what the cinema achieves through cutting: it effaces the apparatus, which, following Metz, "the spectator has behind him, *at the back of his head.*"[1]

A prototype of the subject who identifies with himself in the act of seeing is found in Friedrich's *Wanderer above the Sea of Mists* (figure 14). A solitary figure, positioned squarely within the frame, is seen from behind. His dark shape, along with the sandstone mass supporting him, partly occludes the misty landscape, which, verging on the immaterial, is no less a foil for self-reflection than the mirror in Magritte's painting. *La reproduction interdite* gives literal expression to the dual reflexivity already implicit in Friedrich's composition, which positions the viewer along a severe axis that extends toward the vanishing point, which the wanderer's torso conceals, but on which the diagonals on either side of him converge.[2] This disciplined bi-symmetry runs counter to the advance of post-Renaissance practice as detailed by Norman Bryson. Bryson proposes Johannes Vermeer's *View of Delft* (ca 1660) as a culmination of the shift that had gradually displaced the viewer away from the centric ray, casting him as an "unexpected presence" instead of a fixed subject around whose "act of inspection" all the components of the scene gather.[3] Against this development, which enabled ever more realistic, de-idealized approaches to depicting the world, Friedrich's painting amounts to a regression. It is regressive in the same way that dreams, in Freud's understanding, restore the lost perfection of childhood by enacting the hallucinatory fusion of desire and pleasure.[4] The painting is dream-like, surreal in its manner of brightly outlining the nearly opaque wanderer and his rocky base against the cloud-filled vista, which shimmers before him like a screen.

Friedrich's paintings aren't merely fascinating. They are fascination itself. They suspend the viewer in a state of arrest that is often projected by human figures who, like the wanderer, are centred and seen from behind, motionless before land or sea. They are spellbound, their immobility akin to that of the dreamer as well as the moviegoer.[5] The god-like omnipotence that Metz ascribes to the "spectator-subject" is proper to an early stage of development in which the child does not distinguish between a wish and its gratification. The empiricism on which Friedrich turns his back coincides with the disillusionment that dreams send into remission. Realism is disappointment's synonym. "The fiction film," Metz asserts, "consoles us for things we cannot do."[6] Certain techniques

14. Caspar David Friedrich (1774–1840), *The Wanderer above the Sea of Mists* (1818).

Oil on canvas, 94.8 × 74.8 cm.
bpk Bildagentur/Kunsthalle Hamburg
Photo: Elke Walford /Art Resource, NY

of filmmaking – the "lap-dissolve," for example – emulate the mechanisms of the dream-work (condensation, displacement), forging equivalences between objects, recuperating in each individual operation a momentary union of wish and fulfilment. In affirming that, in film, these equivalences are directly *figured forth*, that is, "without indicating 'like,' 'such as,' or 'at the same moment,'" Metz in effect describes the Romantic emancipation of imagery from discourse. One may speak of an "image-space" (*Bildraum*), which incorporates the subject, and in which metaphors, absolved of their rhetorical duty, acquire, to cite Koschorke, "a purely medial, lyrical presence."[7]

Heinrich von Ofterdingen, the novel-fragment written by Novalis in 1800 and published in 1802, a year after the author's early death, not only presents the dream as an absolute *Bildraum* in which psyche and landscape are one, but also exploits the "medial" potential of dreams in ways that evoke parallels with the cinema, which were theorized over a century later. Set during the Middle Ages, the episodic narrative follows the youthful Heinrich as he and his mother, in the company of travelling merchants, venture southward from their home in Thuringia. His desire to see new and strange lands is stimulated by a dream, in which a mysterious blue flower appears to him. The flower flashes repeatedly before his mind's eye as he stands poised to enter new regions. The novel's figural richness complements its objective impoverishment. Heinrich is always at a threshold, where metaphors proliferate. Here, on the morning of his departure, and from a height that is less topographical than spiritual,[8] he regards the landscape in front of him – a tableau defined by colours, real or imagined, rather than by tangible, determinate features: "He saw himself [*sah sich*] on the threshold of the distance [*Ferne*] into which he had often peered in vain from the nearby mountains, and which his mind had painted with unusual colours [*und die er sich mit sonderbaren Farben ausgemalt hatte*]. He was on the verge of immersing himself in its flood of blue."[9] To a striking degree, Heinrich resembles not only the wanderer in Friedrich's painting but also the hyper-perceptive spectator proposed by Metz – a transcendental subject whose presence "is the condition of the possibility of the perceived."[10] This passage introduces painting as a metaphor for Heinrich's imagination, of which the world that lies ahead of him is a *projection*. Distance is not a spatial quality but one that inheres in things and lends them an aura of unapproachability.[11] The famed flower's blue colour is distance *per se*. Heinrich's longing for immersion repeats the experience of the elaborate dream that precedes his journey.

The novel opens on the youthful Heinrich, lying awake in bed, his mind racing in the wake of tales told earlier the same evening by a visitor of unknown provenance. He eventually falls asleep and dreams a lifetime's worth of dreams – of travels, adventures, battles, capture, love and bereavement, death and rebirth. As dawn breaks beyond his window he grows calm, the imagery in his head clearer and less furtive. He finds himself alone in a forest, where he discovers a deep ravine angling up a mountainside. An opening in the rock leads him along a narrow passageway to a vaulted chamber, its ceiling covered in a light reflected from a basin in which he feels the urge to bathe:

> He felt as if the red sunset were swirling around him; a heavenly sensation poured over his inner being; within him countless thoughts yearned to combine; new, never-seen images arose, flowing into each other and taking visible shape in his presence; and every wave of the sweet element pressed up against him like a soft breast. The bath seemed to him a solution of tantalizing maidens, which took bodily form at the youth's touch [*die an dem Jünglinge sich augenblicklich verkörperten*].[12]

"Intoxicated with rapture and yet conscious of every impression [*und doch jedes Eindrucks bewusst*]," Heinrich swims along the radiant stream that flows from the basin into the rock. Still dreaming, he slips into a slumber, in which he dreams of various experiences before awakening (within his dream) to a different light, "a different inspiration" (*eine andere Erleuchtung*). He finds himself in a meadow beside a spring, which flows upward into the air and dissipates. Mountains with blue veins are visible in the distance; the light is at once bright and soft, the sky limpid, and blue to the point of being black (*schwarzblau*). Beside the pool, amid a host of colourful blooms, stands a single flower of light blue, to which he feels powerfully drawn, and which he contemplates for a good while:

> Finally he was about to approach it when all at once it began to move and change. The leaves glistened and rubbed up against the swelling shaft, the blossom leaned toward him, and the petals formed a blue collar in which a tender face hovered. His sweet astonishment grew at the strange transformation [*Verwandlung*], when suddenly he awoke to his mother's voice and found himself in the room he shared with his parents, which was already awash in golden light.[13]

Heinrich's dream reaches its climax in a transformation for which the lap-dissolve would be the cinematic counterpart: the face of the flower metamorphoses into that of his mother, whose embrace the waking youth blissfully and wordlessly returns. This superimposition of images is commensurate with the mechanism – both cinematic and oneiric – that serves to "abolish the duality of objects" and restore "the short and magical circuits the impatient wish requires."[14] These words, with which Metz summarizes Freud's "primary process," aptly describe Novalis's novel, for Heinrich's journey is an extended "magical circuit," a sequence of substitutions inaugurated by the association of the flower with his mother.[15]

An image-space *par excellence*, the cavern of Heinrich's dream, where thoughts become visually manifest, is a womb in which the idea of the cinema gestates. With its dazzling beams, ignited gold, showering sparks, columns of water, and light both projected and reflected, the subterranean vault looks forward to those attractions alongside which the earliest motion pictures were shown, and which the cinema has almost habitually incorporated as a way of figuring its own prehistory.[16] Likewise, the image of a bath "undulating and trembling with endless colours," or of a fluid that covered the cavern walls and "threw off a faint bluish light" (*ein mattes, bläuliches Licht von sich warf*), is suggestive of certain medial experiments that would translate Heinrich's dream into artistic curiosities. Friedrich, as part of a project planned with the Russian poet Wassilij Shukowski, undertook a series of drawings in chalk on transparent paper (1826–7). These were intended to be displayed by moonlight, to musical accompaniment, and backlit by a candle placed behind a glass bowl filled with water or wine.[17] Friedrich in fact produced a number of transparent paintings where, in the case of the one surviving example, moving the lamp from front to back transforms a placid sunrise into a fiery sunset.[18] These "technologies" may well have been inspired in part by the recent arrival of Louis Daguerre's diorama, though it must be said that Friedrich's canvases had long since come to resemble scrims permeable to light – screens that mark the boundary between the visible and the invisible.[19] In his early oil *Fog* (1807), for example, a sailing vessel at anchor is almost indiscernible in the heavy mist, which fills most of the small painting and lends the whole a feeling of evanescence.[20]

A similar instance of diaphanousness occurs in Percy Shelley's "The Triumph of Life" (1822), in which the speaker describes his "waking dream" as a "strange trance" that casts a shadow "so transparent that the scene came through / As clear as when a veil of light is drawn / O'er evening hills."[21] One reader has characterized the poem as "vitally cinematic," suggesting that it "predicts a history fascinated by the production of images that body forth life."[22] Shelley's enchanted subject takes in the sun as it erupts, "Swift as a spirit hastening to its task": "before me fled / The night; behind me rose the day; the Deep / was at my feet, and Heaven above my head." These lines are conspicuous in their close replication of words spoken by Goethe's Faust as he beholds not the rising of the sun but, with a corresponding reversal, its setting:

> Doch scheint die Göttin endlich wegzusinken;
> Allein der neue Trieb erwacht,
> Ich eile fort, ihr ew'ges Licht zu trinken,
> Vor mir den Tag und hinter mir die Nacht,
> Den Himmel über mir und unter mir die Wellen.[23]
>
> Yet the goddess seems finally to sink away;
> But within me a new drive stirs,
> I make haste to drink her eternal light,
> The day at my front, behind me night,
> The heavens above me and the waves below.[24]

The "view from the summit" (*Gipfelblick*), which Faust's placement might seem to exemplify, represented a certain *embourgeoisement* of sight – an emancipation from the strictures of Baroque spectacle, which guided the eye toward a single, visually compelling and overwhelming object. The growing popularity of panoramas, which centred the viewer on a platform from which to look in *all* directions, and which at times simulated the kind of dramatic landscape evoked by Goethe, Shelley, or even Novalis, was part of a modern mobilization of the viewing subject.[25]

What stands out in the lines just cited, however, and certainly in Friedrich's paintings, is the emphasis on the simplified axis that runs from back to front, from "behind" to "before." To be sure, these various subjects are mobile insofar as their particular vantage points had to be arrived *at*. In this vein, Novalis's dreaming poet-hero must tax himself physically before entering the tunnel that leads into the mountain's interior: "He felt as if he were walking alone in a dark wood. Daylight glinted infrequently through the green mesh. Before long he came upon a rocky gorge [*Felsenschlucht*], which inclined sharply upward. He had to clamber over moss-covered boulders, which some ancient river had swept down from above."[26] The interior vault, which is the nucleus of Heinrich's dream-experience, in fact bears some structural resemblance to a built panorama. But more importantly, it exploits the analogy of cavern to womb along with the corresponding orientation toward the one opening that admits light. Hans Blumenberg speculated that when the earliest savannah-dwellers took shelter in caves, their eyes no longer needed to roam in every direction but were instead concentrated on the entrance, the sole source of both daylight and danger. The cave afforded a security not previously known, one of the benefits of which was deep sleep. The ability to sleep without vigilance was in turn the condition of dreaming – and thus of a creativity not derived from the physical senses.[27] As "guardians of sleep" (to use Freud's expression), dreams revive the experience of cave and womb alike. A tight union of cavern, womb, and dream is forged in the opening pages of Novalis's novel, in which Heinrich appears to dream his own birth.

The lines from Goethe's *Faust* previously cited hint nonetheless at the paradox that to bear oneself is to be unborn. The desire to be free of the fetters of natural childbirth aligns with the ambition of creating life artificially, which is ultimately also the ambition of those who make films. James Whale's 1931 adaptation of Mary Shelley's *Frankenstein, or The Modern Prometheus* illustrates the cinema's habit of projecting its own technical challenges as something more occult and archaic, indeed, Promethean. Faust's own Promethean desire, which is that of being free of all creatural constraints, expresses itself in the exultant vision of a sun that never sets. His wish for transcendence is satisfied through hallucinations fostered by the demon Mephistopheles, who claims to be "a part of the darkness that gave birth to light" (*Ein Teil der Finsternis, die sich das Licht gebar*).[28] With reference to this specific line, Starobinski comments on the broad import of Mephisto's self-conception for post-Enlightenment thought:

> Here, we see not only a return to darkness but darkness itself proclaimed as a universal source: Light is a secondary fount, and the struggle between the two extremes produces the beauty of the world. In this cosmic confrontation, man is not merely the stake or the witness of an event outside himself. He is the field in which the encounter takes place; but he is also the medium through which a transcendence occurs.[29]

Yet this may be the bill of goods with which Mephisto tempts Faust, for Mephisto – like Lucifer a "bringer of light" – leads Faust through a medley of imaginary realms and phantasmagoric scenes that can be looked at but not entered into. He is a master purveyor of illusion, the greatest of which is the disembodied transcendence for which Faust yearns. The godlikeness to which Faust repeatedly lays claim can only be realized virtually, in a spectacle in which the world at hand is replaced by a projected one, or ironically, as with the aborted suicide that would have sent his own birth into remission. The whole of Goethe's Faust-drama, as Helmut Schneider has carefully worked out, can be read as an extended play on the common German turn of phrase meaning "to be born" – "to glimpse the light of the world" (*das Licht der*

Welt erblicken).[30] The disillusionment compressed into the famous sigh (*Ach!*) at the beginning of Faust's initial monologue feeds the impulse to flee his gloomy chamber, where even the sweet light of heaven shows but dimly through the stained glass – a fantasy of aesthetic rebirth that would negate the self-evident existence that is the fruit of natural procreation. The "beautiful images" (*schöne Bilder*)[31] that Mephisto brings forth compensate for that existence and achieve what, again following Metz, films and (by implication) dreams accomplish: they console us for things we cannot do.

Mephisto's aesthetic inventions, then, are "wish-images" (*Wunschbilder*). When during their first encounter he contrives to deflate the overweening Faust, he calls upon spirits to lull his host to sleep with a sung vision of a Mediterranean landscape – a world of gentle sunshine, ripening grapes, and foaming wine. It is a "landscape of predilection" such as the one Roland Barthes finds in an old photograph of a sun-drenched scene in Spain, about which he proclaims: "it is quite simply *there* that I should like to live." "This desire," he continues, "affects me at a depth and according to roots which I do not know."[32] Like the dream, this inviting scene recalls for Barthes the vanished perfection of childhood, awakening in him the Mother, "and never the disturbing Mother." As such, it is devoid of the very *punctum* that otherwise invests the photograph with danger.[33] By characterizing the image as both "docile" and "heimlich," Barthes recalls the argument, made by Odo Marquard, that psychoanalysis was an outgrowth of a strain within nineteenth-century aesthetics, the overriding aim of which was to establish the "safe presence of nature."[34] Landscape is nature seen from a distance and as a whole. It is, following an argument set forth by Joachim Ritter in a key essay from 1962, "the fruit and creation of the theoretical mind," with *theoria* understood in its true sense of "visual contemplation" (*anschauende Betrachtung*).[35] In much the same vein, Richard Alewyn addresses the Romantic conjunction of fear (*Angst*) and desire (*Lust*), and thus the creative ambivalence of which Barthes manages to purify that one photograph ("never the disturbing Mother"). The horror film, Alewyn speculates, is a descendent of the Gothic novel, itself an attempt to bind a residual human capacity for fear whose real, existential objects reason had rendered benign.[36]

Faust summons the Earth Spirit only to cower before the frightful face that appears to him in a red flame. Mephisto, who slips into Faust's study in the guise of a poodle, assumes human shape after taking the intermediary form of a fiery-eyed hippopotamus. In these and similar such instances of the supernatural, of which there are many, Faust describes what he sees, thereby obviating the need for the audience to see it. The didaskalia simply have Mephisto emerging from a mist. In any event, the *Faust*-drama, the actual production of which Goethe did not envision, presents vast challenges to anyone attempting to stage it.[37] When magician-turned-filmmaker Georges Méliès made a handful of films based on the Faust legend, he addressed the technico-magical requirements of the material using a combination of photographic tricks, which he helped pioneer, as well as scenic devices typical of the Early Modern popular theatre.[38] In his *The Damnation of Faust* (1903), which was inspired by Charles Gounod's opera of 1859, a horned Mephisto leads the anxious hero into an infernal grotto, whose interior maw forms a proscenium framing a variety of scenes, including nymphs suspended in a watery cascade and demons prancing amid flames and smoke. The set is reminiscent of the fabulous "Venus Grotto," which Ludwig II of Bavaria commissioned in 1876 to re-create the setting of the first act of Richard Wagner's *Tannhäuser.* From a certain standpoint, Goethe's *Faust*, the first version of which was published in 1790, cries out for cinematic treatment. The same can be said of *Heinrich von Ofterdingen*, a very different example of a similar thing. Visual media such as the magic lantern, the diorama, the panorama, phantasmagoria, or even the novel electronic means by which the Venus Grotto could be bathed in a multitude of changing colours, suggest a genealogy of the cinema – pieces of the history ostensibly predicted by Shelley's *Triumph of Life*, which is fascinated with images and their potential for animation.[39]

Interesting as it may be, the prehistory of cinematic technology is not the object of the present inquiry. The more than five hundred curiosities on film that Méliès produced are less essentially cinematic than Friedrich's motionless compositions in oil. The dance revues and other variety routines that Méliès regularly incorporated into his films were comparable to those which, according to Siegfried Kracauer, the great movie palaces of Berlin used as an anodyne to the cinema, meant to attenuate the power of the images on the screen. Presented on stage before and between film showings as a way of anchoring the audience at the visual periphery, these diversions were meant to keep the audience from "sinking into the abyss" (*damit es nicht ins Bodenlose versinke*).[40] Kracauer's phrasing echoes a general ambivalence toward the screen and the illusory depth that opens up behind it. It also reaches back into a tradition of post-Enlightenment aesthetics that had assigned to art the purpose of keeping nature, in its potential for menace, at bay. To seek nature – to revel in its vital substance – was to hazard oblivion. Thus while Faust, in a state of nocturnal reverie, yearns to bathe in the dew of moonlight, he recoils in terror at the sight of the *Erdgeist*. A dark and irrational conception of nature was in the ascendant. As a consequence, art came to be understood as a kind of protective magic that served to buffer nature's overwhelming power. The aesthetic genius, following Marquard, "paints the devil on the wall in order that he not appear" (*malt den Teufel an die Wand, damit er nicht komme*).[41]

The implied link between demonic and natural forces again recalls Freud, who sought the ancestry of individual neuroses in the apotropaic practices of traditional peoples. The obsessional fear of touching, for example, and the corresponding mania for washing, replicate societal prohibitions, such as those surrounding kings or despots, whose very potency was a contagion to be guarded against. Rulers (*Herrscher*), Freud wrote, were "vehicles of the mysterious and dangerous magical power which is transmitted by contact like an electric charge and which brings death and ruin to anyone who is not protected by a similar charge."[42] There is a hint in this formulation that the sovereign's destructive power would live on in nature, itself a reservoir of ruinous voltage. Sublime nature and absolute monarch are sources of a kindred ambivalence, entities to be feared but also sought out for their powers of healing and renewal. Freud offered examples of the "healing power of the royal touch," much as Friedrich Schelling, a good century earlier, had extolled nature for its *Heilkraft* – its singular capacity to make whole.[43] Freud would cite Schelling's definition of the Uncanny as a feeling that arises when something that should have remained hidden comes into the light.[44] Freud named the Uncanny as a mode of aesthetic experience of unique interest to psychoanalysis. For Schelling, aesthetics had become philosophy's defining pursuit, as acts of artistic expression alone made it possible to "reflect [on] the Unconscious" (*das Unbewusste zu reflektieren*). This Unconscious was none other than nature itself, which resided within the subject but evaded the subject's perceptual grasp. Schelling thus ascribed to the aesthetic imagination the same function that Freud assigned to dreams – that of placing the Unconscious before consciousness as a visible object.

In representational terms, and specifically with regard to depictions of those natural phenomena proper to the Sublime, such projection effects the replacement of actual threats with imagined ones. The difference is not total, however, for the objects that art places before the subject exert a fascination owing precisely to the trace of danger they retain. The ambiguity of these same objects generates the oxymora that pervade Romantic writing, like "fond woe" or "awful majesty." The latter example, taken from *Frankenstein*, captures the experience of a sudden thunderstorm in terms that vibrate with the ambivalence inspired by sovereign power.[45] Barthes's chosen landscape by comparison, however funereal its atmosphere, is unambiguous. It is inviting but not enticing. The sedate Andalusian scene (photographed by Charles Clifford around 1855) conforms to pictorial conventions of mid-nineteenth-century Europe, a time when painters of landscape were mastering effects of light, which, immanently pleasing to their public, had the capacity to console. Willows at river's edge in the lingering glow of evening, for example, might evoke the serenity of a day's toil nearing an end.[46]

How different the inexorably liminal twilight found in so many of Friedrich's paintings and in the Romantic landscape generally! Eichendorff's poem "Zwielicht" ("Twilight") ponders the inner uncertainty that grows with the onset of darkness while inquiring, more literally, as to the meaning of a word that couples fear and suspicion with the colourless, equivocal light of dusk: *Was will dieses Grau'n bedeuten?* – "What is this *Grauen* supposed to mean?"[47] These landscapes, conveyed through paint or in verse, do not offer quiet refuge. They are not places of dwelling but of exile and exposure. If they beckon, they do so ominously. Eichendorff's poem concludes by warning the addressee to guard against sleep: "Be wary, stay awake and chipper!" (*Hüte dich, bleib' wach und munter!*). Friedrich interpellates a viewer who, held squarely in place before a prospect that is manifestly *apart*, is without defences. The viewer is captivated, that is, *held captive* by a fascination that requires of him that he remain still. In this way, the viewer of paintings like *The Wanderer above the Sea of Mists* has something in common with the cinematic spectator, of whom a silent immobility is also required. Metz comments on those moviegoers who, by contrast, rise from their seats, gesticulate, shout encouragement to the hero or threaten the villain. This kind of "affective participation," not unusual in certain cultures or among children, is intrinsically ambivalent. On the one hand, it is a way of committing to the fiction; but once initiated, it actually dissipates the confusion between the on-screen illusion and reality.

These exuberant displays, Metz suggests, are analogous to somnambulism – to motor activity released during sleep. The comparison, which Metz entertains only briefly, suggests itself to *The Cabinet of Dr Caligari*, in which somnambulism not only figures explicitly but also is introduced within the framework of a fairground attraction, a setting comparable to those popular, "unsophisticated" venues in which viewers are prone to addressing themselves verbally and physically to the on-screen action. This behaviour is closely akin to that of spectators at popular dramatic performances, which make no effort to disavow the co-presence of audience and actors. And much as the European theatre after Diderot began to feign unawareness of being watched, the cinema, in its truer, more metropolitan guise, sheds all exhibitionism. The film "*lets* itself be seen without *presenting* itself to be seen."[48]

The uncertainty surrounding the sleepwalker is a variety of the Uncanny. In a theorem cited by Freud in his essay of 1919, Ernst Jentsch attributes the sensation of uncanniness to "doubt as to whether an apparently animate object really is alive and, conversely, whether a lifeless object might not perhaps be animate."[49] This confusion, which marks the experience of the uncanny as a fundamentally aesthetic one, is of a piece with the ambiguity exploited by the Romantics to conjure, say, the disquieting effects of nightfall or sudden changes in the air. Beyond this, the inverted parallelism of Jentsch's formulation lines up with the pronounced *mise en abyme* of Weimar cinema, which is also a structural cognate of Romantic irony. The dream at the beginning of *Ofterdingen*, for example, is revealed to be internal to a mysterious manuscript that Heinrich later discovers in a cave, which itself parallels the inner, subterranean core of his initial, ecstatic vision. Likewise, the final twist of *Caligari* envelops the main fable within a narrative shell, enfolding the twisted style of the former into the naturalism of the latter. The film does not resolve this difference in the doctor's favour ("At last I understand his delusion"), instead gesturing toward the "indissoluble antagonism" in terms of which Friedrich Schlegel explained irony, understood as an endless vacillation between belief and disbelief, between seriousness and jest.[50] And much as Schlegel posits a naïf as an imaginary foil for readers not deluded by the artifice, so Metz proposes a credulous, un-ironic spectator, whose imagined presence in the theatre enables the filmgoer to hover between belief and disavowal without succumbing to the illusion.[51] In this respect, Metz parallels not only Schlegel but also Jentsch (and Freud), yet his ultimate push for disambiguation – for divesting the ostensibly mechanical of every appearance of life – puts him in league with the tradition of thought that would cast life itself as inanimate.

Caligari may be said to extract the essence of cinema from the popular theatrical spectacle and to replace the exhibitionism of the latter with the experience of an immobilized viewer, isolated before an imaginary tableau. The main narrative, framed as the recollection of a man who at film's end is revealed to be mad, begins with Caligari's arrival.[52] The mysterious travelling showman appears in the town of Holstenwall with an "exhibit" – a *Schau-Objekt* – for display at the local fair. The oddity in question is a young man, Cesare, who has been asleep for twenty-three years and who "knows all secrets" – "knows the past and sees the future." "Right before your eyes," Caligari promises the assembled crowd, "Cesare will awaken from his death-like trance." The

15. *The Cabinet of Dr Caligari* (1920), dir. Robert Wiene.

performance, held in a tent on a makeshift stage, has all the hallmarks of popular theatre. A curtain is drawn aside to reveal a coffin-shaped box standing on end, which Caligari proceeds to open with portentous gravity. He rouses Cesare from his long sleep and, in a manner that anticipates Henry Frankenstein of Whale's film, coaxes the dazed figure toward the audience, whose members are prompted to ask questions of him. Alan, a high-strung student who has come to the fair with Francis, his best friend, and Jane, the woman they both love, approaches the stage and asks apprehensively how long he has to live. "Until the break of dawn" (*bis zum Morgengrauen*) – Cesare's answer names the veiled, uncertain light of early morning, leaving the fragile Alan panting with anxiety.[53] Alan meets his fate in the dead of night, however, stabbed by a fiend visible only as a sharp silhouette looming on the wall above his victim's bed (figure 15).

The scene in which Alan meets his death at the hands of a dark shadow has been cited with some considerable frequency in the century following the release of *Caligari*. The "shower scene" in Alfred Hitchcock's *Psycho* (1960), an example so prominent as to be an icon in its own right, attests to the abiding authority of its Expressionist precursor.[54] Beyond this, it underscores the primality of that original scene.

Even *Frankenstein* makes an effort to undo what *Caligari* has done. In a theatrical prelude to the former, the actor Edward Van Sloan, who plays Dr Waldman in the film, steps from behind a curtain and, facing the audience directly, delivers a "friendly warning" on behalf of the film's producer, Carl Laemmle. Offering a preview of the shock that awaits them, the actor suggests that the spectators might not wish to "subject [their] nerves to such a strain." In its overt theatricality, the prologue to *Frankenstein* repeats that of the fairground "cabinet" within which Dr Caligari, on stage before a standing throng, brings his exhibit to life. But whereas Caligari entices, Van Sloan, in the role of chorus, activates the defences of those watching. Addressing himself as to a collective, he disinterpellates the viewer. The unfortunate Alan, by contrast, is isolated – singled out for a death that is decidedly his, decidedly filmic. Asleep in bed, his resistances relaxed, he stirs from his own nightmare only to succumb to it fully.

It is a moment in which cinematic trickery and personal treachery coincide. The main story of *Caligari* is recounted by Francis, whose version of events offers clues indicating that *he* may in fact have a share in Alan's death. In Caligari's tent, for example, he appears to be secretly weighing the opportunity to eliminate his rival under cover of Cesare's dire forecast.[55] He has tried to dissuade Alan from questioning the clairvoyant, whose unsettling response may echo the association, found in Eichendorff's poem, of a friend's duplicity with the sinister ambiguity of twilight: "If you have a friend nearby, / Do not trust him at this hour" (*Hast du einen Freund hienieden, / Trau ihm nicht zu dieser Stunde*). Defying in effect the poem's closing exhortation to stay awake (*bleib' wach und munter!*), Alan dies of the sleep that Cesare personifies. The "death-like trance" from which Caligari rouses Cesare is cousin to the deep sleep whose very possibility Blumenberg attributes to the reduced need for vigilance.[56]

To drop one's guard vis-à-vis external threats, however, is to experience a susceptibility more profound – a vulnerability to disturbances emerging from within. Projection, following Freud, results from the tendency to treat endopsychic stimuli as if they originated outside of the mental apparatus.[57] Dreams conform to a more general mechanism that, by recasting thought processes as sensory perceptions, acts *as if* to confirm the chief tenet of classical empiricism, namely "that all knowledge stems from external perception." Thoughts come to be "actually perceived – as if from without – and are therefore held to be real."[58] Somnambulism, though not well-understood, is related to the "reality testing" whereby the subject distinguishes between external stimuli, which can be influenced by motor activity, and internal ones, which cannot.[59] The legend of early moviegoers fleeing in terror before the filmed image of an approaching train installs such behaviour at cinema's very advent.

Stellan Rye's *The Student of Prague* (1913) represents an advent of its own. Widely considered to be Germany's first "art film," it culminates in a failed attempt at disambiguation.[60] The crisis arises when student and master swordsman Balduin, deceived into selling his physical reflection to a diabolical stranger, stands riveted in disbelief as his own specular image steps out of a full-length mirror and precedes its new master out of the room. The trick, which exposes the space behind the mirror as real, is reminiscent of the generally simple illusions produced by Méliès, though his films strove for the contrary effect, accentuating the surface while diminishing the appearance of actual depth.[61] The surface reassures. But the mirror before which Balduin is otherwise used to practising his expert swordsmanship is a source of disquiet. Both shallow and deep, it doubles for the cinematic screen, which, to revisit Metz's formulation, is a "strange mirror" – one that "returns [to] us everything but ourselves, because we are wholly outside of it."

Balduin dies after firing a pistol at his dispossessed reflection, which at once passes and fails the reality test. The cinema coalesces around such crises of specularity and around an incipient viewer whose vigilance translates not into action but into suspended animation – a state of breathless fascination before a scene that wavers between light and shadow, between life and death. And much as Balduin is brought to a halt before a vacant mirror, so the viewer of Friedrich's paintings is held in place, motionless before a scene whose contraction of perspective conflates surface and depth.

In what is perhaps the fullest and most determined account of German cinema during and after the Weimar period, Thomas Elsaesser observes a contraction of perspective in the films themselves, and this specifically regarding F.W. Murnau's signature juxtaposition of expansive outdoor settings and narrow (psychological) interiors: "Murnau … used two systems (deep-focus sets, and flat, foreshortened spaces) as contrasting alternatives within the same film (*Phantom, The Last Laugh, Faust*), thereby extending the emotional space towards the screen: as suddenly as the depth of a frame opened up, it could, in the very next shot, become suffocatingly close and ominously encroach upon the spectator."[62] Elsaesser follows Janet Bergstrom, who discerns in Murnau a "veiled gaze of contemplation"[63] – an idea that leads Elsaesser to recall and restrict Lotte Eisner's claim that Murnau was influenced by Romanticism and by Friedrich most particularly.[64] In a subchapter whose heading, "Absorption and Theatricality," echoes the title of an important book by art-historian Michael Fried,[65] Elsaesser argues that Murnau "counteract[ed] theatricality by giving the cinema its own distinctive space." This entailed the creation of "a world inhabitable by a very special gaze that can oscillate between the illusionist depth of old stereoscopic photographs, and the pictorial flatness of modernism at its most sophisticatedly 'primitive.'" Elsaesser goes on to insist that even Murnau, the most painterly of German directors, proposed a "visuality" that differed from that of the fine arts – from "the contemplative gaze appropriate to a museum or gallery." He elaborates: "Created by the always changing distribution of light and mass, [Murnau's films] make the viewer vertiginously lose balance, disoriented by the depths modulating into pure surface, and surface undulating into unexpected depth."

This is a fine description, but it is also applicable to the same works of art whose hold over the cinema Murnau was supposedly weakening. The vertiginous destabilization of the viewing subject was, after all, a Romantic ideal. Beyond this, the oscillation between "illusionist depth" and "pictorial flatness" is discernable in Friedrich's works and places them along a trajectory connecting them with modernist painting, in which the assertion of the flat surface was more overt, more deliberate. Discussions of the relationship between the cinema and the fine arts are often hobbled by Benjamin's criticism of the institution of art and its imposition of a devotional attitude on the part of the museumgoer. This meditative stance – the viewer "gathered" before the quasi-sacred work of art – aligns with the absorption theorized by Fried. "A man who concentrates before a work of art," Benjamin wrote, "is absorbed by it."[66] For Fried, however, absorption is a value that arose with Diderot and accords more with a new-found autonomy than with a lingering submissiveness. Elsaesser, who believes that Murnau's filmmaking parted company with both the fine arts and the theatre, sounds a vaguely Adornian note in suggesting that Murnau's innovations exploited, to borrow a phrase from *Philosophy of New Music*, "tendencies of the material":[67] "Murnau's films are also about the possibilities of cinema, trying to discover what forms emerge when inherent qualities of the medium ... are explored as design features of 'other worlds.'"[68]

Adorno invoked Benjamin as part of his characterization of Eichendorff, whose "modernity" was only now (in 1957) beginning to be felt, whose "uncontained Romanticism" at times verges on the "turbulently expressionistic," and in whose poetry an objectified nature is roused to life as language alienated from its meaning.[69] Words "light up" when the poet, whose power is that of *not* resisting the "descending flow of language," brings them into new constellations and associational fields.

This dialectic is behind the "profound paradox": a verse in which the distant blare, in the hush of night, of the mailcoachman's bugle is not *sound* but the "aura of silence." Eichendorff's subject, an "ego that has divested itself of itself," dissolves into the "rustling" or "murmuring" (*Rauschen*) of forests and springs that, destined to die away (*verrauschen*), epitomizes a language finally bereft of meaning but which, in that very meaninglessness, restores the resemblance of things to themselves.[70] In stating that Eichendorff's greatness is to be sought in his enactment of the subject's extinction, Adorno establishes the poet's work as a foil for the bourgeois cult of self-preservation, which has rendered the modern individual as deaf to this poetry as Odysseus's oarsmen to the Sirens.

The idea here is not to enlist Adorno in a discussion of the cinema but to suggest that the dialectic whereby Adorno liberates Eichendorff from the affirmative and endearing triteness of his poetic imagery has a bearing on filmmakers like Murnau, whom Elsaesser portrays as the unsurpassed "lyrical genius" of silent film. Eisner's original proposal – that the techniques developed by Murnau and his German contemporaries "lend visible form to Romantic fancies" – risks trivializing what for the Romantics was already a matter of technique. Another glimpse at Eichendorff confirms the mediatic shift that Koschorke identifies and understands in terms of an "image-stream" (*Bildstrom*), which is emancipated from all descriptive purpose and in which fantasy becomes immersed. The example, from 1826, is titled "Der Abend" ("Evening"):

Schweigt der Menschen laute Lust:
Rauscht die Erde wie in Träumen
Wunderbar mit allen Bäumen,
Was dem Herzen kaum bewusst,
Alte Zeiten, linde Trauer,
Und es schweifen leise Schauer
Wetterleuchtend durch die Brust.[71]

[Human merriment grows still: Then, as if dreaming, the earth, in wondrous concert with the trees, murmurs things of which the heart is scarcely conscious – bygone times, faint grief – and soft shudders sweep through the breast, like lightning unheard from afar.]

Insufficient throughout, this paraphrase is weakest where it would render the adverbial *wetterleuchtend* by means of a simile, the absence of which in the original comports with Koschorke's conferral of absolute status on the Romantic image. The colon at the end of the first line punctuates a moment of motionless audition comparable to that of the paused traveller depicted by Friedrich. Lightning, silent in the distance, modifies the emergence of *leise Schauer*, which, in meaning both "soft shudders" and "gentle showers," aids the passage of affects into natural objects encountered within a landscape that is wholly psychic.[72] The poem, over the course of which syntax unclenches, stages a process similar to that identified by Metz as common to dreams and the cinema, where equivalences are *figured forth*, without the support of "like," "such as," or "at the same moment."

Obstacles to enchantment, the mechanics of grammar relinquish their grip. Eichendorff's imagery is absolved of rhetorical service much as in dreams, as Freud presents them, images are unmoored from their underlying thoughts. The formal regression enacted by both dream and film is for Eichendorff an aesthetic principle. His poem "Sehnsucht" ("Yearning," 1834), whose speaker recalls standing alone at his window, his heart inflamed by the sounds of the night, previews Karl Grune's film *The Street* (*Die Strasse*, 1923), in which a husband, bored with his domestic routine, looks out from his apartment and beholds not the drab boulevard below but the panoply of his desires envisioned as a dazzling montage of nighttime amusements (circus, fairground, and cabaret). However disparate, these examples – a late Romantic poem and a silent film from the 1920s – illustrate Koschorke's claim that the landscape is "no longer a discursive 'view from the window' [*Fensterausblick*]," as it was during the Enlightenment, "but a structured surface over which speech spreads out."[73] In the case of Grune's film, the restless husband will soon follow his own shadow out the door and into a nocturnal world of murderous deceit – a world reminiscent of the one ominously evoked in Eichendorff's "Twilight." "What is this *Grauen* supposed to mean?" The poem is not accountable to the question it poses, which presupposes its own unanswerability. As with the Romantic "image-space" generally, there is no point beyond or behind the frame from which an interpretation is authorized.[74] Koschorke's description of the Romantic landscape as a "structured surface" is germane to Friedrich, who already in the early nineteenth century began what Magritte, in the twentieth, would do in the extreme: explore the nature and workings of pictures while challenging the traditional conception of easel paintings as windows that open out onto the physical world.[75]

Paintings like *The Wanderer above the Sea of Mists*, which divide the subject into the viewer of the painting and the viewer within it, are notable in their analogy to films such as *Caligari*, *The Golem*, and *Warning Shadows*, which station their audience behind spectators within the diegesis, who in turn behold a quasi-filmic spectacle that mirrors the film enveloping them.[76] This structural parallel helps clarify Romanticism as cinema's precedent. Tom Conley, summarizing what Deleuze calls the "perception of perception," evokes "the staging of a space where no immediate center can be discerned, and where, effectively, the atmospheric qualities would stretch out before our eyes."[77] Conley's formulation describes perfectly the experience of Novalis's Heinrich, who is repeatedly positioned before a blue beyond, and who, at the outset of his journey, *sees himself* on the threshold of the far-away (*Ferne*). After arriving at his provisional destination, he looks back in the direction whence he came and, at a companion's prompting, declares: "Into yon distance our path disappears" (*In jene Ferne verliert sich unser Weg*).[78] The circuit this statement completes amounts to an asynchronous face-to-face – a chiasmic inversion consistent with the *mise en abyme* of two juxtaposed mirrors (and the vaporous indeterminacy that opens up within them). The vista that Heinrich presents is like a long shot, in which, following Conley, "[we] relive the birth of visibility itself, we get lost in space, and we refuse to ascertain any causes, effects, or other linkages between the elements floating before our eyes."[79] There is something about the *jen-* ("yon," "beyond") of Heinrich's utterance that echoes Metz's claim that, in the cinema, deixis does not fix identifiable subject positions and that, because of this "impersonality," film as such acquires the status of landscape.[80] To this may be added that a "geography of enunciation," which for Metz *is* the cinema, had already been staked out by the Romantics, whose landscapes provoke reflection on the flatness of the surface, verbal or painted, in relation to the depth of the vista conjured.

Finally, some broad parallels, the pursuit of which informs this project overall: Starobinski, regarding the cosmic struggle between darkness and light, holds that the human subject is not merely witness to an external event but the "medium" in which that struggle takes place; Freud, for whom the ego was "the projection of a surface," described a mechanism that erects an empirical faith in sense-perception as a way of masking the psychical provenance of disturbing stimuli; Elsaesser discerns in Murnau a dynamic interplay of deep focus and flattened depth, the effect of which is that of "extending emotional space toward the screen"; a comparable contraction was already explored by Friedrich, in many of whose paintings the dissolution of the heroic landscape results in the surface being brought oppressively close; painter Gerhard Richter (b. 1932), who found in Friedrich a formal structure on which to base his own abstractions, grants his distant predecessor (and fellow Dresdener) an afterlife in which his paintings shed the inarguably allegorical props found throughout his *oeuvre*: floating cathedrals, crumbling ruins, gnarled oaks, ships at anchor, crosses, graveyards, megalithic tombs, owls, as well as openings – windows, doorways, arches, gates – that indicate the threshold between this world and the next; Eichendorff's poetry, which is likewise supplied with a stock of reusable figures, divests the landscape of all materiality, transforming it, following Alewyn, into an "incorporeal figment of pure movement" (*ein körperloses Gebilde aus reiner Bewegung*).[81] All of these examples represent an involvement with the imaginary that, for Metz, the cinema summons to a heightened degree, because film, he declares, "drums up" perception only to shift it over into its own absence, this absence being "the only signifier present."

Chapter Three

Nightwatching

A brief scene in Murnau's *Nosferatu* (1922) showcases the actions of a custodian tending to a hanging streetlamp (figure 16). The uniformed figure has lowered the large housing in order to kindle its flame, in whose brightening glow he stands for a moment before returning it to a position safely above the heads of passers-by. The sudden illumination reveals the man as kindly, advanced in years, and deliberate in his work. Almost tender in his cradling of the lamp, he is a caretaker in every sense, his labour an antidote to the fear that "crouched" or "cowered" (*kauerte*) in every corner of town. An emblem of reassurance, the scene is counteracted by a shot that occurs not thirty seconds later, in which a gust of wind extinguishes a candle on a bedstand beneath an open window. Something is abroad. Sheer curtains dance fitfully in the breeze as the film's tint shifts from warm amber to a cool blue-green.

Aesthetically rich and self-contained, these two miniatures assimilate the cosmic struggle between light and darkness to the conventions of Biedermeier – the conservative, quietist style that arose in Germany and Austria in the wake of Napoleon's defeat and the Congress of Vienna (1815). Biedermeier poets and painters are known for celebrating the limited ambit of domestic life, the idyllic *Glück im Winkel* ("happiness in the nook") so explicitly jeopardized in *Nosferatu*, which is set in 1838.[1] Carl Spitzweg, the ironically affectionate portraitist of South German provincial life, produced a series of paintings depicting solitary nightwatchmen, their lamps in hand, wandering (as if condemned to wander) the narrow and gloomy streets of otherwise charming townscapes. Some of these small canvases were inspired by *The Nightwatches of Bonaventura*,[2] a novel published pseudonymously in 1804 (the year of Kant's death and Napoleon's coronation).[3] Structured as sixteen "Nightwatches," and narrated by the nightwatchman Kreuzgang, this eccentric and satirical text consists of reflections, often despairing and

16. *Nosferatu – A Symphony of Terror* (1922), dir. F.W. Murnau.

anxiety-fraught, elicited by the lives and scenes to which Kreuzgang is privy as he walks the empty streets announcing the hour. His nocturnal regimen aligns him with Murnau's Count Orlok, who sleeps soundly by day, though the odd bout of insomnia subjects Kreuzgang to the bright, prosaic sunlight of bourgeois life and to the tedious company of the "sleep walkers" (*wachen Schläfern*) who populate that domain.[4] At night, he finds comfort in the echo of his footsteps in the death-like stillness. As the first watch begins, a storm is gathering in the sky; light and darkness vie with each other in rapid alternation, and clouds, disclosing the moon momentarily before hiding it again, sweep past overhead like massive, fantastical figures (*wie wunderliche Riesenbilder vorüber*).[5]

Kreuzgang is gladdened by the occasional sight of a burning lamp, sign of rare nighttime activity akin to his own. In a dingy garret high above the street an impoverished poet, visible at one point as a shadow frozen in tragic attitude, entertains fantasies of immortality, which Kreuzgang delights in deflating with his shouted reminders of passing time. In another room a man lies on his deathbed while his young wife and children keep vigil. A "freethinker," he has refused the last rights, causing the attendant priest to evoke menacingly a Dantesque vision of the inferno beyond. The dying man, in a final stirring of life, is cast as a smouldering candle that flares up suddenly, fed by a nightwind that whistles through one's hair and rattles the rickety window-shutters like the invisible spirit of approaching death.[6] The resemblance to the second shot from *Nosferatu* described above is remarkable, and these first chapters of *The Nightwatches* comprise a study of the aesthetic and dramatic effects of light, both natural and artificial, ethereal and terrestrial. Kreuzgang likens this particular scene to Antonio da Correggio's *Holy Night* (1529–30), in whose "dual illumination" (*doppelte Beleuchtung*) earthly and heavenly rays combine to form a wondrous whole. The same light shines at once into the absolute night that awaits the dying man and into a naive past of faith and poetry (*die dichterische Frühlingswelt des Glaubens und der Poesie*). When the man finally expires, his countenance, grinning in death, is illuminated now and again by flashes of lightning (*Wetterleuchten*), which "convulsed angrily through the wan glow of the candles" (*feindlich durch den matten Schein der Kerzen zuckte*).[7]

A cinematic prescience informs these and other examples, such as when the pale glow of candlelight spreads out through an open door into the night, commingling eerily with the flashes from above while the ghostly murmur of distant mountains grows ever more audible; or when Kreuzgang catches sight of a sleepwalker (*Nachtwandler*) – the town sexton – sure-footed for being asleep, scaling the church spire while the moon appears and disappears through Gothic arches. Throughout, Kreuzgang stages these set pieces in terms of light, careful to specify its source and angle, its relative and changing intensity, its dispersal, its capacity to establish mood and isolate objects. With reference to Correggio, Michelangelo, and others, Kreuzgang summons the *chiaroscuro* that would become a mainstay of Weimar cinematography. Murnau's visual style has been attributed in large part to his time spent working with theatre director Max Reinhardt, who, to cite Eisner, had "mastered all the secrets of lighting." Reinhardt, she expounds,

> had always been fond of clothing shapes in warm light spilling from innumerable invisible sources, of rounding, melting and hollowing surfaces with velvety shadows ... The stage would become a vast expanse bustling with life. Bare wings and curtains would frame the gentle curve of a *Rundhorizont*, a horizon whose concave surface was flooded, first with moonlight, then with brilliant sunlight, then immediately plunged into darkness; stars flickered while a kind of magic lantern covered the sky with moving clouds.[8]

Treatments for which Murnau in particular is known, such as "the phosphorescent halo following the outline of a head and shading out toward the regions of darkness," were already part of Reinhardt's visual repertoire.[9] It might be added, however, that techniques similar to those outlined by Eisner had been worked out a century earlier by Louis Daguerre, whose own paintings exhibit in turn an emphasis on effects – the atmospheric play of moon- or twilight upon Gothic architecture – worked out verbally in *The Nightwatches*. This is demonstrated by his painting *The Ruins of Holyrood Chapel* (1824), and the very title of another of his canvases, *The Effect of Fog and Snow Seen through a Ruined Gothic Colonnade* (1826), not only resembles sights witnessed by Kreuzgang but even presents itself as an exercise in scenography.

The imagery of *The Nightwatches* demonstrates the Romantic revival of the tenebrism used by Baroque artists to heighten tension, deepen space, foster illusions of movement or immateriality, and thus to dramatize the cognate dichotomies of spirit and matter, life and death, and so on. The French painter Georges de La Tour (1593–1652), whose *oeuvre* is a veritable handbook on the mechanics of artificial lighting, affords a uniquely instructive example. La Tour's high-contrast renderings of biblical (and other) scenes are typically lit by a single candle or oil lamp, whose bright flame is completely or partly eclipsed by a hand, arm, or other object. The effect of this compositional tactic is that a certain feature – a forehead, a skull, the leaf of a book or a patch of skin – is accentuated by a softened light, which from the standpoint of the viewer is greater in value than that of its veiled source.[10] In his *Saint Gerome Reading* (1638), to give one example, the bearded figure is shown examining a letter by candlelight. The candle itself is all but invisible behind the page which, creased with folds, is luminous in the candle's radiance, and which reflects a warm glow onto the figure's face while casting a long shadow over the writing table in the lower foreground. La Tour's consistently idiosyncratic approach to lighting results in a quality identified by Eisner as characteristic of Reinhardt's staging, which in turn became a distinctive trait in Murnau, as described here by Elsaesser: "Murnau seemed to prefer light to come into frame from a hidden, covered, or unknown source. Alternatively, he liked to exaggerate the effects of a visible light source, such as Mephisto swinging his lantern in *Faust* or the moonlight casting its pallor on the illicit lovers in *Sunrise*."[11] Comparable moments are legion in *Nosferatu*, the very intertitles of which provide a running commentary on the interplay of light and shadow: "As soon as the sun rose, the shadows of the night withdrew from Hutter as well"; and later, "The spectral light of evening seemed to enliven the shadows of the castle once again." This interval sets the

17. *Nosferatu – A Symphony of Terror* (1922), dir. F.W. Murnau.

stage for the vampire's entrance, at the stroke of midnight, into Hutter's bedchamber. After the door swings open, Orlok advances from the corridor directly toward the camera, his rigidly wooden form interrupting shafts of light that angle down slightly from an unseen source to his right, streaking the air to his left with transparent shadow (figure 17). Hutter has at this point averted his eyes and hidden beneath his bedclothes. The bedpost visible at the lower left indicates that Hutter is not aligned with Orlok's approach. It is the *viewer* toward whom the fiend advances, stepping into the circle of light as into the beam of the projector, whose position the viewer occupies.

Certain of these same compositional elements can be observed in a key scene in Whale's *Frankenstein*, in which the newly animated creature backs through a door into the light, turning stiffly toward the camera to reveal, through an abrupt succession of axial cuts, the deadness in his eyes. An aggregate of parts culled hastily from German films of the previous decade, Whale's monster carries into the era of sound what Deleuze, with direct reference to the films of Murnau, Wegener, and Lang, identifies as the "first principle of Expressionism," namely "*the non-organic life of things*" – a principle "valid for the whole of Nature, that is, for the unconscious spirit, lost in darkness." "From this point of view," he continues, "natural substances and artificial creations, candelabras and trees, turbine and sun are no longer any different. A wall which is alive is dreadful; but utensils, furniture, houses and their roofs also lean, crowd around, lie in wait, or pounce. Shadows of houses pursue the man running along the street."[12] The sets of *Caligari* spring to mind, though Deleuze might well be describing Ludwig Meidner's ink drawing *Figure in the Street at Night* (1913), in which a solitary refugee, dwarfed by building façades heaving with life, is shown fleeing before the aggressive glare of an electric street lamp;[13] or, from the previous year, the succinct narratives that comprise Kafka's *Betrachtung*, in many of which the houses that line the urban streets (*Gassen*), breathless in their silence, are witnesses to shadowy pursuit ("Like a small ghost a child blew in from the pitch-dark corridor, where the lamp was not yet lit, and stood tiptoe on a floor board that quivered imperceptibly").[14]

When Orlok emerges from the corridor, he is isolated by a bright beam whose round shape, surrounded by a dark iris, is centred within the frame, all of which sharpens the severe and primitive symmetry of the shot. The effect of this intense light, following Deleuze, is to make the vampire "burst forth from an even more direct bottomlessness" and give him "an aura of omnipotence which goes beyond his two-dimensional form."[15] Deleuze draws a connection to the Kantian Sublime, the experience of which dazzles and annihilates our organic being and thus enables us to discover within ourselves a spirit that rids us of "*the horror of non-organic life*."[16] He would hereby divide Expressionism from Romanticism: the former, having disavowed the organicism of the latter, sustains the polarity between non-organic life, with its capacity to terrify, and the spiritual-intellectual, which is immune to that same terror. Yet it is not clear how Deleuze would preserve this distinction while arguing, as he does, for the prevalence among the Expressionists (visual artists as well as cinéastes) of a Goethean conception of light.[17] Nor is it apparent why *Nosferatu* should leave the viewer with a feeling of spiritual invincibility. In fact, the idea of a subject who submits voluntarily to the pain of self-reproach (in order to purge himself of its original cause) is suffused with the psychologism to which Deleuze pronounces himself allergic.[18]

The continuum between Romanticism and earlier Weimar cinema is a braided one, often traceable in terms common to contradictory impulses. Deleuze elaborates his understanding of Expressionist film in opposition to "lyrical abstraction," while conceding that Expressionism "can be just as abstract as lyricism." Expressionism, however, "is essentially the intensive play of light with the opaque, with darkness."

The "Expressionist face," he states, may either intensify or reflect light, participating either in the "non-organic life of things" or the "life of the mind" (these being in his view the primary and secondary poles of Expressionism). An example of the latter is Kriemhilde in Lang's *The Nibelungen* (1924), whose "unshakable reflection" forms "a halo around the face, which has become a [phosphorescent, scintillating, brilliant] being of light."[19] This likewise describes the face of the archangel at the beginning of Murnau's *Faust* (1926), whose blinding intensity is offset by the leaden countenance of Mephistopheles, who stands for death and thus for the ultimate victory of the anorganic. (When Henry Frankenstein, upon seeing his creature's hand twitch, shouts repeatedly and excitedly "It's alive!," his cries are sufficiently maniacal to accommodate the ambivalence toward the "non-organic life" of a thing he will eventually endeavour to destroy. His initial, gleeful response recalls Freud's observation that children treat their dolls as if they were living beings, or Benjamin's remark that children mimic not only shopkeepers and teachers but also, just as readily, windmills and trains.)[20]

A variation on the Expressionist face is found at the climax of Murnau's *The Last Laugh* (1924) where the aging (and provisionally tragic) protagonist, stripped of the stature he once enjoyed as the liveried head porter of a luxury hotel, is found crumpled against the wall of the hotel's lavatory, his head encircled by a halo projected by a nightwatchman's lamp. Emil Jannings, who portrayed the porter, returned in von Sternberg's *The Blue Angel* (1930) as the likewise degraded Professor Rath, a once respected schoolteacher who is dismissed after falling for a burlesque performer, whose travelling company he joins. Years later, after suffering the cruellest humiliation, he steals into his former classroom and dies – at the stroke of twelve – his hands clutching the corners of his desk. He is as if crucified; and in a manner reminiscent of *The Last Laugh*, a custodian's lamp casts a halo on the chalkboard behind him. In each film, the nightwatchman follows the round beam of his torch, which flits about in the pitch-blackness like a will-o'-the-wisp (*Irrlicht*). In each, he puts down his lamp and steps into its light to comfort or revive the collapsed figure.[21] In the earlier instance, the lamp is strapped to the nightwatchman's chest, which mirrors cinematographer Karl Freund's reported practice of affixing the camera to his torso in order to simulate, among other things, the porter's unsteadiness on his feet after drinking too much.[22] In *The Blue Angel*, the custodian has a pronounced limp, which causes the light from his hand-held lantern to dart about erratically in the darkened halls and stairways of the deserted school.[23] Both examples recall a scene from Wegener's *The Golem* (1920), photographed by Freund using cameras that were of

18. *The Last Laugh* (1924), dir. F.W. Murnau.

necessity stationary, in which the worried denizens of Prague's ghetto use actual torches to navigate the catacomb-like passageways beneath their quarter. One by one, the torch-bearers hurry past and disappear through a low doorway, where a last, stooped figure pauses to glance behind him, his silvery hair and beard merging with the vaporous light that issues from beyond the door.

White-haired elders reading by candle- or even starlight, a young adept practising alchemy in the glow of a furnace, not to mention a shot-composition that closely replicates the Rembrandt-attributed *Philosopher in Meditation* (1632) – with *The Golem*, Freund proved his mastery of Baroque lighting. Effects like these abound in *The Last Laugh* as well, the newly mobilized camera notwithstanding. Witness the stationary framing of the deposed doorman, aching to conceal his disgrace from his neighbours, as he returns home one evening from his new post as washroom attendant. Entering through a doorway into the open courtyard of his housing block, he is preceded by his shadow, which is cast onto a wall by an unseen source. Bowed and distended, the sharp silhouette rights itself, and the once regal figure steps around the corner and into view (figure 18).[24] Withering ridicule awaits him, culminating in a dizzying, kaleidoscopic montage that distorts and multiplies the laughing faces of the women in his neighbourhood.[25] Twice dismantled, the sad figure returns to his subterranean post, where, near death, he is found by the sympathetic nightwatchman. The latter, unstrapping his lamp and stabilizing it on the washroom sink, moves into the light, which, true to biblical/Baroque precedent, confers dignity upon the meek and downtrodden. In its stillness, this somber *pietà* amounts to a retreat from the cinematic state of the art and its capacity to convey the agitated bustle and fragmentation of metropolitan life.

These various shots are consistent with the dynamic observed in the paintings of La Tour, in which the solitary source of illumination is always diegetic. Divine light does not arrive from the "out-of-field" (*hors-champs*)[26] but emerges from within, enacting a Manichaean exposure of the spirit inherent (though hidden) in the material. In La Tour's *Saint Gerome Reading*, described above, the otherwise opaque fingers holding the letter, which has itself become a carrier of light, are translucent around the edges. The triumph of light amid an excess of shadow is contested by Goethe's Mephisto, who proposes a contrary cosmology grounded in the same polarity: born of darkness, light proudly but vainly challenges the pre-eminence of "Mother Night" and, failing, clings to bodies, emanates from them, and creates through its concourse with the physical a beauty as transitory as those same bodies.[27] Murnau's own *Faust*, roundly criticized for its ungainly recourse to "high culture" and its concomitant flight from the incipient social realism of *The Last Laugh*,[28] is keyed to this foundational passage, as is, one could argue, Elsaesser's keen and concise summation of Murnau's approach to lighting: "The special kind of luminosity that comes from objects being lit and at the same time radiating light, brings forth the illusion of a special kind of 'essence.'"[29] The "high culture" that supplied early Weimar cinema with its materials (and thus with a claim to a certain cultural legitimacy) exists on an historical continuum that includes that cinema, and conforms closely to the extended reach of the nineteenth century. This history courses through the sentence just cited and through the cinematic style it describes, which corroborates the world it would seem to efface. The hero (in both Goethe's drama and Murnau's film), plagued by impotence in the face of plague, and shamed by undeserved veneration, embodies classical reason confronted with its limits. Goethe's Faust, whose habitual midnight wakefulness has often fetched the light of the moon to his lectern (*an diesen Pult herangewacht*), and who discerns the pinnacle of human art and science in the poison he contemplates swallowing, gives voice to the multiple paradoxes of an age whose contrary tendencies, following Starobinski, "intersect in a no-man's-land between night and day, in a cold crepuscular or lunar light, in a place where light is dimmed."[30] First published in 1790 – within a year of the outbreak of revolution in Paris – the *Faust*-drama epitomizes art in its new guise: "a mental spectacle … against a background of darkness," "an adventurous quest that plunged into shadow in search of images whose strange shapes, seen in the light of day, would bear the indelible stigmata of their origin."[31]

At its every turn, *Nosferatu* is an "adventurous quest," yielding up, in the words of one title-card, "eerie visions" (*unheimliche Gesichte*). Undeterred, Hutter resists the modern awareness that "the dividing line between day and night has become an inner frontier."[32] The young man's excited prosecution of his Transylvanian task represents the kind of physical self-exertion that, like somnambulism, serves to project deep-seated anxieties onto external sources. In her own way, his wife follows suit. Apparently pining for her absent husband, an entranced Ellen tiptoes out onto a veranda, her white nightgown shimmering in the moonlight, her arms outstretched in the familiar gesture of a sleepwalker. Perched insouciantly on the narrow balustrade, she crosses from left to right, framed first by a large window draped by a see-through fabric, then by an open door, where she falls into the arms of her host, the family friend and shipowner Harding, who has rushed from his desk to her rescue. The shot of Harding in his dressing gown, carved tobacco pipe in one hand, writing quill in the other, working comfortably by the light of a shaded lamp, is the true image of the Biedermeier habitus – a fortress against the passions that send Hutter galloping into a "no-man's land" where the moon holds sway.[33]

A vision in moonlight, the sleepwalking Ellen personifies the automatism of a desire whose real object, the vampire, manifests the threat that desire poses for the moral and material stability of Harding's world. "Desire has a fear all its own" (*Die Lust hat eignes Grauen*) – so runs a line from a verse by Eichendorff that begins with the change that comes over all things when the deepening sunset envelops the day (*Es wandelt, was wir schauen*).[34] Another of his poems compresses into its single stanza the apprehension that takes hold in the cool light of daybreak, that is, when "the moon puts out its lamp" (*Putzt der Mond die Lampe aus*).[35] The sudden gust that snuffs out the candle in *Nosferatu* (by Ellen's bedside in Harding's home) revives a figure from Eichendorff's poetry, with its familiar stock of elusive coordinates: waxing (or waning) moon, shimmering stars, drifting air, whispering firs, the far-off signal of an approaching mailcoach or roving hunter, the Janus face of solitude. Something is afoot, like the "spectre haunting Europe." The lyrical image, writes Thomas Pfau, is a "volatile symbolic form." The nocturnal breeze that in Eichendorff ripples through fields and forests intimates unrest, a murmuring from afar. Rhetorically and aesthetically, these images portend an awakening on the part of the estranged individual to potentially cataclysmic history.[36] Appropriately, an inescapably Eichendorffian constellation appears in the first story in Kafka's *Betrachtung*, published at the tail end of the long nineteenth century, indeed, in the same year as Thomas Mann's portentous *Death in Venice*: "The moon was already up and in view, a mailcoach drove past in its light. A diffuse wind was stirring everywhere, even in the ditch one could feel it, and nearby the forest began to rustle. One was no longer so eager to be alone."[37]

The moon is the supreme instance of the quality that Elsaesser finds in Murnau, whose films achieve a "special kind of luminosity that comes from objects being lit and at the same time radiating light." Weimar cinema emerged under the aegis of Endymion, as did German Romanticism a century earlier and more. The "eerie visions" that surge up before Hutter when he crosses into Orlok's domain have a benign precursor in Novalis's *Heinrich von Ofterdingen* – dreams that arise under the moon's sovereign watch: "The moon stood in its gentle radiance [*mildem Glanze*] above the hills, and brought forth marvelous dreams in all creatures [*und liess wunderliche Träume in allen Kreaturen aufsteigen*]."[38] The posthumous publication of Novalis's novel-fragment narrowly predated that of the *Nightwatches*, with their opening evocation of storm clouds sweeping overhead like strange, colossal figures (*wunderliche Riesenbilder*), allowing a glimpse of the moon before hiding it again. And as late as 1828 Goethe penned his exquisite apostrophe to the rising moon, which seems "so close" before disappearing altogether, "endarkened" by cloud-masses (*Dich umfinstern Wolkenmassen*).[39] Eichendorff's popular tale *The Marble Statue* (1819) features a carved image of Venus, which, when the hero Florio first catches sight of it, is "sharply illuminated" (*scharf beleuchtet*) by the moon. Seemingly enchanted by its own beauty and grace, the stone figure appears alive. Florio, who looks on while rooted in place (*eingewurzelt im Schauen*), shuts his eyes in ecstasy. When he looks up again, the image has been transformed by the moon, which is now peeking eerily from between passing clouds. In this altered light the figure, deathly pale and motionless, seems to glower at Florio out of empty eye sockets.[40] Neoclassicism and Romanticism combine in the same figure, much as the moon itself, in whose varying light the statue is trans- and disfigured, is both light and matter at once.

These select examples may suffice to indicate a broad literary-aesthetic pattern of exploiting the liminal virtue of moon- or twilight to activate the ambiguity at the heart of the Uncanny, projected in the form of objects that hover between life and death or that vacillate between being "here" and "not-here" (*gar nicht da,* in the words that Goethe addresses to the moon swallowed up by clouds). Kafka's "cinematic" notation of a mailcoach passing through moonlight marks a trajectory along which the moon is gradually robbed of the beneficence conspicuous in the line just cited from Novalis's *Ofterdingen* ("The moon stood in its gentle radiance above the hills ..."). A similar largesse is accorded the moon by Johann Peter Hebel in his *Schatzkästlein des rheinischen Hausfreundes*, the story-filled almanac that Hebel published between 1807 and 1811. The moon, Hebel writes, "brightens our nights with its gentle light, which is the reflection of its sunshine [*der Widerschein von seinem Sonnenschein*], and it watches over the young lads as they kiss their maidens." He goes on to nominate the moon as the "true household friend [*Hausfreund*] of our earth," referring to the titular *ami de maison* who circulates along the upper Rhine, visiting homes, looking in on old acquaintances, and telling tales in which he names himself occasionally as kindly mediator. He "reflects" stories of which he is not the source, and in this way he is like the moon, which Hebel characterizes as the "nightwatchman" of the highest rank (*der oberste Generalnachtwächter*).[41] In his paean to Hebel from 1957, Martin Heidegger consolidates this synonymy of the *Hausfreund,* patron of innocent love, and the moon, whose glow "is neither earthly nor heavenly, but both, which is to say primordially unsundered [*ursprünglich-ungetrennt*]."[42] The moon-as-caretaker serves Heidegger as the true and complete image of the poet (*Dichter*), whose custodial vocation Hebel, having lived in the "bright proximity of language," supremely fulfils. His capacity is that of "transforming everything into the gentle radiance [*den milden Glanz*] of the quietly sounding word."[43]

The image of chaste love – young sweethearts kissing in the moonlight – suggests an idyll of almost Rococo delicacy.[44] Compressed within the simple amalgam of *Haus* and *Freund* is a world that is anything but uncanny, "unhomely" (*unheimlich*). *The Nightwatches of Bonaventura,* contemporaneous with Hebel's earliest stories, provides a foil for the *Hausfreund,* as Kreuzgang's townscape is one in which nightwatchman, moon, and poet are not cognates but distinct, antagonistic entities. Listening to the lonely echo of his own footsteps, Kreuzgang imagines himself the sole survivor of flood or plague and shudders at the comparison before glimpsing, with a certain relief, a lamp glowing feebly from the impoverished poet's window high above the street. Arguably a pallid caricature of Faust, the poet doubles as Kreuzgang's former self. Much the same can be said of three mask-like figures, exposed by a flash of lightning as they skulk along the cemetery wall. Demanding recognition as a kindred spirit, Kreuzgang launches his pike in their direction, only to find, at the subsequent flash, that they have vanished. An act of vigilance analogous to that of the filmgoer who reacts physically to the on-screen action (shouting threats at the villain, etc.), and reminiscent of the pistol shot that Balduin, of *The Student of Prague*, aims at the heart of his evil double, Kreuzgang's gesture is in line with the defensive strategy in which, as Elsaesser argues, Weimar cinema participates (and to whose impotence it repeatedly attests).[45] Such gestures, following Samuel Weber, would defend against the "crisis of perception" that the Uncanny entails. They express the wish "to conserve the integrity of perception" (and thus of the self), which "implies a denial of that almost-nothing which can hardly be seen."[46]

Citing Weber on this count, Elsaesser emphasizes the uncanny power with which, in German cinema of the early 1920s, off-screen space is invested – a power that "forever escapes the protagonists' control." In films like Grune's *The Street* and Murnau's *The Last Laugh*, "there always seem to be more pairs of eyes ... than there are characters on the screen."[47] Viewing positions are not contained within the closed circuit of shot/reverse shot, already codified by American filmmakers, the effect of which is to veil the apparatus and to install a seeing subject in its place.[48] Metz, in his posthumously published *Impersonal Enunciation* (1991), stresses the need to strip the apparatus of "anthropomorphic connotations," which, he submits, are especially "bothersome" in the area of film, "where everything is based on machines." Because it is difficult to relate to "locations of enunciation" except as "instances of incarnation," they take on a "humanoid aspect."[49] Whether everything in cinema is truly based on machines is debatable. Yet the push to differentiate between living subjects and "positions of enunciation" is of a piece with the impulse to thwart the ambiguity from which the experience of the Uncanny arises. In Lang's *Metropolis* (1927), this undecidability divides between the heroine Maria and the treacherous robot supplied with her appearance – a human disguise that falters when one of her eyelids, to disquieting effect, begins to "stick," as may happen with a child's doll whose eyes no longer open and close in unison. In Hoffmann's tale *The Sandman* (1816), which Freud used to illustrate his own conception of the Uncanny, people begin to *affect* spontaneity so as not to be mistaken for mechanical dolls, and this to the point of their supposed spontaneity becoming itself mechanical.

The humour of this latter instance falls under the broad heading of "Romantic irony," the general effect of which is to incorporate authorial machinations within the narrative frame, throwing a spotlight on the underlying conceit or contrivance. *The Sandman* is one example in which the exposure of the fictional apparatus dovetails with that of the insidious machine. Truly, Metz's definition of enunciation – as "the semiological act by means of which certain parts of a text speak to us of that text as an act"[50] – is an apt characterization of Romantic irony (also in its chiasmic formulation). The reflexivity of the cinematic *mise en abyme*, in which films are embedded within films (frames within frames), parallels a key gesture in Romantic literature and thought. Midway in *Heinrich von Ofterdingen*, for example, the young hero is shown an illuminated manuscript, in which he is surprised to find his perfect likeness, though in unfamiliar settings, and in which he recognizes figures from the dream that inaugurates his journey. Dream and manuscript mirror each other, just as *both* mirror the novel in which they are enveloped. The mysterious book is dream-like in the growing murkiness and indecipherability of its images, as well as in the sheepishness Heinrich exhibits when his companions, who have left him to himself, return to discover him in a state of dazed euphoria. The initial dream is itself so involuted that when Heinrich rouses to his mother's embrace, he may still be enclosed within the outer shell of his dream.

The inherently self-alienating reflection that divides the self into subject and object finds literal expression in the pivotal scene of *The Student of Prague*, where Balduin stands motionless and agape while his mirror image, by means of a double exposure, steps out of the looking glass and disappears through the door. In a manner that identifies the mirror as a "supplementary screen,"[51] Balduin is dumbfounded at once by the autonomy of his reflection and by the cinematic trick that makes this doubling possible. In an essay first published within a year of its release, psychoanalyst Otto Rank opens with a discussion of Rye's film, suggesting in passing that the visual technique common to films and dreams might succeed in bringing to light the latent potential of the film's predecessors in literature and legend.[52] Among the film's literary forerunners is Guy de Maupassant's short story "The Horla" (1887), in which the anxious narrator, startled by a perceived presence, turns to face a large mirror and finds it vacant: "The glass was empty, clear, deep, brightly lit, but my image was not in it."[53] While Metz recognizes that the cinema is "rich in specular affinities" – that the mirror enjoys a privileged status in film – he stresses that the mirror and the screen differ essentially in that "the screen does not reflect the viewer's own body."[54] This claim makes for an especially apposite foil for *The Student of Prague*, in which, as with "The Horla," it is the *mirror* that does not reflect the subject's body. Balduin's experience inverts the situation described by de Maupassant's narrator, who believes his reflection to have been eclipsed by the invisible yet impermeable phantom named in the story's title. A trait of the vampire becomes an attribute of the self, which in certain scenarios the fiend may be thought to duplicate. When in *The Student of Prague* the Lady Margit, whom Balduin is courting, realizes that her suitor's reflection is absent from the mirror in her sitting room, her alarmed discovery closely resembles that made by Jonathan Harker in Bram Stoker's *Dracula* (1897): "But there was no reflection of [the Count] in the mirror! The whole room behind me was displayed; but there was no sign of a man in it, except myself."[55] In Murnau's loose adaptation of Stoker's novel, it is more a matter of shadows than of reflections, though *Nosferatu* embodies an observation made by Harker, namely that Dracula and his shadow appear to move independently of each other. At the film's climax it is Orlok's disembodied shadow that looms at the top of the stairway while slowly extending an arm to open the door to Ellen's bedroom.

Murnau employed various pre-cinematic techniques at critical junctures in his narrative: the vampire's stealthy, almost avian emergence from the hold of a ship is rendered through stop-action photography; earlier, when the fiend advances along a corridor directly toward the camera, his forward movement is indicated by the abrupt succession of two still photographs, the second of these taken at much closer range than the first. The effect is startlingly primitive for a filmmaker capable of the most seamless and fluid transitions. At these crucial moments, Murnau's film *decomposes*, exploiting what is inherently undead about the medium that cinema displaced. Writing on Francis Ford Coppola's *Bram Stoker's Dracula* (1992), which includes an extended episode at a turn-of-the-century cinematograph, but which also exploits the vampiric potential of the photographic medium, Garrett Stewart observes how such a "convolution of visual technology" provides for a structure that enables contemporary culture to "flirt with the elegiac mood in heritage films even while celebrating the supremacy of the present." Cinema, he writes, "promotes its own representational agenda by recovering the naïve ruptures that greeted its arrival on the scene of mere photography."[56] The climax of *Nosferatu* thus constitutes a mediatic regression. The composition not only mimes the tonal inversion of a photographic negative but also revives an old theatrical technique whereby low-angle lighting was used to project human figures as shadowy giants. Photography in the original sense, this method recalls the ancient account of the origin of painting as provided by Pliny the Elder: a young woman traces the outline of her lover's shadow on the eve of their separation.[57] The classical fable in turn points to the *camera obscura*, which inflects *Nosferatu*, in which the fiend is vanquished *photographically*, that is, through exposure to daylight.[58]

Weimar cinema is crowded with examples in which allusions to the cinema and its forebears are cinematically realized, as when, in *The Golem*, Rabbi Loew causes Ahasverus (the "wandering Jew") to appear magically on the wall of the imperial palace, or in *The Street* when the middle-aged protagonist, lying on his couch while his wife prepares dinner, studies the fluttering shadows on the bright ceiling above him and pictures an illicit encounter. In Arthur Robison's *Warning Shadows* (1923), guests at an aristocratic soirée are treated to an extended shadow-puppet performance arranged, in the tradition of *Hamlet*, to dramatize and heal a marital rift. Caligari's fairground curiosity is itself a prototype of Wiene's film, the bulk of which stages the mental distortions of its frame-narrator, whose very psyche constitutes a secondary screen.[59]

Impugning any such conflation of the apparatus of the cinema with that of the psyche is Friedrich Kittler, who castigates those who have attempted to "scrutinize a banal mass media for an unconscious symbolic." Liberal in his disdain, Kittler reserves a special measure of asperity for Rank, who allegedly found his way to the literature of the double by way of *The Student of Prague*, in which he believed to find confirmation of a literary phenomenon that film had in fact superseded. Golems, Kittler proclaims, are "stupid doubles" not only of human beings whose nervous systems had been replaced by the technical medium of film but also of "sheepish" readers who, a century earlier, had been systematically prompted to recognize themselves in the "magic mirror" of literature.[60] Whereas the enchanted mirror of previous epochs "revealed gods or demons," the post-Enlightenment reader found a reflection of generic traits ostensibly shared by all human subjects. The double, Kittler asserts, is not the projection of unconscious turmoil, as Freud and Rank would have it, but the product of literacy campaigns launched around 1800; the "light in the study" is the working condition of the double who, significantly, "turns up at writing desks."[61] A mainstay of the Romantic-Fantastic, the figure of the double "populates the literary record since and *only* since" the era that began with Goethe's *Wilhelm Meister* (1795) and Fichte's *Wissenschaftslehre* (1797). (Yet Dante, anno 1308, declares himself traumatized by the sight of an infernal shade, swinging its own severed head like a lantern: "Truly I saw, and seem to see it still." Divided in two yet miraculously one, "it made a lamp *of* itself *for* itself.")[62] But no matter when the literary double originated, it disappeared once the cinema and psychoanalysis – in tandem – implemented and validated "all of the shadows and mirrorings of the subject."[63] (If

Kittler's claims are true, then Kafka's "Unmasking of a Confidence Trickster," in which the narrator recounts his attempts to free himself one evening of the stranger who "had pressed himself unbidden into my company and led me for two hours through the narrow lanes," represents a last gasp of the literary *Doppelgänger*.)[64]

An early example of Kittler's "sheepish" reader is Novalis's Heinrich, stunned to behold his own spitting image in the pages of that indecipherable manuscript. The strange volume not only mirrors Heinrich's original dream but also is found in a cave like the one in which the dreaming youth, suspended in a quivering bath, is entranced by visual projections of his innermost thoughts. Novalis, who elsewhere stated that the written word caused visible worlds to unfold within the reader, is already, in Kittler's view, allied with a tradition of hallucinatory tricks, including those that enabled Wegener's rabbi to conjure a film (within a film) to distract an emperor.[65] Such tricks are for Kittler nothing more than "strategies of power," functions of a technical apparatus that Rank, believing film capable of performing dream-work, failed to unmask. Perhaps. But self-denial is at the heart of the cinema, which strives to restore the integrity of perception and thus of a subject effectively dismembered by the spinning blades of the projector's shutter – the source of flickering shapes like those that tantalize the reclining protagonist of *The Street*. Grune's film, which opens as a technical *tour de force*, resolves in favour of bleak realism and of a defeated adventurer's return to a world bereft of illusion. The errant figure is a mundane and irrevocably bourgeois successor to Goethe's Faust. Frustrated habitué of the writing desk, and heir to Luther, who claimed to have "fought the devil with ink," Faust is himself vulnerable to a diabolical agent who summons illusion in the interest of disillusionment.

Kittler's wariness of such comparisons stems from the belief that the truth of the cinema is to be found in its technological, not its aesthetic moment. Similarly, Metz's disavowal of a transcendental subject in favour of codes (endearing to those with a fascination for cybernetic logic and for schematic mappings of "sources" and "targets"), translates into an interdiction of deixis, that is, of utterances that anchor perception in corporeal self-apprehension. For Metz, disembodied enunciation comports with the ideal of impersonality: "the 'enunciator' incarnates itself in the only body that is available, the body of the text, that is to say, a *thing*, which will never be an *I* and is not empowered to switch roles with some *YOU*, and which is and remains the source of images and sounds."[66] This short-circuiting of reciprocity follows the ban on anthropomorphism that Metz inherits from a long tradition of science in which the disillusioned subject (which the Cartesian subject is by definition) adapts to the rigidity of a nature that has been moulded to the requirements of exact knowledge. Jonas described this ban in terms of a "strict abstention from projecting onto [nature's] image our own felt aliveness."[67] Science sheds the last vestige of animism when understanding is purified of "the force-experience of [one's] own body in action."

The ideal of objectivity requires, in the tradition of Hume, that internal impressions not be "read into" the record of things. In the name of this ideal, knowledge grounded in the subject's "inner mode of affectedness," which enables the mind to map the sequence of disparate events onto a causal nexus, is invalidated.[68] In keeping with the project of preventing the world from "[intruding] dynamically into its testimony," *sight* comes to be exalted as the physical sense least vulnerable to the flood of stimuli. The power of vision is that of the "distancing of its object from the perceptive function." The organ of subjective self-disengagement, the eye substitutes image for effect, the distance inherent in the former being the necessary condition of imitation.[69] In thrall to the visual, imitation keeps its object fixed in space and at a remove. It is distinct from – even contrary to – mimesis, which constitutes an involvement with an Other not fully demarcated from the self. Continuous with mimicry and magic, mimesis is closely akin to the animism whose every last trace modern thought had struggled to expel. This expulsion is consistent with the "mimetic taboo" that for Adorno is coeval with repression as such.[70] The primacy of sight during the Age of Reason completes the isolation of objects from subjects, which, in the process of being objectified, are severed from one another. "[Even] the human being," to quote from *Dialectic of Enlightenment*, "becomes an anthropomorphism for human beings."[71] By excluding force from the field of what can be admitted as knowledge, science neutralizes that by which our own suffering and that of others is known to us. This progressive distancing of the object from us and from one another undercuts true mimesis, summarized here by Robert Hullot-Kentor: "Mimesis … is the affinity of subject and object as it is felt in one's knees on seeing someone else stumble on theirs."[72]

This affinity is eroded by certain theorists of narrative, such as Käte Hamburger, who uphold the decrees of classical epistemology by construing the correspondences of narration as functional (impersonal) rather than relational (personal). Hamburger, to whom Metz declares himself substantially indebted, discredits the term "narrator" as a "personifying expression."[73] If true mimesis is grounded in the affinity just described, then literary fiction is effectively *non*-mimetic, as the narrative function (*Erzählfunktion*) does not represent an experiential field verifiable "with the aid of [the reader's] own *tactile image*." In fiction, according to Hamburger, the reality of a representation "cannot be corroborated via the image of the reader's own physical presence." Adverbs of space and time "relinquish the deictic, existential function," whereby "temporal or spatial perception is reduced to a conceptual level."[74] With reference to Hamburger's claim that fiction is defined by the absence of an "I-Origin," Metz renews his criticism of those who would project a "human presence" in place of "this hollowed-out thing."[75] For Hamburger, "all art media narration" thrives on the *impression* of a fictive narrator, that is, "the impression of a 'person' who posits himself in a relationship not only to the figures he creates, but to the reader as well."[76]

Hebel's *Hausfreund* exemplifies what Metz, echoing Hamburger, describes as fiction's felt obligation "of reconnecting the narrated story to those fictional I-Origins that are the characters."[77] One might venture here that the epithet "well-disposed" (*geneigt*), which Hebel affixes to his reader, constructs a subject whose sympathetic temperament bends him literally (involuntarily) toward the writer. This same disposition is found throughout Spitzweg's paintings (to be taken up later), in which kindly figures almost invariably bow toward another person or thing and, in leaning forward, exhibit the very affinity that defines mimesis. It is found in such formulations as "our good fellow from Tuttlingen,"[78] by means of which the *Hausfreund*, recounting the experiences of a simple tradesman, affirms a particular, locally coloured *sensus communis*. The *Hausfreund* also positions himself in relation to the reader through periodic gestures of self-reference. Two examples, in the first and third person respectively, occur at the beginning and end of the tale "Secret Beheading," in which a small-town executioner is summoned by a mysterious tribunal to decapitate an anonymous victim:

> Whether on the morning of June 17th the headsman of Landau prayed the sixth petition of the Our Father with devotion, I cannot say.
>
> That is the story of the headsman of Landau, and it would grieve the *Hausfreund* if he could name the poor soul who had to pass into eternity by so bloody a road.[79]

Twin concessions to non-omniscience, these statements bookend the account in which the headsman is driven blindfolded through the night to a building where, eyes still bound, he is led along passageways and up and down stairs to a candlelit chamber, at the centre of which the doomed figure, masked and sobbing, sits before an assembly of veiled judges. The blindfold signals the impartiality of justice but also the limited comprehension of the executioner, who gauges the distance and duration of the overnight journey by the motion of the carriage and the sounds of owls, roosters, and morning bells. The experience is relived by Stoker's Harker, who, confined to a windowless room deep within Dracula's stronghold, is attuned to the change in the air that, like the incoming tide, heralds daybreak; and by Murnau's Hutter, who is fetched by coach into Orlok's sphere at speeds so precipitous as to prompt the bewildered passenger to shield his eyes from the view.[80] In Hebel, the blindfolding restores the headsman to a level of embodied perception in which the effort-motion experience, to cite Jonas, supplies "the dynamical links in the sequence of observed events."[81] Hebel's "well-disposed reader" is conscripted into a set of spatial and temporal coordinates shared by the *Hausfreund* and the executioner, this by means of a deictic phrase – a veritable road-sign – that indicates the point at which the headsman is first intercepted, and to which he is eventually returned: "an hour this side of Nanzig" (*eine Stunde herwärts Nanzig*). The *Hausfreund*, whose capacity for sympathy is evident, the reader, whose favourable disposition may cause him to lean slightly toward the storyteller, and the reluctant headsman himself, whose visual (and moral) disorientation is corrected through an enhanced perceptual grounding – all are instances of embodiment supported by the deictic positioning within a common time and space. The recurring demonstrative *Merke* ("Mark"; "Note"), whereby the *Hausfreund* induces the reader to regard things from where he stands, is a rhetorically more explicit example of this general practice, in which utterance assumes carnal form.

To be sure, the persona of the *Hausfreund* is not inert but rather mutates in keeping with the enunciatory requirements of the narrative.[82] The intent here is not to refute the broader narratological claim, as advanced by Hamburger and Metz, but to recognize its alignment with the general course of epistemology, which posits a purely theoretical (as opposed to practical) subject, self-sufficient in its construction of the world as a perceptual whole.[83] Many histories are implicated here. Writing on Albertian perspective, Bryson describes the emergence of a practice of painting in which "the eye contemplates the world alone." The painter's gaze, he writes, "arrests the flux of phenomena, contemplates the visual field from a vantage-point outside the mobility of duration, in an eternal moment of disclosed presence." Maintaining that Western painting is "predicated on *the disavowal of deictic reference*," Bryson defines deixis as including "all of those particles and forms of speech where the utterance incorporates into itself information about its own spatial position relative to its content (here, there, near, far off) and its own relative temporality (yesterday, today, sooner, later, long ago)."[84] The impulse to obliterate all traces of the painter's physical labour – effects of the artist's *here and now* – corresponds historically with the epistemological regime that would deny, in the name of pure reason, the body and its testimony. In what can be read as a direct and historically emblematic refutation of this trend, Herder, writing in 1770 on the plastic arts, contended that the viewer of a piece of sculpture does not experience the work strictly as an object of sight. Rather, the eye serves as an organ of the hand, restlessly exploring the sensuous contours of the sculpted human form, enabling one to see "as if one were touching" (*als ob man tastete*).[85] Herder invites his reader to imagine a viewer "rooted" (*eingewurzelt*) before a carved Apollo, changing his position, regarding the figure from every possible vantage point, experiencing physically a beauty and fullness of form that is essentially corporeal. His insistence that such formal beauty cannot be grasped through mere sight is echoed by Jonas's more foundational claim that the body's capacity for movement is a constituent of seeing – that "we would not be able to 'see' if we had not previously moved." He thus defines vision as "the part-function of a whole body which experiences its dynamic involvement with the environment in the feeling of its position and changes of position."[86]

The belief that vision of the world is conditioned on the possession of a body capable of moving itself in and through space has implications not only for the cinema but also for the modern technological means that afforded seeing subjects new levels of mobility.[87] The invention of the hot-air balloon (1782) and the introduction of passenger trains (ca 1825) are examples of these, though Petrarch's account of his taxing assault on Mont Ventoux in 1336 is already a powerful testimony to the dependency of sight on locomotion. Already in its earliest phase, the cinema was entangled in the history and technology of the railway, with cameras placed on tracks or even mounted on trains proper.[88] Indeed, the legend of those Parisian spectators who in 1896 fled their seats for fear of being struck by an approaching locomotive stages the birth of the cinema as a violation of the tradition of thought that would purify sight of all bodily self-awareness. More than two decades later, the cinema was still absorbing this imagined trauma. Witness Wegener's Rabbi Loew, who seeks to foreclose any affective response as he prepares to "screen" his spectacle of Jewish exile ("No one shall speak or laugh, lest they incur some horrible disaster").

An aesthetic birth as much as a technological one. Herder's account of the viewer comprehending the carved body of Apollo in terms of his own is true to the aesthetic regime that began to emerge around 1750.

Well before Rilke explored a variation of this theme in 1908, *empathy* had taken its place in the lexicon of art history. His "Archaic Torso of Apollo" (also to be taken up later) describes an ancient marble figure the slope of whose shoulders cues the viewer to the artist's own centre of gravity, by means of which the sculptor was able to intuit the distribution of the figure's weight. Such empathy is of a piece with the sympathetic involvement (*Beteiligung*) that Ernst Bloch attributed to Hebel.[89] The disposition that Hebel himself ascribes to his reader (*dem geneigten Leser*) exemplifies mimesis in the deepest sense, understood as the bond between subjects grounded in a feeling of shared frailty. "Shuddering is the best part of humanity" (*Das Schaudern ist der Menschheit bestes Teil*).[90] Bloch is here echoing Goethe's Faust, who, seeking his own humanity in the company of humans, embodies the will to find fulfilment in the here and now. Bloch's thesis that an anticipation of what is yet to come is necessary to penetrate the potential of what is close at hand has a parallel in Erich Auerbach's claim, with respect to Christian eschatology, that the promise of fulfilment is anchored not in allegory but in experiences that are historically palpable and concrete – that "the origins of prophecy seem to lie in the politico-religious spontaneity of the people."[91] An eruptive social energy, otherwise thwarted by the classical separation of genres, found a conduit in the vertical dynamism of biblical narrative, in which misery, signalling divine favor, catalyses transformation: "precisely the most extreme circumstances, in which we are immeasurably forsaken … give us, if we survive them, a personal stamp which is recognized as the product of a rich existence."[92] Misery and compassion inform the tenebrous scene in *The Last Laugh* where the nightwatchman discovers the former porter slumped against the washroom wall. Bowing over the listless figure, the nightwatchman leans in close, as if to hear a dying confession, and places a tender hand upon the broken man's head (figure 1).

An even deeper sense of martyrdom pervades the sombre finale of *The Blue Angel*. The custodian, limping vigorously as he pursues the former professor through the darkened halls of the empty school, not only "incarnates" a "position of enunciation" but also tethers it to the tortured locomotion of a body that is its own obstacle. This physical stigma makes the caretaker the suitable source of the empathy of which the tragically degraded and betrayed Professor Rath is the ultimate vessel. In a kind of deposition, the caretaker tries in vain to pry loose the dead man's hands, which clutch the corners of his desk as if nailed fast. Jannings's ponderous head appears in the end as an object at once illuminated (by the custodian's lantern) and emitting light (the resulting halo). The "dual illumination" invoked in *The Nightwatches* by Kreuzgang, who shudders to behold the dying man enlivened suddenly like a candle inflamed by an unexpected draft, summons the Baroque technique that would eventually provide a model for so much of Weimar cinema. The dynamic contrast of light and dark is itself a carrier of the paradox, likewise discernable in these films, of a theology that looks for signs of the utmost grace in the wrenched joints of the body crucified – the contrary of the gentle bending of the torso in Rilke's poem. Rilke's closing enjoinder to "change your life" echoes Nietzsche's view (utterly inimical to this theology) that the impulse to change and transform may stem from a superabundant power "pregnant with the future," but also, on the opposite hand, from a "hatred of the ill-constituted, disinherited, underprivileged."[93] According to Donald Gordon, this tension (more than any stylistic factor) is what animated the work of the Expressionists, who, especially after the First World War and the political despair that followed, had to "pit their antigens of hope against the long odds of real suffering."[94] That even Nietzsche could implicate himself as the object of the supremely deictic *Ecce homo* is a fair measure of the capacity of the Christian passion to contain this tension. Lovis Corinth produced a painting of Christ presented to the jeering throng (*Ecce Homo*, 1925), and Jannings's Professor Rath, in a scene that foreshadows his ultimate debasement, is introduced – to whistles and catcalls – from the celebrity box of the seedy venue into which he has blundered. The spectrum of attributes named by Nietzsche – ill-constituted, disinherited, underprivileged – is comprehensive in its coverage of the many figures discussed here, including the "last man" of *The Last Laugh*, who *inherits* improbably in a reversal of fortune heralded by the biblical assurance that "the last shall be first" (Matthew 19:30).[95] After the scene in the lavatory fades to black, a scrolling text declares that here, "at the site of his humiliation" (*an der Stätte seiner Schmach*), the old man would normally be expected to live out his remaining days in abject toil. The "author," however, has taken pity on him and provided the film with an alternate ending. A newspaper notice then reports that the washroom attendant has become the accidental heir to a visiting millionaire who died in his arms.

This explicitly mechanical intervention illustrates strikingly the enunciation that Metz defines as "the semiological act by means of which certain parts of a text speak to us of that text as an act." It is the *author* who is "well-disposed," his engagement modelled on the compassion exhibited by the nightwatchman, a character of his own creation, though in this case the "author" is himself a character within the narrative frame. A fictional I-Origin to be sure, he gives body to an overflowing and contagious empathy. The much-derided shift from social tragedy to comedy, which Jannings is said to have urged on the film's producers, is in truth driven by the requirements of a genre whose salvational thrust entails the acceptance of a defining flaw. Jannings would himself carry such a flaw into his portrayal, in Gustav Ucicky's *The Broken Jug* (1937), of the club-footed Judge Adam, a figure whose comical self-incrimination proceeds, in the vein of his biblical namesake, from having "stumbled" (*gestrauchelt*). His ultimate reincorporation, likewise a requisite of the genre, is consistent with the mimesis characterized earlier as "the affinity of subject and object as it is felt in one's knees on seeing someone else stumble on theirs." His congenital imperfection aligns him with the hobbled custodian of *The Blue Angel*, in whom the "effort-motion experience" is most palpable, his limp a mark of life's hard labour.[96]

Chapter Four

A Pause in the Action

There is a scene in *The Talented Mr Ripley* (1999), Anthony Minghella's adaptation of the novel by Patricia Highsmith, where Ripley, his back to the camera, is shown gazing out over an inlet of the Mediterranean (figure 19). Walter Murch, who edited Minghella's film, remarks on the challenge of deciding how long to sustain the shot before cutting to the next: "How long do you hold it? You hold it for as long as the thoughts you imagine Ripley is thinking can be held."[1]

A gestural equivalent of thought, this particular moment amounts to a pause in – or respite from – the succession of joined shots by means of which motion passes over into the medium and is enacted by it. Murch, whose editorial approach aims generally at easing the displacement of one visual field by another, here admits of the fundamental antagonism between reflection and the inherent restlessness of cinematic montage. He indicates as well a certain mental rapport wherein the viewer, though without necessarily knowing what Ripley is thinking, sees that he is lost in thought. A pensive close-up might well have been used to similar effect. Yet Ripley's physical orientation, legible as introspection and aligned with that of the filmgoer, implicates the latter in a longing for equilibrium. The vast and relatively empty expanse of sea and sky affords a refuge from the welter of stimuli characteristic of modern life, of which the constantly shifting cinematic frame is a constituent. This brief hiatus in the action corroborates the full sense of the German verb *innehalten*, which means "to pause" and connotes a *holding in*.[2] Erich Auerbach argued that a particular verbal syntax was especially suited to "the dramatization of an inner event, an inner about-face."[3] This figure of reversal gives a cue as to how such an event – a moment of recognition, say, or regret – might be staged as a visible gesture.[4] Perhaps the most monumental "about-face" in cinema occurs at the end of François Truffaut's *The 400 Blows* (1959), where the young and troubled

19. *The Talented Mr Ripley* (1999), dir. Anthony Minghella.

Antoine, after gazing briefly seaward, turns and steps toward the camera, staring defiantly into the lens just as the frame – the very last of the film – magnifies and freezes (20). In its dynamic frontality, this famous shot is at variance with the one from Minghella's film, which is far more typical of what has become a commonplace in the cinema – a shot that evokes quiet self-confrontation. The contentious daring with which Antoine turns to meet the viewer's gaze contrasts with the introversion of those lone individuals who, facing away from the camera, search their souls, weigh decisions, nurse memories, or contemplate roads not taken.[5] Seldom are these shots followed by a reverse shot. In them, syntax is momentarily suspended. Almost mournful in their nostalgia for the autonomous frame, they impose a stillness at odds with a medium of which movement is the defining feature.[6]

A vein of thought within the history and theory of the cinema has long held that film did not come into its own until it ceased trying to assimilate to the conventions of painting and took full possession of its uniquely mechanical character. Benjamin famously counterposed the emancipated spectator of film to the museumgoer, isolated before the work of art, "collected," as it were, in a kind of devotional silence.[7] The residual sacrality surrounding the traditional artwork constituted a certain distance in proximity, familiar to the wanderer who, resting on a summer's afternoon, traced with his eye the far ridge of a mountain

20. *The 400 Blows* (1959), dir. François Truffaut.

range or a branch of the tree in whose shadow he lay.[8] Benjamin's vignette is distinctly Romantic, as is the shot of the solitary figure, seen from behind, motionless before a distant horizon. Yet for Benjamin a cinema that was true to its historical moment would confirm the general tendency within modern, mass society to bring things closer, to replace visual contemplation with tactile apprehension, and to dissolve cultural objects in favour of physical participation. In this, Soviet cinema was exemplary, having become, he believed, a *praxis* in the true sense of the word.[9]

Sergei Eisenstein's *Battleship Potemkin* was released in 1925. In the same year, F. Scott Fitzgerald published *The Great Gatsby*, a novel whose setting is one of commuter trains and speeding automobiles – of post-war freneticism and metropolitan energy. Indeed, narrator Nick Carraway's newfound affinity for New York reflects a sensibility forged in the era of film: "I began to like … the satisfaction that the constant flicker of men and women and machines gives to the restless eye."[10] But amid all the flash and clamour Fitzgerald summons this hushed nocturne, in which Carraway first catches sight of the enigmatic millionaire next door, standing in the dark at water's edge:

> The silhouette of a moving cat wavered across the moonlight, and turning my head to watch it, I saw that I was not alone – fifty feet away a figure had emerged from the shadow of my neighbor's mansion and was standing with his hands in his pockets regarding the silver pepper of the stars. Something in his leisurely movements and the secure position of his feet

> upon the lawn suggested that it was Mr. Gatsby himself, come to determine what share was his of our local heavens.
>
> I decided to call to him. Miss Baker had mentioned him at dinner, and that would do for an introduction. But I didn't call to him, for he gave a sudden intimation that he was content to be alone – he stretched out his arms toward the dark water in a curious way, and, far as I was from him, I could have sworn he was trembling. Involuntarily I glanced seaward – and distinguished nothing except a single green light, minute and far away, that might have been the end of a dock. When I looked once more for Gatsby he had vanished, and I was alone in the unquiet darkness.
>
> (20–1)

In its ruminative quiet, this passage would appear out of place in the novel's agitated world, yet the scene is cinematic in the fluid dynamism that ultimately leaves the narrator to himself, uneasily interpellated before the distant and faintly luminous object of Gatsby's desire. A silent complicity is fostered by means of the "involuntary" alignment of Carraway's gaze with that of Gatsby, who comes into view only after Carraway, his eyes following the path of a prowling cat, rotates his head.[11] Their lyricism notwithstanding, these lines provide for a veritable shooting script, carefully accounting for such key components of *mise en scène* as lighting, framing, the disposition of figures in space, their movements and gestures, and so on.

The Great Gatsby has thus far been adapted for the screen five times. The first of these films was made in 1926, as if the novel couldn't wait to shed its literary carapace.[12] In the most recent version, directed by Baz Luhrmann in 2013, the encounter just described is made to conform to the same set of compositional habits observed in the shot of Tom Ripley: Gatsby is seen from behind, standing at the end of his own dock, with one hand extended toward the light that beckons from the opposite shore. That light, which has the appearance of an emerald-green will-o'-the-wisp, is revealed in a reverse close-up to be a mechanical beacon. According to Benjamin, the close-up in film allowed everday things, which had otherwise "floated along unnoticed in the broad stream of perception," to be isolated and precisely analysed.[13] Franco Moretti has identified a comparable disenchantment already in the late eighteenth- and early nineteenth-century novel, in which "metaphors are completely ousted by analytical predicates."[14] The shot of the beacon in Luhrmann's film aptly illustrates how close photographic scrutiny dispels the quasi-sacred breath surrounding objects, of which in the film industry – this again according to Benjamin – the personality of the star had become the new vessel.[15] Fitzgerald's novel is in fact provided with such a personality – a young *ingénue* who attends one of Gatsby's extravagant parties on the arm of her doting director. Daisy and Tom Buchanan, Carraway's cousin and her husband, stare at this "gorgeous, scarcely human orchid of a woman … with that particularly unreal feeling that accompanies the recognition of a hitherto ghostly celebrity of the movies" (105).

Sitting "in state" under the watch of her protector, the starlet enthralls even those for whom Hollywood and Broadway represent an unprecedented vulgarity. Her presence *qua* presence implies distance in proximity – an unapproachability the director himself violates when he stoops to "kiss at her cheek." Carraway's recollection culminates in a *tableau vivant*, which he and Daisy take in as they stand side-by-side: "Almost the last thing I remember was standing with Daisy and watching the moving-picture director and his Star. They were still under the white-plum tree and their faces were touching except for a pale, thin ray of moonlight between" (106–7). The Romantic overtones of this "picture" can be stressed through comparison with Eichendorff's poem "Mondnacht," mentioned earlier, in which the gentle "kiss" of moonlight causes the earth to effloresce dreamily in a "glimmer of blossoms" (*Blütenschimmer*).[16] This comparison may for the moment serve to suggest how a novel from 1925, in whose protagonist Carraway acknowledges a "romantic readiness" and "a heightened sensitivity to the promises of life" (2), taps the cinematic potential of Romanticism's image-repertoire. The two moonlit scenes referred to here (Gatsby gazing out over the "dark water," Nick and Daisy standing together in quiet contemplation of the starlet seated beneath the white plum) may again put one in mind of Friedrich and his misty or twilit scenes in which human figures – alone, in pairs, or (less commonly) in groups of three and four – assume meditative poses as they face away from the viewer and toward a land- or seascape. His *Man and Woman Contemplating the Moon* (figure 2) is an iconic example, having adorned the paperback cover of many a gothic novel. Featured are a man and woman, her arm on his shoulder, motionless beside a leafless oak, gnarled and partly uprooted. The ancient tree is uncannily animated in death, its roots reaching toward the couple like fingers. Opposite, the rising moon and the "evening star" (Venus) expand in the luminous mist.

Apparelled for travel by foot over wooded terrain, the man and woman in Friedrich's painting inhabit a world that could not be more remote from Gatsby's, the denizens of which, in Carraway's words, are "herded … along a short-cut from nothing to nothing" (106). But that world of 1922 – sleek, fast, and throbbing with danceable jazz – is also at odds with itself. If the tendency of the modern age is to bring everything close and subject it to touch, Gatsby remains in thrall to the magic conferred by distance. Carraway, who admires in Gatsby a commitment to the ideal, has a sense of this when he first sees his neighbour peering out over the water in the moonlight. The green light glowing from afar is the metonym for the woman in the interest of whose acquisition he has acquired everything else. Yet on another moonlit evening five years earlier, he had hesitated before kissing her for the first time – before "wed[ding] his unutterable visions to her perishable breath" (110). Reunited with her now in Nick's company, he shows her the world from his vantage point, indicating the direction from which that green light shone:

> "If it wasn't for the mist we could see your home across the bay," said Gatsby. "You always have a green light that burns all night at the end of your dock."
>
> Daisy put her arm through his abruptly, but he seemed absorbed in what he had just said. Possibly it had occurred to him that the colossal significance of that light had now vanished forever. Compared to the great distance that had separated him from Daisy it had seemed very near to her, almost touching her. It had seemed as close as a star to the moon. Now it was again a green light on a dock. His count of enchanted objects had diminished by one.
>
> (92–3)

By the time Fitzgerald published *The Great Gatsby* in 1925, narrative cinema had achieved a high level of technical and artistic facility. This was rather less the case in 1912, when Thomas Mann published *Death in Venice*, the first sentence of which presages the same catastrophic war from which Gatsby's world had vigorously emerged. It is even more surprising, therefore, to discover passages like the following, found toward the end of Mann's novella, which seem to accommodate certain advanced practices of filmmaking:

> But as [Aschenbach] dreamt his way into the void, the horizontal shoreline was suddenly intersected by a human form and, summoning his gaze back from the infinite and bringing it into focus, he saw none other than the beautiful boy coming from the left, walking past him in the sand.[17]

The cinematic import of this passage, in which the delicate youth comes into focus as he strides "into frame" before his somnolent admirer, is insistently realized in Luchino Visconti's 1971 adaptation of Mann's novella. Repeated shots of the boy, his back to the camera, silhouetted against sea and sky, exploit what is already filmic about the German Romantic pictorial canon. Friedrich's *Moonrise over the Sea* (1822) is another example of his work, which typically features men and women, seen from behind, transfixed before a horizon or vacant expanse (figure 21). Gustav Aschenbach and Jay Gatsby, both of whom harbour a resistance to "incarnation," are both seen trembling before such vistas. Different as the two men may be, each is captivated by objects the perfection of which makes them not objects but articles of belief. The green light is Gatsby's counterpart to the blue flower that fascinates and enflames the young hero of Novalis's *Heinrich von Ofterdingen*. A beacon in its own right, the flower flashes within him like distant lightning (*Wetterleuchten*).[18] It is contiguous with the "blue flood" in which Heinrich longs to immerse himself, which in turn prefigures the drowning of the maiden in whom, at the end of his initial journey, he discovers the flower's ultimate avatar. Heinrich thus strikes out from home with a presentiment of the sheer grief that overtakes him finally when, in a severe and desolate mountainscape, he looks back in the direction from which he has come and wishes simply to dissolve: "He wanted to cry himself into the distance [*sich in die Ferne verweinen*] so that no trace of his being would remain."[19]

The pull of oblivion that Heinrich feels is likewise felt by Mann's Aschenbach. His vision blurring as he "let his eyes run over the sea's great expanse," the weary writer is aware of the "desire to take shelter from the demanding diversity of phenomena in the bosom of boundless simplicity" – a desire to "repose in perfection."[20] This perfection eludes Gatsby, who, in Carraway's judgment, "paid a high price for living too long with a single dream." Adrift in his own swimming pool – in the hours and minutes before being murdered by the man who believes him culpable in his wife's death – the disillusioned millionaire takes stock of his surroundings, which are harsh in their disenchantment. The starkness of these impressions, which Nick imputes to Gatsby, verges on the surreal:

> He must have looked up at an unfamiliar sky through frightening leaves and shivered as he found what a grotesque thing a rose is and how raw the sunlight was upon the scarcely created grass. A new world, material without being real, where poor ghosts, breathing dreams like air, drifted fortuitously about.
>
> (161)

The exhaustion that leaves Gatsby resigned to his end echoes the last gasp of the *ancien régime* in France, with its particular cult of dazzling

21. Caspar David Friedrich (1774–1840), *Moonrise over the Sea* (1822).

Oil on canvas, 55 × 71 cm.
Alte Nationalgalerie, Staatliche Museen zu Berlin
HIP/Art Resource, NY

ornament and unchecked expenditure. Implicit in Gatsby's demise is the principle acknowledged by those doomed voluptuaries who understood, to cite Starobinski, "that desire, with its endless quest for pleasure, yearns broodingly to end, to find rest, to soothe the weariness of time with death."[21] The order that met its fate after 1789 had evolved a style of fleeting effect and infinite, opulent distraction synonymous with the "demanding diversity of phenomena" from which, more than a century later, the fictional Aschenbach seeks refuge. Of course, the Rococo had already found its negation in those Romantic conjurations of empty reaches of sea and sky, of glowing or waning light, and of receding ships or approaching storms. The twentieth-century American painter Mark Rothko invoked the Romantics explicitly, and he would name the preoccupation with death as a requirement of art. In almost the same breath, however, he emphasized the importance of sensualism and of "a lustful relationship to things that exist."[22] This sounds contradictory, though Freud had speculated some decades earlier that the span of biological life was determined by the interplay of contrary forces – the *élan vital* and the death-drive. The latter he defined as the impulse, inherent in all living things, to return *in due course* to the original, inanimate state that preceded the first stirring of life.[23] The human desire to recover this original state corresponds to the source of religious sentiment, which Freud's friend Romain Rolland characterized as "a sensation of 'eternity,' a feeling as of something limitless, unbounded – as it were, 'oceanic.'"[24]

Rothko is best-known for his large paintings composed of figureless fields of richly hypnotic colour – unevenly edged rectangles whose horizontal positioning orients the viewer as before a landscape. Rothko urged that his works be hung near the floor, thereby placing the viewer, who was expected to stand close to the canvas, almost literally at the threshold of an immensity akin to the "boundless simplicity" that calls to Aschenbach. Such modern works of art counteract the distraction that Benjamin welcomed. They answer the need felt by Aschenbach to "repose in perfection," the longing for which is likewise a defining motive of German Romanticism. In the novel-fragment already discussed, Novalis exalts those of a poetic sensibility for whom, paradoxically, "contemplation" (*Betrachtung*) is itself the "activity" (*Tätigkeit*), and who recuse themselves from life's "immeasurable spectacle" (*unermessliches Schauspiel*) in order to grasp its spirit.[25] "No unrest impels them outward" (*Keine Unruhe treibt sie nach aussen*): Novalis's formulation is remarkable in its broad consonance with Freud's account, which in turn reverberates darkly through Rothko's practice of, in the words of Robert Rosenblum, "[locating] the beholder at the brink of a resonant void."[26]

These works thus presuppose and generate a response for whose verbalization *Death in Venice* supplies a proper compendium. The following lines describe Aschenbach's slow approach, by steamship, to the city of his dreams:

> The rain had ceased; the awning had been taken down. The horizon was now visible in its entirety. The vast disk of the barren sea stretched out beneath the turbid dome of the sky. But in empty, unarticulated space our senses lose the capacity to articulate time as well, and we sink into the immeasurable.[27]

In this brief excerpt, the Romantic predilection for the infinite and indeterminate melds with the dissipation, characteristic of modernism, of objects and matter.[28] A disintegration may be observed in Piet Mondrian's *Pier and Ocean* (1915), closely contemporaneous with *Death in Venice*. The painting's very title intones the "oceanic" even as it names objects but vaguely discernable in the abstract interplay of horizontal and vertical indices (figure 5).[29] In the morbid climax of Mann's novella, the boy's "intersection" of the "horizontal shoreline" draws Aschenbach back from "the monotonous mist of barren space" – the "nothingness" that, at the disruption of his Apollonian reverie, becomes the true and final object of his yearning.[30]

The Venice in which Aschenbach collapses and dies has become the febrile swamp about which he, while still in Munich, had fantasized with a combination of "terror" and "enigmatic craving." This sinister attraction is reminiscent of that certain "fascination of the abomination" which, according to Charlie Marlow of Joseph Conrad's *Heart of Darkness* (1899/1902), took hold of those ancient Romans who had come to face the natural and human savagery of Britannia.[31] Aschenbach's "hallucination," as it is characterized, may in fact recall the oppressively virulent worlds – the Belgian Congo as well as Roman Britain – so vividly described in Conrad's novella:

> His [Aschenbach's] desire sprouted eyes, his imagination, as yet unstilled from its morning labors, conjured forth the earth's manifold wonders and horrors in his attempt to visualize them: he saw. He saw a landscape, a tropical quagmire beneath a steamy sky – sultry, luxuriant, and monstrous – a kind of primordial wilderness of islands, marshes, and alluvial channels ...[32]

As with the jungle into which Marlow ventures, the exotic and primeval world of Aschenbach's imagination offers the dangerously enticing prospect of a Dionysian "un-selving" (*Selbstentäusserung*), to use Nietzsche's coinage.[33] And whereas Marlow's European companions are unfailingly on edge as they scan the "heavy and motionless foliage" for "rolling eyes," Marlow himself admits to a "thrill" at the "terrible frankness" of the noise issuing from the riverbank, and if the throbbing frenzy of indigenous dance and song is plausibly Dionysian, so too is Marlow Odysseus-like in his determination to sail safely past temptation: "You wonder I didn't go ashore for a howl and a dance? Well ... I had to watch the steering and circumvent those snags, and get the tin-pot along by hook or by crook" (38).

At once threatening and seductive, the vision of self-dissolution – of engulfment by a prodigious and monstrously fecund nature – is offset by the studied efficiency of the technically focused, though technology itself is subject to the same engulfment. Marlow has entered a world in which pieces of abandoned machinery are strewn about like animal carcasses and in which his African crewmen employ the flotsam and jetsam of the European presence as fetishes and propitiatory charms. By reverse parallel, European art had begun to appropriate African sculpture to apotropaic purpose. Carved masks and figures, such as the ones that Picasso first encountered in 1907, were found to possess, in Hullot-Kentor's synopsis, "a formal capacity to direct the violence of life back against its own violence."[34]

Marlow's countenance in fact takes on the appearance of the indigenous figures whose faces he likens to "grotesque masks" (17), as exemplified by one young man, who in dying looks up at Marlow, his "sunken eyes … enormous and vacant, a kind of blind, white flicker in the depths of the orbs which died out slowly" (20). This now metaphorized "dying of the light" prefigures the death of Marlow's Congolese helmsman, struck by a spear thrown from the riverbank. Helpless onlookers feel themselves "enveloped" by the light emanating from the helmsman's eyes until a frown creeps briefly over his face and lends it a "sombre, brooding and menacing expression." The poor fellow's expiration is signalled by a fluid, alliterative passage into the material negation of vision – an emptiness that evokes the original sense of *vanitas*: "The lustre of inquiring glance faded swiftly into vacant glassiness" (47). This evanescence echoes an initial tableau in which Conrad's frame-narrator evokes the dusk over the banks of the Thames as they run "out to sea in vanishing flatness," much as the helmsman's "death-mask" has its precursor in the "mournful gloom brooding motionless" over London itself (7). The narrator's subsequent comparison of the haze to "a gauzy and radiant fabric … draping the low shores in diaphanous folds" (8) appeals to a Romantic phantasmagoria, as does the oft-quoted passage in which the same narrator likens the allusive meaning of Marlow's tale to "one of these misty halos that, sometimes, are made visible by the spectral illumination of moonshine" (9).[35]

Figurality prevails where "analytical predicates" suffer the fate of the machinery rusting in the tall grass along the river. Metaphors suspend experience between proximate terror and "inaccessible distance" (58), while spatial depth is contracted into the vast and empty tableaux that arrest the beholder in attitudes of hushed captivation. Marlow's "fascination of the abomination" mirrors the "holy dread" found in Freud and, before him, Coleridge.[36] The "deep Romantic chasm" proposed in the latter's "Kubla Khan" offers a compressed prototype of the dark interior into which Marlow travels in search of the infamous Mr Kurtz (the abomination that fascinates *him*): "A savage place! as holy and enchanted / As e'er beneath a waning moon was haunted / By woman wailing for her demon-lover!"[37]

Rothko faulted the Romantics for their focus on "exotic subjects" and "far off places," emphasizing the importance of the familiar and commonplace, which in archaic times were capable of transcendence. He stated that for him "the great achievements of the centuries in which the artist accepted the probable and familiar as his subjects were the pictures of the single human figure – alone in a moment of utter mobility."[38] This has been wrongly construed as an allusion to the lone wanderers in certain of Friedrich's paintings, such as *The Wanderer above the Sea of Mists* (figure 14)[39] – a figure that haunts *Death in Venice* via the recurring reference to Aschenbach as "the solitary traveler."[40] Yet Aschenbach's own extended reflections on classical beauty and grace, which he sees embodied in the boy, whose self-containment reminds him of the famous sculpture of a youth absorbed in the act of teasing a thorn from his foot, provide a better clue as to the actual, classically archaic object of Rothko's interest. The "*moment* of utter mobility" he names is accurate to the heedless divinity immortalized in the innocuous gesture of removing the thorn. It is also consistent with what Rancière has called "the pensive image," the constitutive indifference of which Hegel ascribed to the Olympians. To illustrate this attitude, Rancière recalls Winckelmann's pre-Hegelian analysis of the Belvedere Torso: "For Winckelmann, this torso was Hercules resting, Hercules serenely thinking about his past exploits, but whose thought was itself wholly expressed in the folds of the back and stomach whose muscles rippled like rising and falling waves. Activity has become thought, but thought itself has passed into an immobile motion, similar to the radical indifference of the sea's waves."[41]

Rancière, for whom the "pensive image" is one in which action has been suspended, here in effect summarizes what is oxymoronic about Rothko's "moment of utter mobility." Rothko's paintings, by his own account, partake of the melancholy into which modern art, in response to a general profanation, has sunk. Those familiar and probable objects are no longer capable of transcendence, and Rothko's call for the destruction of "the finite associations with which our society increasingly enshrouds every aspect of our environment" is not inconsistent with Novalis's plaintive aphorism: "We *look* everywhere for the indeterminate [*das Unbedingte*], and always *find* only things [*Dinge*]."[42] Note: Aschenbach is horrified when the beautiful youth smiles back at him – knowingly, it seems – and his extreme disquiet is of a piece with Gatsby's apprehension that a world in which he finally possessed Daisy would be emptied of all magic.

The decidedly pensive shot of Tom Ripley looking out to sea closely replicates one that occurs in *Apocalypse Now* (1979), Coppola's momentous interpretation of *Heart of Darkness*. Murch, who edited the original film, later restored an extended segment (for the *Redux* of 2001) in which the patrol boat escorting Captain Willard into

Cambodia happens unexpectedly upon a French plantation.[43] Forgotten by time, the compound, implacably guarded by Legionnaires, emerges out of the heavy fog, which gives the boat itself a ghostly cast as it lists silently upstream. Crouching at the prow with his back to the camera, Willard – Marlow's counterpart – peers through binoculars as the landing and its defenders take shape. The scene has been well-rehearsed. Witness the point in *Death in Venice* where Aschenbach's steamer enters the lagoon just as the fog is lifting: "He stood at the foremast, gazing into the distance, watching for land … Then, to the right, the flat coastline hove in sight." Or Friedrich's painting *On the Sailing Ship* (1818/20), which pictures a young man and woman, holding hands, seated on the forward deck of a sloop returning to shore (figure 22). The lean of the mast and the taut diagonals of the rigging amplify the appeal of the straight and level horizon, above which distant church towers and civic structures, as well as ships at harbour, are rendered in faint detail.

Evident in Friedrich's work generally is a tendency toward the abstraction that modern painting was to perfect. Gerhard Richter, a Dresden-born painter who conceives much of his work as an homage to Friedrich, makes the case for abstraction in terms consistent with the Romantic quest for the ineffable:

> [Abstract paintings] make visible a reality we can neither see nor describe, but whose existence we can postulate. We note this reality in negative terms: the unknown, the incomprehensible, the infinite. And for thousands of years we have been depicting it through surrogate images such as heaven and hell, gods and devils. In abstract painting we have found a better way of gaining access to the unvisualizable, the incomprehensible; because abstract painting deploys … all the resources of art, in fact in order to depict nothing."[44]

Heart of Darkness and *Death and Venice*, with their repeated emphasis on "vanishing flatness" and "boundless simplicity," hint at the genealogy that would connect those Romantic compositions to modern abstraction. Rosenblum, who first elaborated this connection, describes Rothko's work in terms germane to Conrad's narrative: "horizontal divisions evoking the primordial separation of earth or sea from cloud and sky, and luminous fields of dense, quietly lambent color that seem to generate the primal energies of natural light."[45] This same separation of sea and sky is already part of Mondrian's *Pier and Ocean*, in which, along with the suggestion of waves sparkling in sunlight, a sense of spatial recession counterbalances the unavoidable flatness of the painting.

22. Caspar David Friedrich (1774–1840), *On the Sailing Ship* (1822).

Oil on canvas, 71 × 56 cm.
Hermitage, St. Petersburg
HIP/Art Resource, NY

With Mondrian's composition in mind, as well as Rosenblum's reference to the "primal energies of natural light," it is especially interesting to contemplate the sight that greets Marlow upon his arrival at one of his company's outposts:

> A jetty projected into the river. A blinding sunlight drowned all this at times in a sudden recrudescence of glare.
>
> (18–19)

The image is haiku-like and recalls Eisenstein's attempt to find in Japanese poetry a model for the editing of film: "From our point of view, these [poems] are montage phrases. Shot lists. The simple combination of two or three details of a material kind yields a perfectly finished representation of another kind – psychological."[46] The abrupt redundancy of "jetty projected" is consistent with Eisenstein's "dialectical" approach to montage, which aimed at exploiting "collisions" between shots but also within individual shots, which he likened to the separate explosions within an internal combustion engine. Eisenstein's ideal is the clear contrary of the "pensive image" that, following Rancière, serves to "thwart the logic of the action."[47] In describing a sunset in which sea and sky "were welded together without a joint" (7), Conrad's frame-narrator evokes the aesthetic opposite of a practice aimed at disarticulating shots and "shattering" the frame by, in Eisenstein's formulation, "plunging [the dry quadrilateral] into the hazards of nature's diffuseness."[48]

Such hazards abound in Marlow's Congo, where even the light, like the vegetation, is irrepressibly virulent. The cannibalism feared by Marlow's fellow Europeans distils the voracious gaze of the African bush. Repeatedly, Marlow and his companions are overtaken by the glow or brooding shadow of a riverscape, their attitude mirroring the uneasy stillness of the prospect.[49] They are stunned by that "sudden recrudescence of glare" (19) as if by the glowering Medusa, whose eyes retain their ability to petrify even after – or especially after – they can no longer see. The severed head of the Gorgon shares its mask-like power with the shrunken heads placed on poles in a half-circle around Kurtz's hut. No longer simply organs of vision, the eyes become sources of fascination. Roger Caillois, with respect to a "magical tendency" in the biological world, devotes much attention to eye-spots (*ocelli*), such as the markings on the wings of butterflies that seem to mimic the eyes of predatory birds.[50] Caillois argues that these markings fascinate and frighten not because they resemble organs of sight but because they seem to be watching even though they are not eyes. Of particular interest are owls: unlike the eyes of virtually all other birds, those of owls are frontally positioned, their pupils dilated and fixed in orbit. Moreover, they are surrounded by a golden ring and by feathers that accentuate their roundness and exaggerate their size. "The eyes of these birds are thus turned into ... huge concentric circles, motionless and shining."[51]

Friedrich's *Landscape with Grave, Coffin and Owl* (1837/8), a study in pencil and sepia, is a remarkable pendant to those many figures seen from behind (figure 23). The owl, given its uncanny ability to rotate its head, is uniquely suited to the tropism endemic to a story – Marlow's – in which the platform of the narrative is the deck of a boat that, over the course of the telling, shifts on its mooring with the turn of the tide.[52] This turning is also germane to the novella's apotropaic aspect, of which those severed heads on posts are particular examples. Their purpose is to "turn away," in the sense of "warding off." Its association with death notwithstanding, the owl in Friedrich's drawing is notably more amusing, its wide-eyed, comical dimension exaggerated by its central, frontal positioning. The tall thistles in the foreground allude to the expulsion from Eden, as does the serpentine coil of rope, reaching outward as if threatening to entangle a viewer already susceptible to enchantment. A visual metaphor, the rope's form looks forward to that of the river unwinding out of the African interior, as described by Marlow, who is likewise "charmed" when he first glimpses it on a map in a shop window. He is, in his own terms, "fascinated," captivated before the map, as he is later "arrested" before a sketch in oils done by Kurtz. That little picture – of a woman holding a torch against a sullen background – is true to the manifold tenebrism that makes of light an *interruption* and casts Kurtz himself as the diabolical "bringer of light."

Friedrich's drawing, one of many featuring owls, caskets, grave-markers, and grave-digging implements, bears a similarity to the *Scherzi* of Giambattista Tiepolo, which often include a plurality of owls (figure 24). In his recent study of this eighteenth-century Italian master of mythological and biblical scenes, Roberto Calasso observes throughout the painter's *oeuvre* a striking plethora of "poles, flags, pennants, tree trunks, stakes, staves, masting, branches, and halbherds." It is a feature found also in Friedrich's drawing, with its criss-crossing planks and shovel handles, and it may be thought that Friedrich, who had a similar propensity for painting the masts and riggings of ships, the mullions of windows, and even the occasional easel, was compelled wherever he looked to find the sort of structure of which Mondrian's *Pier and Ocean* is a more abstract rendering. Calasso's explanation of this remarkable

23. Caspar David Friedrich (1774–1840), *Landscape with Grave, Coffin, and Owl* (1836–7).

Sepia over pencil, 38.5 × 38.3 cm
bpk Bildagentur / Kunsthalle, Hamburg
Photo: Elke Walford / Art Resource / NY

24. Giambattista Tiepolo (1696–1770), *Scherzi di Fantasia* (frontispiece) (1743–57).

Etching, 22.6 × 18.2 cm
Metropolitan Museum of Art, New York

habit of Tiepolo's is reproduced here at length for its arguably Conradian concern with immensity and emptiness:

> For Tiepolo, [these slanted trunks] are the matrix of painting. Why? So irrepressible is Tiepolo's sense of the boundless, overmastering nature of space – a sense he allows to issue freely from his painting – that we are led to presume that those intrusive posts, those trunks or poles or staves that appear everywhere without any plausible explanation, serve to mark and explore the immensity of the atmosphere. They are tokens of the momentary, fleeting order needed by that which happens in order to detach, isolate, and confine itself to space, in order to make a lucky escape from the terror of that which contains [infinity] within itself ... Except for the sky, an entity whose "enigmatic instability" can only be attested to by clouds ... Every place is fit to be divided, wounded, etched by what – to use a generic collective – we might call *poles*. Tiepolo is the first and foremost painter of poles. They are his phrasing, they mark the tempo of the musical articulation of space. In a transient and irregular way, the poles serve to demarcate portions of space. Without at least a hint of a frame there is no image, but at the same time only a boundless immensity can be the background against which the image stands out.[53]

These various references to a "matrix" composed of poles, their function being that of dividing space into "portions" and creating a pattern akin to "musical phrasing," may again put one in mind of Aschenbach's observation that "in empty, unarticulated space our senses lose the capacity to articulate time as well, and we sink into the immeasurable." Likewise, Calasso's inference of a "terror" provoked by "infinity" recalls the *horror vacui* captured astonishingly in Rilke's "Island of the Sirens" (1907), in which Odysseus seeks to re-create in words a terror arising not from the Sirens' song but from an expansive calm that eerily proclaims the *possibility* of their singing – a silence that causes the anxious crewmen to lean into their oars. And with an eye to those poles and stakes, which, everywhere in Tiepolo, compose a bulwark against "enigmatic instability," recall how Homer's Odysseus cleaves for nine days to timbers disgorged by the vortex Charybdis. Enigmatically, too, the "pilgrims" in Conrad's *Heart of Darkness* – the white managers and agents encountered by Marlow – are repeatedly described as constantly and inexplicably brandishing "long staves." They're never seen without them ("I verily believe they took these sticks to bed with them" [28]). Their importance may lie in the tactile assurance they provide, much as the book Marlow finds on certain pedestrian points of seamanship, in providing him with "something unmistakably real," makes him "forget the jungle" (39).

But Tiepolo's *Scherzi* are remarkable for their irreality. Calasso expands on the near omnipresence of snakes in these etchings – snakes that crawl, that coil around staffs or the twisted trunks of dead trees, and that, in keeping with a certain biblical exhortation, are burnt. Relevant episodes from the Bible are named, such as when Aaron's rod turns into a snake when cast upon the ground before the Pharaoh, or when Moses, whose people are beset by venomous snakes, commands them to contemplate the bronze figure of a serpent – "a gesture that marks the discovery that evil can be cured by its image."[54] In this gesture one may recognize the aforesaid "capacity to turn the violence of life back against its own violence." But what dazzles about these *Scherzi* is a blanching daylight so insistent that the owls confer upon it a sense of inverse extremity, rather like that "sudden recrudescence of glare" remarked upon by Marlow. (*Glare* in fact is precisely what these owls do.) What one sees in these images is that shadowless time of day, noontide, when Pan plays upon his pipes and incites the "panic" in which, citing Horkheimer and Adorno, "nature suddenly appeared to humans as an all-encompassing power ... and trapped the human gaze in the fakery of sorcerers and medicine men."[55] Marlow's gaze is enchanted, and his fascination leads him to the experience of an extreme he characterizes in a way that makes it superfluous to go on – as "a vision of greyness without form ... and a careless contempt for the evanescence of all things" (69).

At the close of Conrad's novella, Marlow and his company, their small craft anchored on the Thames, face silently into an effulgent gloom whose description is remarkably adequate to many a canvas of Rothko's. At the same time, that "careless contempt for the evanescence of all things" would contradict the American painter's belief that "a lustful relationship to things that exist" was required of all artists. The "vision of greyness without form" may likewise evoke the abstract "nothing" that Richter opposes to the "surrogate images" of demons and deities with which art has long sought to give shape to what cannot be seen. These figures, like the monsters that fill the empty regions of old maps, perform the role that Moretti (following Paul Ricoeur) ascribes to metaphors: they express the unknown while keeping it at bay.[56] The severed heads posted around Kurtz's riverside hovel exercise the same defensive magic. All but one of these gruesome masks face inward, but the single *extroverted* head is the one Marlow sights through his spyglass first. The discovery, he reports, made him recoil suddenly "as if before a blow" (57). Marlow puts down his glass, thereby causing the head that seemed "near enough to be spoken to" to leap away from him "into inaccessible distance." Such distance – in its very inaccessibility – is for both Aschenbach and Gatsby an ideal, and even more so for Novalis's grieving protagonist, who longs "to cry himself into the distance, so that no trace of his being would remain." This desire simply to disappear conforms to what Caillois calls the "withdrawal of life to a lesser state," which is for him the real purpose of mimicry in the natural world: to defend not against death but against an excess of life. An "inertia of the *élan vital*" is apparent in Friedrich's subjects, who appear frozen before often silent expanses, as well as in shots like the one of Tom Ripley gazing out over the water. Comparable moments, in which the turning point is a matter of introversion, were and remain legion in the cinema. Within the medium in which "Action!" is the defining command, then, a contrary tendency becomes briefly visible – an inclination toward the state of complete and perfect, brooding repose.

Marlow's recollection of scanning the dense tangle along the riverbank for "rolling eyes" suggests that the fear of cannibalism projects the dread of being "devoured" by darkness and of being seen by what one cannot see. Caillois speculates that the "magical ascendancy of night and dark," indeed, the "fear of the dark," derives from the threat that darkness poses to the boundaries of the self. "The feeling of mystery we feel at night," he suggests, stems from the fact that the self is "permeable to the dark," which "enfolds, penetrates and even passes through" the subject.[57] An attaché of Surrealism, Caillois published these thoughts in 1935. In 1937, Walt Disney released *Snow White and the Seven Dwarfs,* which both realizes the cinematic potential of Friedrich's paintings and anchors the fear of the dark, precisely as Caillois understands it, in the expressive conventions that would consolidate as what came to be known as *Schauerromantik* – a Romanticism that revelled in the sensation of shudders and chills.[58] A precursor to this is Goethe's early poem "My Heart Pounded" ("Mir schlug das Herz"). Most likely written in 1771, this *Lied* conjures an impassioned nocturnal ride on horseback. Bearing witness to the rider's passage into night is a towering oak, looming in a mantle of rising mist above the spot "Where darkness from the thicket peered / With a hundred black eyes" (*Wo Finsternis aus dem Gesträuche / Mit hundert schwarzen Augen sah*).[59] In *Snow White,* the heroine flees into the forest, where, in a manner reminiscent of Friedrich's *Man and Woman Contemplating the Moon* (figure 2), the finger-like roots and branches of dead and toppled trees threaten to snag the terrified princess, and where glaring eyes not only multiply but at one point even come to resemble the wings of butterflies. With the arrival of daylight, the numerous blinking eyes that watch over the exhausted child, asleep in a clearing, resolve into the most benign of woodland creatures – squirrels, chipmunks, bunnies, and so on. Conventions of the idyll afford refuge from the dangers of unmediated nature, which the film casts in terms of the fear of being seen.

Not long after the release of *Snow White*, Disney presented *Fantasia* (1940), which mined a rich reserve of recognizably Romantic motifs while flirting with modernist abstraction. Recall that Worringer had argued in 1907 that abstraction represented a general impulse in art – one that served to reinforce the contours of the self against a nature that threatened to devour it. (Snow White faces the literal threat of being eaten by her stepmother, of whom the forest, animated by evil intent, is a vivid projection.) Abstraction, Worringer believed, isolated objects from one another and placed them on a spatial plane apart from the viewer, thus affording the subject a desired sovereignty. But consider Gatsby, his feet planted securely on his lawn as he gazes out over Long Island Sound. Nothing proclaims sovereignty more than this, yet Carraway perceives that Gatsby is trembling, consumed by a passion that transforms a mechanical beacon into something that has him firmly in its grip. This overvaluation is true to the mental state described by Freud in which a desire that draws things close is potentially also a fear of what cannot be defended against. This fear induces Marlow to drop his spyglass, causing that shrunken head to retreat abruptly into "inaccessible distance." His startled recognition that the grizly posting is at once "food for thought and also for vultures" (57) accords with the distinction between the figural and the starkly objective. "We *look* everywhere for the indeterminate and always *find* only things" – Novalis's signature concession indicates the disenchantment brought about by the modern tendency to view things at close range, of which the modernist flattening of the visual field is a part. Worringer ascribed the impulse to abstraction to a "dread of space" (*Raumscheu*), which the practice of depicting objects in their material individuality served to counteract. One lesson of psychoanalysis, however, is that nothing is truly remote – nothing truly "inaccessible." For Freud, the "telepathic disregard for spatial distance" was an attribute of the "primitive" mind (and thus of the mind as such), which had the power to "[comprehend] what lies apart both in time and space … in a single act of consciousness."[60] This reads like a summary of modernism, which in its essence understood that the objects devised to ward off powers were themselves powerful, as if charged with electricity.[61] Such also is Friedrich's intuition. His work summons great distance while drawing it unsettlingly close. His viewers, held in quiet thrall before a space devoid of tangible objects, and of "analytical predicates," have their heirs in Aschenbach, Gatsby, and especially Marlow and his sailing companions as they silently contemplate banks of clouds gathering beneath a sombre sky.

Chapter Five

Facing the Image

An iconic shot from *The Cabinet of Dr Caligari* displays the "zigzag delineations" that, according to Siegfried Kracauer, pervaded Wiene's film and aligned it with Expressionist art (figure 25).[1] The film's famous sets, with their sharp angles, flattened shapes, and flaring shadows, exhibit an unmistakable kinship with the paintings and woodcuts of such notable contemporaries as Ernst Ludwig Kirchner and Karl Schmidt-Rottluff. While provocatively unnaturalistic, this style has in this instance the effect of animating the rooftop setting, which mimics the peaks and crevasses of a rugged mountainscape. The angles of the chimneys, windows, and gables, and especially the deep cleft between the plunging rooflines at centre, permit this frame to be mapped onto Friedrich's *Rocky Ravine in the Elbe Sandstone Mountains* (1822), in which diagonals also predominate (figure 26). The chimney flues re-create in slant and number the finger-like outcroppings in Friedrich's canvas; at the same time, they resemble, in their quadratic flatness, shapes found in paintings by Kazimir Malevich and László Moholy-Nagy.[2]

These stylistic features, "strongly reminiscent of Gothic patterns," led Kracauer to wonder whether Lyonel Feininger, known for his angular and prismatically layered paintings of medieval churches, town squares, and seascapes, had collaborated with those artists credited with designing the sets (Hermann Warm, Walter Röhrig, and Walter Reimann).[3] Although he hadn't, his work is singular in its testimony to the modernist afterlife of the Romantic vision. Of all artists affiliated with German Expressionism, Feininger exhibits the greatest apparent debt to Friedrich, many of whose works, to cite Rosenblum, are "virtually reborn" in Feininger's own.[4] His *Bird Cloud* (1926) is one of many that, like Friedrich's *Monk by the Sea*, places a tiny human figure before an empty expanse of water and sky (figure 27). The "transparent

25. *The Cabinet of Dr Caligari* (1920), dir. Robert Wiene.

overlay" of pellucid, crystalline shapes characteristic of Feininger's art allows Friedrich's work to show through as a veritable underpainting.[5] Imposing a greater stringency on Friedrich's already austere image, Feininger displaces the monk to the far left and brings the coastline into tight parallel with the horizon, the precision of which is accentuated by the sharp vertical at the centre of the composition. The bright triangles of the origami-like cloud are also evocative of the sails of the ships that appear in other of Friedrich's works, not to mention the stylized patterns that, in *Caligari*, simulate patches of sunlight or the reflected glow of candles and street lamps.[6]

As if to superimpose one painting over another, Feininger conflates forms and motifs distributed throughout Friedrich's catalogue. In both paintings, the low horizon, which extends to – and seemingly beyond – the edges of the picture, places the viewer before an ambiguous space. In *Monk by the Sea*, the void that expands before the solitary figure confronts the viewer with an almost oppressive flatness (figure 6). Friedrich had originally placed two ships in the middle ground but later painted them out, ridding his composition of the intermediary objects essential to the

26. Caspar David Friedrich (1774–1840), *Rocky Ravine in the Elbe Sandstone Mountains* (1822).

Oil on canvas, 94 × 74 cm
Osterreichische Galerie, Belvedere, Vienna
HIP / Art Resource, NY

27. Lyonel Feininger (1871–1956), *Bird Cloud* (1926).

Oil on canvas, 43.8 × 71.1
Harvard Art Museums/Busch-Reisinger Museum,
Purchase in memory of Eda K. Loeb

illusion of graduated depth.[7] The disquiet that many of his contemporaries professed to feel before this canvas is consistent with the same loss that the interplay of absence and presence serves to mitigate. Oblivion, which is both the threat and promise of *Monk by the Sea*, is an incitement to self-assertion.[8] This ambiguity comports with the paradox of solitude, just as the monk's vocational privation is echoed by the severity of his surroundings. The ships that Friedrich deleted from his controversial painting reappear in other of his seascapes, though these vessels, suspended between harbour and horizon as between life and death, often verge on immateriality. Hinting at the compulsion with which Feininger seemed to repeat Friedrich's practice, Rosenblum conjures the mystery of ships that are neither here nor there: "Again and again, Feininger locates us, as Friedrich had done, on the very fringe of the sea, so that we can contemplate the soundless movements of ships that, like Flying Dutchmen, seem to be phantom vessels headed for ports that belong more to the geography of the spirit than of the earth."[9]

28. *Nosferatu – A Symphony of Terror* (1922), dir. F.W. Murnau.

Rosenblum's discussion is restricted to painting. However, his fine evocation of ships moving soundlessly seems haunted by Murnau's *Nosferatu*, which features a phantom vessel of its own, gliding past the camera as it spirits its sinister cargo toward an unsuspecting Baltic port. Murnau's film draws much of its imagery from Friedrich, an assortment of whose paintings and drawings are condensed, for example, in the shot of Ellen as she awaits the arrival of the same ship. Striking a mournful pose while seated among the dunes, she is flanked by half-toppled crosses, which appear feeble in the face of the vampire's irresistible approach (figure 28).[10]

Monuments to sailors lost at sea, these crosses have numerous precursors in Friedrich, whose work displays the "cruciform symmetry" that Rosenblum detects in Mondrian's *Pier and Ocean* (figure 5).[11] This and similar studies by Mondrian interpret the tradition of Dutch dune painting, a seventeenth-century genre whose influence can be seen in those works by Friedrich that were in turn incorporated into the shot of Ellen by the sea. These include numerous sepia-toned or coloured drawings of coastal burials, of crooked grave-markers planted in sand, of human figures gazing out toward empty horizons, as well as empty

29. Caspar David Friedrich (1774–1840), *View through an Embankment onto the Sea* (1824).

Watercolour and pencil on vellum, 24.7 cm × 36.5 cm.
bpk Bildagentur/Staatliche Museen zu Berlin, Kupferstichkabinett
Photo: Jörg P. Anders/Art Resource NY

horizons without human figures (figure 29).[12] The oval format of Mondrian's painting accommodates the unbounded horizon-line familiar from *Monk by the Sea* (itself heir to that Dutch tradition),[13] and while it has been linked to Madame Blavatsky's "cosmic egg,"[14] it more obviously mimics the shape of the human eye and as such is homomorphic with the image created by the "iris" that opens on the shot of Ellen.[15] At first sight, *Pier and Ocean* is distinctly flat, especially when seen alongside the work of a filmmaker known for his depth-of-field. But this apparent flatness yields to a sense of embodied dimension that expands toward the viewer, just as the seeming abstraction discloses a horizon as well as a fixed structure extending outward. A vanishing point can be detected within the disciplined binarism of horizontal and vertical marks, which suggest the play of sunlight on waves as they disintegrate into wavelengths.[16]

A digital prescience is on display in *Pier and Ocean*, the culmination of a suite of studies known as the "plus-and-minus" series.[17] These monochrome drawings, the format of which is almost exclusively elliptical, are of church façades as well as dunes and waves – a range that implicates the features of Gothic design and the motions of the sea in the same living complex of rhythm and balance. Less than a decade earlier Worringer had argued that Gothic architecture did not represent an organic style but rather one in which abstract mechanical principles had "come to life."[18] Worringer's formulation has a liberal resonance not only for modernism but also for the cinema of the same period, in which a mechanically enabled animation frequently found its way into a film's very plot. *Caligari* is a prominent and influential example of an early motion picture in which this coming to life is incorporated into the fiction. Like *The Golem* and eventually *Metropolis*, Wiene's film is a forerunner of Whale's *Frankenstein* (1931), in which the dream of restoring the dead to life merges fully with a popular, pseudo-Gothic vision.[19]

Reaching its climax at a windmill, Whale's Hollywood horror classic completes a circuit. Framed against an ominous evening sky in potent chiaroscuro, the turning mill cites a Dutch pictorial tradition that extends back to Rembrandt and includes Mondrian, who through 1907–8 specialized in tenebrous, twilit portraits of mills, farms, and sundry riparian scenes. The "sails" of the windmill – four perpendicular spars – supplied the artist with a model for the "cruciform symmetry" of *Pier and Ocean*. In turn, that skein of vertical and horizontal lines had precursors in various paintings of trees lining riverbanks. The strong verticals of the evenly spaced trunks and the dense mesh of branches and twigs have the effect of emphasizing the surface while diminishing the sense of spatial recession.[20] A comparable faceting is found in Friedrich's paintings of ships at anchor, in which the criss-cross of masts and yards forms a virtual forest, lit from behind by the last glimmer of sunset.[21] Certain of Friedrich's canvases confront the viewer with a barely penetrable web of intersecting forms, more typically a thicket or network of tree branches. As in Mondrian's riverscapes almost a century later, these patterns have the effect, following Koerner, of "confound[ing] any ordered progression of vision into depth."[22]

It is interesting to consider the formal insistence whereby so many of Friedrich's compositions allow the eye to wander, to explore the edges of the painting, and to experience the painting itself as a material object in space. Rosenblum, however, after explaining the abstract discipline whereby Rothko, like Friedrich, "locates the beholder at the brink of a resonant void,"[23] emphasizes a kindred spirituality, invoking the iconoclastic programs common to Judaism and Protestantism. The figural richness of his critical language would seem to resist the disarticulation of sign and image, as does his tendency to find, for example, the "structural skeleton" that lies beneath the rhythmic balance of Mondrian's *Pier and Ocean*.[24] This suggests a negation of the very negation intrinsic to the religion that, quoting Horkheimer and Adorno, "brooks no word that might bring solace to the despair of all mortality."[25] Rosenblum in fact adheres to the tendency to read those Romantic paintings allegorically even while neglecting the decomposition, inherent in allegory, of image and idea.[26] It is worth underscoring the kernel of modernism that has long fixed critical attention on Holbein's *The Ambassadors* (1533), with its split perspective and ultimate refusal of consolation. When the anamorphic skull floating in the foreground is suddenly recognized, the "dread objectified in the fixed image" pierces consciousness to reveal the anemia of art that is content to reproduce what already is.[27] In his analysis of Holbein's painting Lacan emphasizes how "as subjects, we are literally called into the picture, and represented here as *caught*."[28] This experience of "imaginary capture" is related to that of the organism that, likewise captivated, assimilates to the stillness of its natural surroundings. Caillois (a reference point for Lacan) refers to such mimicry as a "magical tendency" in the biological world,[29] and this magic may in turn be construed as an attribute of an art that did not simply aim at imitating nature but, more primordially, sought to influence nature through its likeness.

The feral undertow of captivation is explored and to an extent theorized by Freud at a step in his analysis of the "Wolfman" ("From the History of an Infantile Neurosis," 1918). The analysis turns on a dream Freud's patient reported having as a young boy – an anxiety dream within which (not *from* which) he awoke to see the window at the foot of his bed fly open. A walnut tree, leafless in winter, stood just beyond the window, a clutch of white wolves perched among its boughs. A drawing furnished by the patient shows five wolves, which, by his account, remained silent and motionless, their ears perked up and pointed forward (figure 30).[30] Fearing that he would be devoured, the patient awoke and for minutes was unable to shake the feeling that the dream had been real. Freud isolates the stillness with which the animals appeared to watch the boy and interprets this as a projection of the rapt attention with which he, at a yet younger age, had observed his parents performing intercourse "in the manner of beasts" (*more ferarum*). Freud's conjecture of this "primal scene" places psychoanalysis within the wider compass of modernism, in which, citing Adorno, "[archaic] layers have come into our field of vision that were hidden."[31]

With an emphasis on "instances of attentive looking and motionlessness" (*Momente des aufmerksamen Schauens und der Bewegungslosigkeit*),[32] Freud understands the wolves' silent vigilance as an inverted distortion

30. Sigmund Freud, "From the History of an Infantile Neurosis" (patient's sketch, 1918).

of the agitated movement supposedly witnessed by the child in his parents' bedroom. At the manifest level of the dream, however, such inversion allows also for a reciprocal viewing akin to the "dyadic reversibility" of the gaze that, for Bryson, "returns that of the viewer as its own object."[33] Dream and drawing alike confront the child with his own act of looking, much as the wolves personify Lacan's "eye filled with voracity."[34] The child's frozen attitude is true to the hypnotic power of painting – a power found in "even those [pictures] most lacking in what is usually called the gaze, and which is constituted by a pair of eyes." Lacan himself invokes the tradition of Dutch landscape, and it may be that the presence of the gaze is felt most uncannily in paintings focused on the materials of camouflage – trees, grasses, undergrowth, stones – and in which "any representation of the human figure is absent."[35]

The experience recounted by Freud's patient – this instance of "attentive looking and motionlessness" – re-enacts the break with a tradition that exploited the window as a device for framing nature and keeping it at a safe remove. The preference for a clearly bounded view of the world is of a piece with the primacy accorded sight during the Enlightenment. Eisenstein's vanguard embrace of the conflict between "the dry quadrilateral" of the film-frame and "the hazards of nature's diffuseness" underscores the issue at the heart of the aesthetics of rationalism.[36] The conception of the easel painting as a transparent window onto the physical world came to be ironized by certain modernists, most particularly Magritte, who used window casements and mirror frames to challenge this same conception.[37] A kindred though less explicitly ironic gesture is found in Goethe's *The Sorrows of Young Werther* (1774) where Werther and Lotte stand before a window gazing out onto the remnants of a thunderstorm. Overcome by sentiment, Lotte takes Werther's hand and, eyes moist, exclaims "Klopstock!," naming the poet whose popular ode "Die Frühlingsfeier" (1759) describes a landscape redolent with spring and blessed by rainfall.[38] Beyond serving as a kind of erotic currency that passes between Lotte and Werther, Klopstock's poem is itself a window that opens up within Goethe's novel. How different the anxiety-dream relayed by Freud, in which the window exposes the dreaming child to threats harboured by a dark nature within! Behind the eighteenth-century preference for clear and formally circumscribed images of nature lay an impulse similar to the one that, for Worringer, gave rise to abstraction, understood as a source of calm "in the face of the monstrous confusion of the world-picture" (*angesichts der ungeheuren Verworrenheit des Weltbildes*).[39] Consisting in the isolation of objects in space, abstraction satisfied an abiding human need for distinct boundaries – a formal defence against a luxuriant nature whose limitless undifferentiation threatened the borders of the self.[40] Freud's case study was written at the outset of the First World War and published four years later, one year before "The Uncanny" (1919), and two years before *Beyond the Pleasure Principle* (1920), whose publication coincided with the release of *Caligari*. Freud's own interest in the cinema was negligible.[41] Yet his analysis of the young patient, petrified before the scene beyond his window, complicated the problem of spectatorship just as German art-cinema was getting off the ground.

Friedrich's *Rocky Ravine*, introduced earlier along with a shot from *Caligari*, embodies Eisenstein's juxtaposition of "the dry quadrilateral" of the frame to "the hazards of nature's diffuseness." No painting is more patently devoid of rectilinear structures than this dramatic record of geological upheaval, epic erosion, and the cycles of growth and decay. Ancient roots, clutching at rocks like tendrils, flow from both sides toward the narrow path, which disappears into the invisible gorge. The sloping embankments in the foreground reinforce the V-shaped fissure beyond which the path sinks from view. These dark masses offset the towering sandstone formation, diaphanous and surreal in the bright glow of the vapour surrounding its base. The unusual landmark, the so-called *Felsentor* along the Elbe southeast of Dresden, is familiar from Friedrich's earlier *Wanderer above the Sea of Mists* (figure 14). While the vantage point has shifted, *Rocky Ravine* achieves a similar contraction of space, obscuring the middle-ground while bringing distant objects closer. The straight diagonal of the dead spruce – one of many obstacles to both eye and foot confronting the viewer – draws attention to the painting's right-hand edge by projecting past it.[42] Here as elsewhere, Friedrich disavows the established approach to landscape that rendered the material limits of the canvas less obtrusive by supplementing them with corresponding objects within the painted scene (trees, stone columns, etc.). *Monk by the Sea* is a more radical experiment, in which the dissolution of structure collapses spatial fields into the painted surface and brings it oppressively close.

Kracauer discerned in *Caligari* a similar, though certainly more extreme, vacillation between two- and three-dimensional representation: "Space now dwindled to a flat plane, now augmented its dimensions to become what one writer called a 'stereoscopic universe.'"[43] Kracauer is citing Herman George Scheffauer, a German-American poet and translator whose writing on Expressionism is itself abrupt and forceful.[44] Writing in 1924, when the film was still quite recent, Scheffauer claimed *Caligari* for a "revolutionary" conception of space as something "plastically felt." He described the film as a work in which "[the] plastic is amalgamated with the painted, bulk and form with the simulacra of bulk and form." Space acquired both mass and vital energy. Backdrops became actors. Perspective served not to position the spectator vis-à-vis the spectacle but to "penetrate and transfix him with its linear life."[45] Scheffauer's proposal of an intensified sense of space (*Raumgefühl*) and of a corresponding treatment of space as "sculpturesque" resonates with Noël Burch's more recent account of how early cinema gradually renounced the decorated surface in favour of a "haptic space" – a three-dimensional arena that could be entered into.[46] This shift entailed the tempering of geometrical perspective and the suppression of the extreme depth celebrated by Scheffauer. In his compact but important discussion of *Caligari,* Burch noted "a kind of self-conscious return to the major features of the primitive cinema (and especially the autarchy and fixity of the primitive tableau in preference to the 'realism' of modern editing)." Unique in Wiene's film was the simultaneous presence of two contrary visual regimes, one defined by the graphic and essentially flat artificiality of the sets and backdrops, the other by the staging of depth in which actors move "along the axis of the lens and perpendicular to the picture plane."[47]

31. *The Cabinet of Dr Caligari* (1920), dir. Robert Wiene.

Burch positions himself in critical relation to certain members of the *Tel Quel* group (Baudry and others), for whom the monocular technology of photography constituted a kind of "original sin" that reaffirmed Albertian perspective at the expense of the "*avowed surface* of modernism."[48] Clement Greenberg also alludes to the biblical fall when he links the three-dimensional treatment of volume by fifteenth-century painters to a "profane appetite for the round."[49] The foremost champion of painting that "openly [confessed] the physical nature of the canvas and of the paint,"[50] Greenberg offers Sassetta's *Journey of the Magi* (ca 1435) as an early example of a work that had not yet fully sacrificed the hieratic surface of the Gothic to Renaissance illusionism.[51] Sassetta's small panel shows a train of colourfully clad pilgrims on foot and horseback. Behind them lie two barren hills, across which a number of trees are unevenly and sparsely distributed. Flat, truncated, leafless, and black to the point of seeming charred, these shapes are transported almost five hundred years later to the sets of *Caligari*, where they appear, in Kracauer's words, as "treelike arabesques that were *threats* rather than trees" (figure 31).[52]

While less conceptually driven, Scheffauer demonstrates the more reliable sense of how, in *Caligari*, depth-of-field breaks free of the geometrical constraints of classical perspective. For Burch, space becomes "haptic" by means of perspective, which satisfied that "profane appetite for the round" by endowing objects with an apparent tangible fullness. Whereas the stylized flatness of Wiene's sets are, in Burch's estimation, "primitive," the film's staging of depth is consistent with a model, derived from Lumière, that adapted perfectly the Albertian program.[53] For Scheffauer, it is not the objects but the space between them that comes to life. His invocation of the "stereoscopic universe" ("a world of intense relief and depth") into which the viewer of *Caligari* is plunged is thus consistent with the optical experience of the stereoscope proper.[54] For Jonathan Crary, this experience was characterized by the uneasiness prompted by the stereoscope's distension of space. The optical mechanism by which the stereoscope constructed the illusion of space often resulted in an uncanny impression of emptiness, which the makers of stereocards sought to counteract with photographic images of sculpture galleries and object-filled parlours – images that simulated the "material plenitude that bespeaks a nineteenth-century bourgeois horror of the void."[55] This *horror vacui* is the close equivalent of the *Raumscheu* specified by Worringer as the state against which abstraction served as a defence. Crary describes the experience afforded by the stereoscope in terms of an inversion whereby the atmosphere surrounding material things became tangible, even as the objects themselves grew immaterial:

> We are given an insistent sense of "in front of" and "in back of" that seems to organize the image as a sequence of receding planes. And in fact the fundamental organization of the stereoscopic image is *planar*. We perceive individual elements as flat, cutout forms arrayed either nearer or further from us. But the experience of space between these objects (planes) is not one of gradual or predictable recession; rather, there is a vertiginous uncertainty about the distance separating forms. Compared to the strange insubstantiality of objects and figures located in the middle ground, the absolutely airless space surrounding them has a disturbing palpability.[56]

Crary could well be describing Friedrich's *Wanderer*, whose subject stands in nonchalant defiance of that "vertiginous uncertainty," and in which the space separating the planes of the composition literally condenses. This painting, which predates the first stereoscope by some twenty years, is a true demonstration of that sense of "in front of" and "in back of." The wanderer stands out with almost surrealistic clarity against the luminous vapour. Together with the pyramidal mass of rock on which he is poised, he forms a dark plane, flattened by high contrast, as if simply superimposed over the scenery. What is technically the middle ground of the painting is already placed at such a distance as to make the hills and high summits beyond all the more remote.[57]

What Crary described as the anxiety-inducing structure of the stereoscopic image is already a working principle in this and other of Friedrich's paintings, including *Rocky Ravine*, in which the gulf that separates the viewer from the natural spectacle is at once a source of awe and an enticement to enter, even *disappear*, into the landscape. Crary points to the parallel "realisms" of the stereoscope and painting, suggesting that both "were equally bound up in a much broader transformation of the observer."[58] It is important to add not only that Friedrich's work was already enacting a stage in this transformation, but also that the stereoscope itself had important technical precursors. Indeed, it shares certain features with an earlier visual device, namely the seventeenth-century Dutch perspective box. The most accomplished of these were made by Samuel Van Hoogstraten. Some may hasten to insist that the perspective box was an affair of painting, not photography. Yet the perspective box is itself a camera and was already a part of the culture that was working out, in theory and practice, many of the optical principles of photography. At the same time, these experiments, which required an astounding combination of artistic and geometrical virtuosity, were designed to reveal the technique behind the illusion of depth. Van Hoogstraten's perspective boxes were rectangular wooden chests roughly two feet deep. Their interior surfaces were painted with anamorphically distorted renderings of domestic spaces. When viewed through a carefully placed aperture, the distortions are resolved, the separate faces of the box appear continuous, and the miniature setting seems life-sized. Most importantly, furnishings, columns, and other objects, all of which are painted on flat surfaces, "stand free within the fictive space."[59]

Both the stereoscope and the perspective box play with the dual optic that Burch finds in *Caligari*, whose visual program divides between the deliberate exposure of artifice, on the one hand, and, on the other, its effacement. A comparison with the perspective box is useful especially in that the scenes depicted within them have the quality of empty stage sets. In Wiene's film, the surfaces on which people stand and walk, whether inside or out, are *floors*, conspicuously flat and level. This makes for a stage-like effect, as exemplified by the first indoor shot of the film, in which Alan is introduced.[60] As the scene opens, the moonstruck student is shown standing by a desk in his room, examining a book by lamplight. The room is largely vacant. The far wall is featureless apart from a window, which, though square, displays a non-rectilinear grid of cross-pieces. Light from the window and the lamp casts a quilted pattern of overlapping patches on the floor, the sharp angles

32. *The Cabinet of Dr Caligari* (1920), dir. Robert Wiene.

of which are reflected in the shadow-shapes on the wall.[61] Standing in the near foreground is a ladderback chair, so close to the camera that only the high wooden back is visible above the lower edge of the frame (figure 32).[62] Its proximity to the camera serves to pull the spectator into the frame while exaggerating the depth of the space and making Alan, who is standing toward the back, appear small. He will presently move toward the chair, resting his arm on it as he continues to read. His mind focused on his book, he jostles the chair with his elbow – a haphazard collision that makes the viewer aware of the chair's stand-alone materiality in this realm of light and shadow.

Unable to concentrate, Alan rushes to the window, distracted by the loud bustle of the fair that has just come to town. His face bright with excitement, he dashes for his hat and coat, leaving the frame entirely for a full seven seconds. The viewer is thus confronted with a motionless shot of the empty room, in which the chair is the one truly tangible object. Benjamin would liken Eugène Atget's exposures of deserted Paris streets to crime scenes, "photographed for the purpose of establishing evidence."[63] In fact, the scene just described will soon be a crime scene, in which the same chair exhibits a certain evidentiary weight.[64] That very night, after his fateful encounter with a sideshow somnambulist, Alan is murdered in his bed. The killer is visible only as a silhouette, projected on top of another quilt-like pattern of overlapping shapes. Pieces of white fabric have been fastened to the wall to suggest the tactile glow of the candle that Alan had placed on the chair, which now stands beside his bed (figure 15). Mute witness to a murder, the chair is seen once again the next morning when Francis, Alan's closest friend (but also his rival in love), is called to the scene.

The scene of Alan's room is effectively a reverse-shot, hallucinated by Francis, the mad narrator of this story. In the previous shot Francis, his eyes fixed maniacally on a point beyond the camera, introduces Alan by name *as if* he were beholding him. The scene that follows is thus explicitly the embodiment of Francis's addled gaze, which is remarkable in a narrative not determined by the shot/reverse-shot formation. Yet the viewer, who now sees what Francis, himself a viewer, envisions, is interpellated by the extreme perspective that is presumably a reflection of Francis's troubled mind.[65] For Burch, the patently artificial and stylized sets of *Caligari* reach back into an earlier phase of cinematic history in which spectators found reassurance in a screen that proclaimed its own decorative flatness. Worringer, in an argument now familiar, held that the working loose of individual forms from the space that unites them was a response to the perceived threat of engulfment.[66] Friedrich's *Rocky Ravine*, which invites the viewer to imagine entering a landscape that is objectively uninviting, expresses an ambivalence vis-à-vis the prospect of being swallowed up. The dark underside of the all-consuming embrace, this threat is at the same time the ultimate enticement. Rosenblum, who finds Friedrich's tragic spirit of isolation resurrected in the late works of Van Gogh, observes in both painters the tendency to subject the beholder to the "extremities of space" – to make the beholder feel "paralyzed before the forces of nature." In his *Crows over Wheat Fields* (1890), notorious for having been painted just weeks before the artist's death, Van Gogh inverts linear perspective with the result that "the rush of orthogonals ... from near to far suddenly converges on the viewer."[67]

The inversion described here is consistent with that "dyadic reversibility" of Albertian perspective, whose "*logic* of representation," Bryson argues, "changes the viewer himself into a representation, an object or spectacle before his own vision." *Wanderer above the Sea of Mists* rehearses this logic, whereby "the body [is returned] to itself in its own image."[68] The post-Renaissance tradition of painting had gradually displaced the viewer to the side of the centric ray, installing the viewer as an oblique and somewhat clandestine witness to a scene that appears innocent of inspection. By placing the wanderer at its exact centre, Friedrich's painting sends this development into remission. Art historians who insist on understanding Friedrich as a religious painter are confirmed to the extent that the wanderer is positioned *processionally*, centred and fixed by the axial alignments of a quasi-sacred space of mystery.[69] Archaic perspective returns with a vengeance. The sloping backs of the hills on either side of the wanderer are presumably parallel to the picture plane, yet they are *read* as orthogonals that narrow toward the vanishing point, which, in being eclipsed by the figure, secures both him and the viewer as presences around whose gaze the whole is composed.[70] In anticipation of the "zoom effect" in photography, the extreme wide angle at which these "rays" open toward the viewer fosters an impression of contraction and acceleration.

Friedrich's most dedicated opponent was the critic F.W. Basil von Ramdohr, discussed earlier, who in 1809 castigated the painter's *Cross in the Mountains*, unveiled the previous year and intended as part of an altarpiece in a private chapel. The painting features a cross with a gilded carving of Christ placed on a pyramid-shaped outcropping of rock similar to that shown in *Wanderer above the Sea of Mists*. Flanked by fir trees, the barren summit eclipses the rising sun, the limpid rays of which fan out in geometrical regularity against a deepening sky. Ramdohr found much to fault in this work, including the disregard of aerial perspective. Of greater significance is the complaint that *Cross in the Mountains* presented an aggregate of impressions and moments that could not be synthesized from a unitary point of view or point in time. The mountain is painted at close range, yet the artist would need to have stood on another peak of comparable height to capture the view from the angle shown. Light falls on objects in a manner incongruous with the low angle of the sun. Strains of Lessing's *Laocoön* can be detected in Ramdohr's dismissal of art works that stir "pathological" emotions in the viewer, as well as in his insistence that the visual arts, in contrast to music, dance, and poetry, move their audience by means of "forms that stand still" (*stillstehende Formen*).[71]

This last tenet implicates film as painting's antagonist-to-come, and indeed, Ramdohr's criticism helps isolate what is quite arguably cinematic about paintings that, like *Cross in the Mountains*, refuse the viewer a stable, empirically definable platform. In *Large Enclosure* (1832), the shallows of the river Elbe seem to bend down toward the edges, as if distorted by a wide-angle lens, while the flat surface of the braided channel falls away beneath the spectator, who views the scene from a height to which no physical elevation corresponds.[72] These and many other paintings provoke the question as to *where* one would have to stand in order to take in the particular view. The filmgoer, though constantly repositioned with regard to abrupt shifts in framing, is not plagued by this question, which is nullified by the ubiquity conferred on the viewer by the camera, with which the viewer identifies. Metz clarifies this subjective alignment with the apparatus in terms that enable us to associate the cinematic spectator with, say, Friedrich's exalted wanderer or the unpictured viewer of *Cross in the Mountains*:

> Without this identification with the camera certain facts could not be understood, though they are constant ones: the fact, for example, that the spectator is not amazed when the image "rotates" (= a pan) and yet he knows he has not turned his head. The explanation is that he has no need to turn it really, he has turned it in his all-seeing capacity, his identification with the movement of the camera being that of a transcendental, not an empirical subject.[73]

Koerner, for whom the "halted traveller" in *Wanderer above the Sea of Mists* is a transcendental subject, closely echoes Metz's account of the viewer whose constitution of the spectacle ("it is I who make the film") has its mechanical analogue in the projector, which the viewer "has behind him, *at the back of his head*."[74] "The *Rückenfigur*," Koerner asserts, "is so prominent in the composition that the world seems to be an emanation of his gaze."[75] This judgment conforms to Friedrich's oft-quoted enjoinder to the aspiring artist: "Close your bodily eye [*leibliches Auge*] so that you first see the image with your spiritual eye."[76] Friedrich's exhortation amounts to a simplified defence of "intellectual intuition" (*intellektuelle Anschauung*) – spontaneous knowledge independent of sense perception. Kant disputed the possibility of such knowledge, maintaining that to know something independently of sensible experience was to create it.[77] Kant's "realism," as it were, is undone not only by the Romantic concept of the imagination but also by the "omnipotence of thoughts" (*Allmacht der Gedanken*), the belief in which Freud identified as a component of narcissism. The narcissist, like the child, does not distinguish between a desire and its gratification: to want something is enough to bring it forth.[78] Metz, following Baudry, affirms that the experience of watching a film restores the viewer to the "sub-motor and hyper-perceptive state" of the child.[79] Such wakeful stillness is familiar from the primal scene ostensibly witnessed and repressed by Freud's "Wolfman" – a scene to which Metz also refers in describing the paradox of a viewer splayed between intimacy and separation: "For its spectator the film unfolds in that simultaneously very close and definitively inaccessible 'elsewhere' in which the child *sees* the amorous play of the parental couple."[80] This *inaccessible elsewhere* is suggestive of the Romantic ideal of indeterminacy, much as the paradox outlined by Metz is endemic to those of Friedrich's paintings that collapse distance into proximity and place the viewer at the brink of an untouchable void. Typically "frozen in contemplation,"[81] Friedrich's viewing subjects display the same "attentive looking and motionlessness" with which Freud's dreaming analysand and the wolves beyond his window regard each other. The patient's attitude of silent awe is in turn comparable to the paralysis felt by the beholder before certain canvases of Friedrich or Van Gogh, as if "before the forces of nature."

This state of extreme physical arrest, as Rosenblum understands it, results from "the *rush* of orthogonals ... suddenly [converging] on the viewer."[82] So described, the effect is to undo the mathematical construction that, according to Erwin Panofsky, Albertian perspective erected in place of "psychophysiological" space.[83] If empathy is psychophysiological, then art that conforms less to the criteria of strict geometrical perspective is the *less* abstract – the more likely to summon a visceral or motor response. Such a reaction figures prominently in the lore surrounding the advent of motion pictures: in January of 1896, at a screening of the Lumière brothers' minute-long *L'Arriveé d'un train*, members of a select Parisian audience reportedly rose from their seats and fled before the moving image of an approaching locomotive. The report is thought to be apocryphal.[84] Nevertheless, it is worth noting how quickly the slowing train fills the left half of the frame and how close to the tracks the camera is placed. Maurice Merleau-Ponty alludes to this famous shot in an essay on Cézanne, whose work evinces an awareness that monocular perspective, in painting or photography, distorts the magnitude of actual objects as their distance from the viewer grows or diminishes:

> By remaining faithful to the phenomena in his investigations of perspective, Cézanne discovered what recent psychologists have come to formulate: the lived perspective, that which we actually perceive, is not a geometric or photographic one. The objects we see close at hand appear smaller, those far away seem larger than they do in a photograph. (This is evident in films: an approaching train gets bigger much faster than a real train would under the same circumstances.)[85]

The train approaching along tracks that angle just to the viewer's left underscores the exposure that is the effect of a construction that positions the viewer as a corporeal presence opposite the spectacle.[86] The anecdote of the frightened spectators may well be fictitious, but a trauma imagined is still traumatic. Subsequent practices intended to replace the illusion of depth with a flat surface constitute a flight, stylistically achieved, from desire. The "carefully sustained ambiguity" that Burch observes in *Caligari* reflects an ambivalence, more generally characteristic of modernism, toward objects in space. The "profane appetite for the round" that Greenberg ascribed to painters of the Renaissance would seem to implicate Cézanne's "fiercely prehensile eye," as Lawrence Gowing has called it.[87] Cézanne's apples, melons, vases, and pots epitomize the haptic, yet the technique whereby the painter invested these objects with a tangible volume served at the same time to acknowledge "the brute flatness of the surface."[88] Gowing finds in Cézanne a "dichotomy of style" roughly equivalent to the fundamental polarity around which Worringer built his argument (and which, again, Eisenstein articulated with respect to cinematography): "There was an opposition between the bulging, biomorphic rhythms, which are half-destructive, and the light, yet calculated precision with which color patches are built along parallel lines into rectilinear structures."[89]

The menace suggested by this landscape also complicates the nostalgia for the womb (and the attendant susceptibility to tyranny) of which, in Kracauer's analysis, German cinema of the Weimar era was broadly symptomatic. For Kracauer, these films reflected an instinctive submissiveness resulting from the prolonged German dependency on feudal paternalism – a social-psychological trait reinforced by postwar economic conditions.[90] His criticism implicates the German Romantics, to whom a generation of commentators, Georg Lukács among them, was inclined to attribute regressive political tendencies.[91] Eisner likewise believed Expressionist cinema to be descended from Romanticism, though her analysis was more narrowly characteralogical: the strong contrasts of light and dark typical of Weimar films were to be explained in terms of the "Faustian soul" and Nordic man's commitment to gloom. Novalis, who sought solace in "the dark maternal bosom of this dream- and death-dispensing night," exemplified for Eisner the German preference for darkness and twilight – a predilection she explained with the help of Oswald Spengler: "Daylight imposed limits on the eye and created corporeal objects. Night dissolved objects, daylight dissolved souls."[92]

The dissolution of the soul by light is more extensively explored by Blumenberg, who proposes that the upright gait unique to humans makes for a singular sense of vulnerability and exposure. The result is an acute sensitivity to light – an inveterate aversion to the medium of our emphatic, species-specific visibility. As a consequence of this inexorable feeling of defencelessness, humans are susceptible to the temptation to "return to the cave."[93] A "prop of Romanticism,"[94] the cave offered the first humans refuge from the "realism" of the open landscape and thus from a life monopolized by the avoidance of danger. This distance from the exigencies of survival first afforded the possibility of deep sleep, which made dreaming possible. The mother, whose womb the protective security (*Geborgenheit*) of the cave replicates, serves, like the dream itself, as the guardian of sleep – as the guarantor of a creativity independent of sensory experience. Once forced on the savannah to roam constantly in all directions, the ever-vigilant eye is now fixed on the cave's opening, which becomes the sole source of daylight and fear.[95] The seeing subject assumes an attitude of immobilized concentration, a silent watchfulness akin to that of Freud's Wolfman before the open window at the foot of his bed.

This "attentive looking and motionlessness" has its distant precursor in Plato's parable of the cave, with its fettered prisoners, unable even to turn their heads, watching shapes of humans and animals artificially cast on the walls before them. Baudry presents Plato's cave-scenario not only as "the approximate construct of the cinematographic apparatus" but also, beyond that, as "the text of a signifier of a desire which haunts the invention of cinema."[96] What Plato's parable and the cinema have in common is "the wish to construct a simulation machine capable of offering the subject perceptions which are really representations mistaken for perceptions."[97] The regressive aim of such an apparatus is the recovery of a state in which the satisfaction of desire is strictly hallucinatory – in which the subject (like those immobilized prisoners) has not yet learned to distinguish representations from perceptions. The peculiar capacity of the cinema to produce an "impression of reality," which dreams also produce, uniquely enables it to revive in the viewer an experience of archaic gratification. Baudry draws his understanding of the dream-state largely from Freud, who observed that the unconscious, to the extent that it is ever figured in dreams, is typically located underground. Baudry's opening salvo – "One always returns to the scene of the cave"[98] – could well serve as a motto for Blumenberg's extended reflection on the ubiquity of the cave-metaphor. Blumenberg mentions the cinema only in passing but comments on the non-coincidental contemporaneity of the cinema and psychoanalysis, the latter having metaphorized the mechanism of "projection" essential to the former. A dream's meaning, Blumenberg argues, is merely the by-product of its function, which is not primarily "indicative" but "projective-illusory." To focus on the content of a dream is to miss its more essential purpose, which is that of casting endopsychic disturbances as threats from without. Baudry sounds a complementary note, impugning those students of the cinema who are distracted by the content of films and the technical specifics of their making. He argues that "in order to determine the *raison d'être* for the cinema effect," one should instead "examine the position of the subject facing the image."[99]

Paintings like *Wanderer above the Sea of Mists* and *Rocky Ravine* do just this. Is there something arguably cinematic about these paintings? For one thing, they presuppose a viewer who, like Plato's prisoners, cannot help but face forward. Contrary to Koerner's claim, these paintings are addressed to a gaze, not a glance, the gaze corresponding to an *advertency* that is all the more forceful in images in which a wanderer, fixed squarely within the frame, faces away from the viewer. The stillness these paintings impose on the viewer is implied even in paintings in which no *Rückenfigur* is pictured. In *Early Snow* (1828), for example, a rutted road bends through a clearing and vanishes before a dark stand of tall conifers (figure 33). Like the path in *Rocky Ravine*, the road disappears around a turn in the middle distance, which has the effect of drawing the background toward the picture plane. Koerner assumes a generalized viewing experience in which the subject participates corporeally in the view. His reading of *Early Snow*, to adopt Worringer's lexicon, is empathetic: "I am the first to enter this wood; no footprints mar the uniqueness of my experience."[100]

Koerner invokes Heidegger's *Holzweg* – the overgrown woodcutter's trail that disappears abruptly "in the untrodden" (*im Unbegangenen*),[101] though one is also put in mind of Robert Frost's "The Road Not Taken" (1916) and of the traveller forced to choose between two forking paths, both of which "lay / In leaves no step had trodden black." Mutedly Romantic, Frost's verse contains a late example of a wanderer brought to a halt before an ambiguous prospect:

> Two roads diverged in a yellow wood,
> And sorry I could not travel both
> And be one traveler, long I stood
> And looked down one as far as I could
> To where it bent in the undergrowth;[102]

Frost's famous poem ultimately proposes a subject whose character is the sum of his sacrifices ("I shall be telling this with a sigh / Somewhere ages and ages hence"). A full century earlier – in the very year that

33. Caspar David Friedrich (1774–1840), *Early Snow* (1827).

Oil on canvas, 43.8 × 34.5 cm
bpk Bildagentur/Kunsthalle Hamburg
Photo: Elke Walford/Art Resource, NY

Friedrich painted his solitary wanderer – Lord Byron had placed his own ambivalent pilgrim before an atmospheric tableau:

> I stood in Venice, on the Bridge of Sighs;
> A palace and a prison on each hand:
> I saw from out the wave her structures rise
> As from the stroke of the enchanter's wand:[103]

Divided between contrary emotions, the speaker is centred before this Venetian variant of the "sea of mists." The bridge, enclosed and fitted with small windows meant to grant condemned prisoners their last glimpse of earth, is an apparatus in its own right – the architectural medium of an apperception mapped onto the cruciform *bi*-symmetry of the human body. The prolonged but provisional pause of Frost's poem ("long I stood") contrasts with Byron's proclamation of self ("I stood"). The compromise at the heart of realism is likewise a foil for the gossamer vision of Venice's "proud towers" rising before the traveller "[at] airy distance."[104] And whereas the speaker of Frost's poem enters into the foot-worn setting, the implied traveller of *Early Snow* stands frozen before the near blackness that yawns between the road and treetops. Koerner summons and identifies with a subject who imagines entering into the painted scene. Appropriately, his first-person, present-tense account reads like a dream-protocol, performing – in compliance with Baudry's mandate – the examination of the subject vis-à-vis the image:

> A path leads into the wood before me. I trace it with my eye: a white painted surface that rises vertically from the bottom of the canvas, but which, as I cling to it with my gaze, stretches forth as a horizontal path. I see into the canvas as if into a wood; my eye goes forth into this picture of an entrance as a stone would fall to earth. Entering the wood, my eye can trace many paths. Straight ahead, bare tree trunks give way to darkness. (189)

In keeping with the oneiric character of this "deposition," *abstraction* (the awareness of the flat canvas) yields to *empathy* (the credible illusion of spatial depth), representation collapses into perception. This does not mean that the requirements of realism have been satisfied. Instead, they have been suspended, neutralized by the hallucinatory character of an image that is unreal in its hyper-reality. The clarity of Friedrich's paintings, with their sharp outlines and transparent pigments, is often severe. Much as the dreaming subject is immobilized before a projection that is manifestly non-haptical, the viewer of *Rocky Ravine* or *Early Snow* is brought to a standstill.

Freud's patient, whose "attentive looking and motionlessness" mirrors that of the wolves peering in at him through his bedroom window, embodies a Romantic commonplace: a subject held in silent thrall before an overwhelming nature. A defining example is found in Wackenroder's Joseph Berglinger, discussed earlier, whose biography constitutes its own brand of psychopathology.[105] Here again is the friar's account of the youthful Joseph's experience of sacred music:

> Expectantly, he would await the first sound of the instruments – and when it came bursting forth, mighty and sustained, shattering the dull silence like a storm from Heaven, and when the sounds swept over his head in all their grandeur, then it was as if his soul spread great wings, as if he were rising up from a desolate heath, as if the curtain of dark cloud were dissolving before his mortal gaze and he were soaring up to the radiant Heavens. Then he would hold his whole body still and motionless, fixing his eyes unmoving on the floor.[106]

Burch, incidentally, proposes that music, which in the early days of cinema was performed live, served to create a "higher space" by isolating the individual filmgoer from the noise of the projector and fellow spectators.[107] The fairground – site of both the early cinema and Dr Caligari's sinister sideshow – is precisely the cacophonous setting that Joseph is described as having fled. That "higher space" is heir to the vaulted interior of the church, itself analogous to the "radiant Heavens" to which Joseph felt transported. The metropolitan movie palaces that supplanted the temporary, often makeshift structures in which films were once shown came to resemble Baroque theatres, if not churches, their lavish decor extending the spectacle that appeared on the screen.[108]

A venerable precursor to this moment is found in a scene from Goethe's *Faust*, first published in 1790 ("Forest and Cavern"). Having, like Wackenroder's Joseph, fled human company, the agitated hero summons imagery of a violent storm, as well as of the cave that affords him safe harbour. Once the external threat abates, the secrets of his inner world, newly revealed to him, are projected phantasmagorically as moon-shadows and radiant mists:

> Und steigt vor meinem Blick der reine Mond
> Besänftigend herüber: schweben mir
> Von Felsenwänden, aus dem feuchten Busch,

Der Vorwelt silberne Gestalten auf,
Und lindern der Betrachtung strenge Lust.[109]

And when before my gaze the moon rises
in soothing clarity:
Silver shapes of forgotten time
float upward from the rock walls, from the damp bush,
softening the severe pleasure of contemplation.[110]

This imagined scene effectively stages Blumenberg's hypothesis of human prehistory. The cave shelters the subject from the elements, which persist as objects of pure sight; their greatly reduced immediacy determines their "diaphanous mediality."[111] Such "silver shapes of forgotten time" may recall Marcel Proust's *tempes perdue*, raised by Blumenberg as emblematic of the paradox that defines the beginning of the novel as such. The inception of consciousness – the moment of awakening – is itself inaccessible to the conscious mind. The novel's beginning is the release from everything that "lies at one's back" (*im Rücken liegt*).[112] The cave, with its one opening onto the outside world, provides for the forward-facing attitude characteristic of modernity – an orientation that aligns Friedrich's wanderer with the cinematic spectator.[113]

The first volume of Proust's *À la recherche du temps perdu* (1913) begins with the insomniac-narrator attempting to recollect the slumber from which he has awakened and to which he finds himself unable to return. The above lines from *Faust* corroborate Blumenberg's proposal that deep sleep was possible only after humans came to dwell in caves. Wakefulness, and the habit of sleeping "with one eye open," are chronologically prior conditions. Yet even the state that just precedes waking eludes the grasp of experience. It is known only by the disturbance that brought it to an end. The same modern age that engendered the novel, Blumenberg claims, begot the notion of traumatic birth, which at base is the idea that every living thing is marked by the rupture of its sudden emergence from its anorganic substrate.[114] The end of the novel, like death itself, undoes the disequilibrium of its beginning. All life is insomnia. Dreams only expose the sleeping subject to the forgotten horrors of waking life. Freud's Wolfman dreams of lying awake in bed. Proust's Swann, who in sleep "come[s] under the thrall of one of [his] childish terrors," wakes himself up to escape the fingers of his great-uncle, who used to torment him as a boy by pulling at his curls.[115]

Not surprisingly, the horror film takes shape under the sign of insomnia. *Caligari* features the somnambulist Cesare, who after twenty-three years of death-like sleep is summoned to tell fortunes and to accost slumbering victims in their beds. Count Orlok, the vampire of Murnau's *Nosferatu*, is habitually awake nights but during the day, as he tells his wary guest, sleeps "the deepest sleep." Cesare's literary forebear, the creature of Mary Shelley's *Frankenstein*, begins his own narrative by remarking on the very aporia named by Blumenberg – that one can ill recollect what is beyond the reach of memory: "It is with considerable difficulty that I remember the original era of my being."[116] Startled awake, convulsed to life by the "spark of being" with which his maker has infused him,[117] the creature inherits the insomnia of his creator while harbouring an incipient sense of death as the one true cure for the thoughts that trouble sleep.[118]

An artificial child, Frankenstein's creation passes through the successive stages of Rousseau's subject, from "savagery" to erudition, from innocence to a consciousness plagued by self-knowledge and imprinted with the myriad cruelties of human society. Remembering what could never be the object of memory, he recalls the dullness of his first impressions and an initial, strong aversion to light:

> By degrees, I remember, a stronger light pressed upon my nerves, so that I was obliged to shut my eyes. Darkness then came over me, and troubled me; but hardly had I felt this, when, by opening my eyes, as I now suppose, the light poured in upon me again. I walked, and, I believe, descended; but I presently found a great alteration in my sensations. Before, dark and opaque bodies had surrounded me, impervious to my touch or sight; but I now found that I could wander on at liberty, with no obstacles which I could not either surmount or avoid.[119]

Acute photosensitivity is a quality the creature shares with Plato's prisoner, who upon being "freed from [his] fetters and compelled to … lift up his eyes to the light" recoils at the glare, which leaves him "unable to discern the objects whose shadows he formerly saw."[120] In Whale's 1931 adaptation, a comparable experience is condensed into the words with which Frankenstein heralds the creature's emergence from within the castle's unlit interior: "So far he's been kept in complete darkness. Wait till I bring him into the light." When the creature first appears, he is seen from behind, his angular frame filling that of the door as he shuffles backward into the room before turning to search the scene with listless eyes. As if coaxing a child to take its first steps,

34. *Frankenstein* (1931), dir. James Whale.

Frankenstein guides the creature to a chair and bids him sit. Pleased at the creature's comprehension, he draws open a window high overhead. The creature casts his gaze gradually upward, then stands and stretches his long, slender arms toward the light. When after a few moments Frankenstein reshutters the window, the creature, noticeably crestfallen, is left in shadow, reaching vainly for the vanished sun (figure 34). With a questioning gesture of his hands he addresses his maker, who directs him back to the chair. The camera now pans from the creature's face down to his hands, which motion pleadingly toward the man he knows as his father.

However limited the artistry of Whale's production overall, these discrete moments, in their mute poignancy and power, incarnate the spirit of Expressionism. The diagonal suture visible on the creature's right wrist is a reminder of his having been cobbled together out of lifeless limbs and organs. Some years earlier, Wiene's *Hands of Orlac* (1924) told the story of a celebrated pianist whose hands, badly injured in a railway accident, are surgically replaced with those of a freshly executed murderer. The transplanted hands, or so the pianist believes, remain subject to the evil will of the dead criminal, and the film becomes a character study of a man increasingly alienated from parts of his own body. The same conflict is explored throughout the oeuvre of Austrian Expressionist Egon Schiele, who frequently portrayed himself as if struggling with unseen adversaries. His arms and hands, as if invisibly bound, are painfully racked and contorted. Oversized and arthritically misshapen, the hands are at times positioned beside or near the face in physiognomic parallel. Writing on Schiele's "mannerist" use of gestures to convey the "nightmarish and monstrous aspects of the self," Salomon Resnik discerns a kinship to psychosis, wherein "fragments of hallucinated objects of the inner world or the contents of the body come to inhabit our surrounding landscape, including the natural human landscape." The "body image" – the picture the mind draws of the body – is projected as "iconographic scenery."[121] Indeed, the young trees found in many of Schiele's landscapes – twisted, splayed, and often tied to stakes – exhibit the tortured disfigurement of his self-portraits.

Much as the creature of Whale's film embodies the same "nightmarish and monstrous aspects" that compose Schiele's self-image, so the creature of Shelley's novel models the self-directed disgust that was the Austrian painter's stock in trade. A textbook example of narcissistic injury, Shelley's creature comes to see himself as a "monster" after glimpsing his reflection in a pool and comparing himself to the family in whose proximity he has been hiding:

> I had admired the perfect forms of my cottagers – their grace, beauty, and delicate complexions: but how was I terrified when I viewed myself in a transparent pool! At first I started back, unable to believe that it was indeed I who was reflected in the mirror; and when I became fully convinced that I was in reality the monster that I am, I was filled with the bitterest sensations of despondence and mortification. Alas! I did not yet entirely know the fatal effects of this miserable deformity.[122]

The creature in Shelley's novel is the product of education, albeit self-education. His counterpart in Whale's film is brutally simple. He snarls and bellows, even laughing at one point, but he never develops the ability to speak. His muteness, starkly offset by his master's effete elocution, bears the essential silence of early cinema into the era of sound. To be sure, the experiment of the cinema, of which *Caligari* is a paramount example, is largely absorbed by *Frankenstein*, reproduced thematically while being neutralized filmically. Sharply angled walls and trapezoidal windows are no longer a matter of modernist style but instead serve a credible rendering of the "Gothic" – a setting in which the high contrast of Expressionism seems naturally at home. Yet Frankenstein's castle reverberates but dimly with the Expressionist penchant for the Gothic proper. Worringer's assessment of Gothic architecture has already been mentioned. Art historians like Heinrich Wölfflin argued that criticism had wrongly subjected medieval art to the standards of the Renaissance, faulting the former for the absence of three-dimensionality and studied proportion. Contending that medieval art was driven by a more abstract purpose, Wölfflin stressed those qualities that early twentieth-century painters came to embrace: the expressivity of line, the restlessness of form, the prominence of the surface, rhythmic freedom, the unnaturalistic use of colour, and so on. With respect to the eleventh-century manuscript known as the *Bamberg Apocalypse*, Wölfflin noted the emphasis achieved by deliberate distortion, as when, in order to accentuate the importance of a manual gesture, the hand is made disproportionately large.[123]

These properties are found in Mathias Grünewald, a German painter of the early sixteenth century whose work, rediscovered in the nineteenth, became a point of reference for many Expressionists. His Isenheim Altarpiece (1512–16), with its unprecedentedly graphic and pathos-laden rendering of the crucifixion, championed a residual Medievalism in the midst of the Northern Renaissance. Grünewald's Christ, his flesh gangrenous, his shoulders (as in Schiele) violently dislocated, appears utterly starved, yet the horizontal beam of the cross bends downward at the improbable heft of the wasted corpse. The figure's hands, cupped tensely around nails in frozen spasms of pain, exhibit an Expressionist potential fully realized in *The Hands of Orlac*, in which the tormented pianist regards his own knotted fingers in terrified awe.[124]

Shelley's creature, in comparing himself unfavourably to the "grace, beauty, and delicate complexions" of the cottagers, identifies himself as the antithesis of the neoclassical ideal. In Whale's film particularly, the creature is the popular embodiment of the self-alienation that is the condition of modern art – the contrary of the classicism in which, following Worringer, the human form and the phenomenal world partake of a common organic vitality. His is a fragmented self. Denied the *imago* onto which he would map his own physique, the creature personifies the turbulence of the storm from which he drew life. The contrary of classical proportion and ease of movement, he is, to adopt Lacan's phrasing, "the automaton in which, in an ambiguous relation, the world of his own making tends to find completion."[125] He exhibits not only a minimal control over his own limbs but also a frustration at the sheer *impotence* of his thoughts. His hands express his helplessness throughout, such as when he finds himself powerless simply to wave off his tormentors. In the end, the cinema's definitive monster is left shrieking in uncomprehending terror as the mill, which the townspeople have set ablaze, crashes down around him. Last seen pinned beneath a massive timber, he is a true *corpus dolente*.

At certain points in Whale's *Frankenstein*, then, an iconography of martyrdom surfaces. These moments are isolated, also in the sense of their being framed and magnified by the cinematography, which sets them apart and marks them as meaningful. Their genealogy is tangled. The motifs are derived in part from a long tradition of painting, in part from a closely contemporary current in the arts that drew new vigour from that tradition, and in part from a cinema that, for a time, gleaned its visual vocabulary from both.[126] Wiene's *Caligari*, in which the "zigzag delineations" of the set-design are assimilated to the human frame, incorporates an Expressionism that had already incorporated the medieval conventions of sacred suffering. Just before Cesare, the fugitive sleepwalker, collapses and dies, he lingers upright as if crucified (figure 35), his contorted posture mimicking the form of those starkly menacing trees while recalling that of Schiele in his *Self-Portrait as St Sebastian* (figure 36). These homologous figures attest to a common stock of available images. More fundamentally, they foreground the symmetry whose paradigm we carry within our bodies as the cross we have to bear.[127] *Rocky Ravine* is a clandestine portrayal of the body, not only because of its petrified intimation of a human hand but also because of the somatic challenge the painting poses. With reference to another of Friedrich's paintings, Koerner summons the disequilibrium of self and world effected by the work's disintegration into "jagged, helter-skelter fragments of horizontals and verticals juxtaposed."[128] The painting in question (*Winter*, 1807–8) is a snowy landscape featuring the broken and weathered remnants of a medieval monastery amid the twisted ruins of ancient oaks. Trees and Gothic façades (along with sea waves) were the materials of Mondrian's "plus-and-minus" series, and Koerner's formulation provides a foil for the "cruciform symmetry" whereby the Dutch artist lent his compositions a pervasive sense of balance – a sense anchored in corporeal self-experience. Where the ambient world is otherwise an echo of the subject's own felt wretchedness, as embodied by Schiele as well as Frankenstein's creature, Mondrian's abstractions counteract that "monstrous confusion of the world-picture" named by Worringer. In its mirage-like quality, Mondrian's *Pier and Ocean* is consistent with the phantom support onto which the human animal maps its upright orientation. Indeed *Pier and Ocean,* to borrow Lacan's language, is "pregnant with the correspondences that unite the *I* with the statue in which man projects himself."[129]

35. *The Cabinet of Dr Caligari* (1920), dir. Robert Wiene.

36. Egon Schiele (1890–1918), *Self-Portrait as St Sebastian* (1914).

Poster for Schiele's Exhibition at the Arnot Gallery (1915)
Vienna Museum
HIP / Art Resource, NY

Chapter Six

Necessary Advances

In an attempt to explain how the cinema evolved into a storytelling medium so quickly following its inception, film editor Walter Murch, who has already been mentioned in these pages, cites the influence of three figures: Thomas Edison, Ludwig van Beethoven, and Gustave Flaubert. Edison's inclusion in this trio is self-explanatory. Beethoven's rather less so. But the dynamism of cinema, Murch affirms, is heir to the innovations that set Beethoven apart from his immediate predecessors – the often rapid rise and fall in volume, the expansion and contraction in instrumentation, and the overall thematic restlessness: "When you listen to Beethoven's music now and hear those sudden shifts in tonality, rhythm, and musical focus, it's as though you can hear the grammar of film – cuts, dissolves, fades, superimposures, long shots, close shots – being worked out in musical terms." The structural volatility that Beethoven introduced coincided with a new emphasis, in the *belles lettres* of the nineteenth century, on the details of ordinary life. Enter Flaubert, "who will spend a whole page evoking tiny sounds and motes of dust in an empty room." The explosion of form in music and the unprecedented scrutiny of the commonplace in literature were not integral to a unitary development but separate currents that eventually "surged together within the physical framework of film."[1]

The intuitions of this working filmmaker find their philosophical reinforcement in Rancière, who likewise understands the cinema as a "union of contraries." Parting company with those modernists who deduced the nature of cinema from its technical means and, consequently, embraced it for its utopian potential, Rancière identifies the cinema with an "aesthetic moment" that is neither reducible to the machine of filmmaking nor limited to the cinematic medium. He proposes a dialectics wherein two contradictory forces combined to form the inherently paradoxical nature of film. To begin with, there was the aestheticist regime that proclaimed the originary power of the imagination and, as the nineteenth century progressed, de-emphasized figuration in favour of the artistic process. Beethoven, in whose work that process is frequently audible, was a seminal agent in a history that freed music from its subservience to fable or textual program and eventually from the centuries-old habit of employing the resources of music to simulate human passions. The ultimate retreat from tonality was contemporaneous with the early years of the cinema, which, in a manner that ran counter to modernist aestheticism, revived the conventions of plot and character, thus appearing to counteract the true and unique aesthetic capacity of this revolutionary medium. Deemed a betrayal by some, this reversion is prefigured in Flaubert, whose desire to write a novel of pure style was realized in one devoid of style, "stripped of every trace of the writer's intervention and composed instead of the indifferent swirl of specks of dust and the passivity of things with neither will nor meaning."[2]

Erich Auerbach had long since extolled Flaubert's subjective self-effacement – the novelist's seemingly artless ability to "bestow the power of mature expression" on the unremarkable material of a hollow existence (Emma Bovary's).[3] Yet the result is not a "splendor of the insignificant," as Rancière characterizes it, for the mundane objects and circumstances that Flaubert describes are themselves volatile, indices of "a grey and random human destiny [moving] toward its end." Writing on Beethoven's late style, Adorno states that it is within the subject that the objective catastrophes of history achieve their full radiance.[4] In a similar vein, Auerbach holds that Emma's situation, however poorly she comprehends it, is suffused with a light that issues from her experience and her perceptions of it (484). In modernist novels, by contrast, subjectivities become unmoored from external events, which are themselves fragmented and "loosely joined" (545). Within the history of the novel then, there is also a "late style," characterized by an erosion of chronology and a disarticulation of external and internal processes.[5] With respect to the paragon afforded by Virginia Woolf, Auerbach observes how easily one could assume that the writer had sought to "exploit the structural possibilities of film in the interest of the novel" (546). For Auerbach, however, the radically dissociative character of Woolf's *To the Lighthouse* (1927) represents a potential inherent in the genre itself. The cinema, with its unique capacity to condense space and time, had only served to heighten the novel's sense of the spatial and temporal restrictions imposed on it by the instrument of language.

The novels of German Romanticism, Auerbach notes, challenged these limitations, if but tentatively – a fact that supports Rancière's contention not only that the cinema existed as an *artistic* idea well prior to its *technical* advent but also that it owed its genesis to an essentially Romantic program that rejected traditional mimesis in favour of creative vision. The cinema is only apparently the heir to realism, and realism itself, in literature as well as in art, was made possible by what Odo Marquard, commenting on Hegel, termed *die Entschränkung des Kunstfähigen*, that is, the delimitation of that which is suitable for art.[6] What in both Flaubert and narrative cinema would appear to be a submission to the mundane is paradoxically the result of an aestheticism that found the potential for beauty (or meaning) in everything. Rancière stresses this paradox common to both, yet he cautions against concluding that Flaubert constructed certain scenes – as when Emma stands at a window absorbed by the sight of garden trellises toppled by a storm – as "film-shots," maintaining instead that these "frames" strive to achieve "the dream-like stasis of painting."[7]

But is this "dream-like stasis" a characteristic of *all* painting, or is this itself not proper to the aesthetic moment of which the works of Caspar David Friedrich are exemplary expressions? Friedrich painted his *Wanderer above the Sea of Mists* in 1818. In the same year, Mary Shelley published *Frankenstein*, and Byron his lines on Venice, while Hegel delivered a draft of his lectures on aesthetics at the University of Heidelberg. Friedrich's *Wanderer* and so many of his works seem emblematic of Hegel's view that the purpose of painting was that of "making visible to sense what is withdrawn from sense [*den Sinnen entrückt*]."[8] In its reduction of three dimensions to a planar surface, painting divests the material object of the corporeal independence that defines the sculpted figure, which, as an embodiment of spirit, is complete in itself. The work of sculpture is indifferent to the spectator, who can view the figure from any angle or position; a painting, by contrast, exists for the "fixed point, i.e., for the subject apprehending it." Painting dissolves the spatial self-sufficiency of the object, which, relieved of its third dimension, enters into a far more intimate relation with the spectator, who finds in the painting an externalized reflection of his own inner life. Painting transforms the depicted world into pure appearance, which becomes the means of visual self-apprehension. And because painting "is concerned not only with the subjective inner life as such but ... with the inner life as *particularized* within," it must expand its domain of suitable objects to include "anything and everything in which a man as an individual subject can take an interest or find satisfaction."[9]

In what Hegel thus understood to be a "necessary advance" over sculpture, painting is intrinsically receptive to the "prosaic" conditions of which prose proper was to become the true conduit.[10] With Hegel at his back, Auerbach traces the origins of literary realism, as supremely exemplified in *Madame Bovary*, to an ancient disturbance in the elevated classical style. This style, in which actions are effectively purified of their material circumstances and, indeed, of the "vital processes of life," lost its hold with the rising influence of the Bible, in which individuals, often of lower birth, are embroiled in a dialectic of debasement and exaltation. In characterizing the modern realist novel as "a chronologically well-ordered total treatment which accompanies the subject from beginning to end … and emphasizes the great turning points of destiny" (548), Auerbach pinpoints the respective virtues of the Homeric and biblical styles. The former, being equipped with a vast and differentiated repertoire of grammatical and syntactical devices, enables the coherent and comprehensive arrangement of people, things, and episodes in their spatial and temporal relations and in terms of their relative magnitude. This subtle and precise management of detail goes hand in hand with the lives of individuals who, like Odysseus, seem nobly inert, untransformed by the trials and hardships they endure. Biblical narrative, by contrast, consigns to shadow everything but the most essential and pivotal. The more rudimentary syntax of biblical language is consistent with the incipient realism of these stories, which turn on sudden, dramatic reversals that thrust ordinary lives into history.

A key aspect of Auerbach's schema is forecast in Rilke's "Archaic Torso of Apollo," from the second volume of the *New Poems* (1908). Largely a loose cataract of clauses held together by conjunctions and relative-pronoun constructions, the poem – a sonnet – concludes with an isolated and stark exhortation:

> Wir kannten nicht sein unerhörtes Haupt,
> darin die Augenäpfel reiften. Aber
> sein Torso glüht noch wie ein Kandelaber,
> in dem sein Schauen, nur zurückgeschraubt,
>
> sich hält und glänzt. Sonst könnte nicht der Bug
> der Brust dich blenden, und im leisen Drehen
> der Lenden könnte nicht ein Lächeln gehen
> zu jener Mitte, die die Zeugung trug.
>
> Sonst stünde dieser Stein enstellt und kurz
> unter der Schultern durchsichtigem Sturz
> und flimmerte nicht so wie Raubtierfelle;
>
> und bräche nicht aus allen seinen Rändern
> aus wie ein Stern: denn da ist keine Stelle,
> die dich nicht sieht. Du musst dein Leben ändern.[11]

We cannot know his legendary head
with eyes like ripening fruit. And yet his torso
is still suffused with brilliance from inside,
like a lamp, in which his gaze, now turned to low,

gleams in all its power. Otherwise
the curved breast could not dazzle you so, nor could
a smile run through the placid hips and thighs
to that dark center where procreation flared.

Otherwise this stone would seem defaced
beneath the translucent cascade of the shoulders
and would not glisten like a wild beast's fur:

would not, from all the borders of itself,
burst like a star: for here there is no place
that does not see you. You must change your life.[12]

The poem seems specific in its contradiction of Hegel's claim regarding sculpture, namely that "a person's own subjective inwardness" was "not revealed in the sightless figure [*blicklose Gestalt*], nor can such a figure convey a concentrated expression of inner life."[13] The adjuratory coda could well serve as Emma Bovary's epitaph, though Rilke's sonnet, in conditioning this reversal on the truncation of classical form, suggests an unexpected vantage point from which to reconsider Auerbach's monumental account of the mimetic impulse in Western literature. "Archaic Torso of Apollo" predates *To the Lighthouse* by almost twenty years, but Rilke and Woolf have, to follow Auerbach's take on the latter, a common approach to the objective world. Flaubert's subjects are still anchored in that world. The movements of their minds are integral to the novel's "plan." In Woolf, random events in the outer world serve merely to set internal ones in motion: a brown stocking, innocuous in itself, is sufficient to launch a succession of interiorized reflections. That stocking is akin to the many objects around which Rilke's "thing-poems" gather. His poetry frequently seems on the verge of assimilating to the prosaic world and to prose *per se*, in the face of which the sonnet-form struggles to persist. The poem states the circumstance under which objects appear as affairs of the mind.[14] While the marble torso is a classical bulwark against the atomized modern world, that world insinuates itself into the figure's profile through the analogy of the lamp – a "candelabra" that, whatever its nature, can be mechanically dimmed (*zurückgeschraubt*). As good an example of modern aestheticism as one can imagine, Rilke's sonnet is itself a "union of contraries," one that inevitably, in Rancière's formulation, "draws our attention ... to the glimmer of the epiphany and the splendor of pure reasonless being."[15]

Modernism placed its hopes in such splendour and believed the cinema to be made for the new technical moment – an art-form in which fables would dissipate and yield to the dance of matter or the play of light.[16] But Rancière, arguing that the cinema had of necessity reinstated the very narrative conventions the aesthetic age had worked to erode, resists the modernist claim that the cinema had discarded "the arrangement of necessary and verisimilar actions that lead the characters from fortune to misfortune, or vice versa, through the careful construction of the intrigue [*noeud*] and denouement."[17] Rancière's formulation recalls Auerbach, for whom the precise architecture of fully exteriorized actions and situations, found prototypically in Homer's *Odyssey*, has its footing in a highly advanced grammar: "a large number of conjunctions, adverbs, particles, and other syntactical tools, all clearly circumscribed and delicately differentiated in meaning, delimit persons, things and portions of incidents in respect to one another" (6). The precise delineation of order, sequence, hierarchy, and priority, made possible by a virtuoso facility with the basic parts of speech, was of minimal concern to a grammatically subversive modernism. Energy eclipsed causality, and even Henry James evolved a "late style" in which, citing Hugh Kenner, "subject and verb are 'there' but don't carry the burden of what is said."[18] An indifference to syntax was the new ardour. Kenner, remarking that Ezra Pound mined the Ancients for "non-consecutive arrays" and "constellated words," likewise noted a mounting interest in fragmentary forms, such as torn bits of old papyri or the dismembered marbles in museums, prized all the more for being incomplete.[19] Witness Rilke's "Archaic Torso," in which the elements of syntax – "and yet," "like," "in which," "now," "otherwise," "nor," "otherwise" (a second time) – stand out as the exposed ligaments of a poem whose near disintegration (into prose) leaves the sonnet-form intact but empty. The poem, in which a vision of bodily (self-)coherence outshines what would otherwise be experienced as stunted deformity, is also a vague reminder that the Greeks derived the terms of both grammar and prosody from parts of the anatomy (*pous, daktylos, arthron, colon*, etc.).[20]

The contrast between a realistic representation, carefully structured and sequentially consistent, and the less coherent, temporally compressed narrative typical of modernism parallels a distinction drawn by Freud, for whom the difference between the latent dream-thought and the manifest dream-content is by nature syntactical. The task of analysis is to restore the "conjunctions" that the dream-*work*, intent on thwarting traceable associations, labours to disable. In the following passage from *The Interpretation of Dreams*, Freud describes the dream-thought using terms identical to those that Auerbach later applied to the realist novel and especially to its distant forerunners. His subsequent evocation of the dream-content truly vibrates with artistic movements still to come:

> The different portions of this complicated structure stand ... in the most manifold logical relations to one another. They can represent foreground and background, digressions and illustrations, conditions, chains of evidence and counter-arguments. When the whole mass of the dream-thoughts is brought under the pressure of the dream-work, and its elements are turned about, broken into fragments and jammed together – almost like pack-ice – the question arises of what happens to the logical connections which have hitherto formed its framework. What representation do dreams provide for "if," "because," "just as," "although," "either-or," and all the other conjunctions without which we cannot understand sentences of speech?[21]

As with Auerbach, whose *Mimesis* appeared nearly a half-century after *The Interpretation of Dreams*, Freud borrows his vocabulary from art history ("foreground and background") as well as rhetoric ("chains of evidence and counter-arguments"); and by way of analogy, he will go on to summon the difference between the visual and the verbal arts: dreams, like paintings, lacked the ability that language affords to express logical relations.[22] But the question Freud poses at the end of the paragraph just cited is of greater potential relevance for the cinema: What representation do *films* have for "if," "because," "just as," "although," "either–or," and so on?

Rancière poses a cognate question, and this with respect to Murnau's *Tartuffe* (1925), adapted from the play by Molière of the same title. Written and first staged in 1664, Molière's comedy is about an aristocrat, Orgon, who has fallen under the spell of a religious charlatan, the eponymous Tartuffe. Orgon invites the imposter into his home and even determines to marry his (horrified) daughter to him. The family contrives to expose Tartuffe's parasitic designs, causing Orgon to bear clandestine witness to a scene in which the vile hypocrite exhibits his lust for Elmire, Orgon's wife. The successful execution of this "mousetrap" does not resolve the play, whose happy outcome results instead from an intervention by the king. Murnau's film, however, turns on the moment when Tartuffe, believing himself unobserved, relaxes his performance, revealing his body as one conspicuously out of place in Orgon's noble household. For Rancière, the manner of this resolution goes to what is distinctive about the cinema: "Molière's Tartuffe is done in by words, by the predilection for seducing with words common to the priest and the lecher. What equivalent power does silent film have at its disposal to animate, and betray, the silhouette, to lead it to lower its guard?"[23]

Rancière's analysis of Murnau's *Tartuffe* corroborates his general thesis concerning the paradoxical nature of the cinema. The cinema became what it had to become by breaking the circuit between its technical capacities and its aesthetic calling, "[using] its artistic procedures to construct dramaturgies that thwart its natural powers" (11). Expressionist *par excellence,* Murnau marshalled the resources of the cinema only to frustrate the enchantment that is film's unique quality. The villainous interloper is a shadow whose power is inseparable from the gloom he inhabits. To defeat him, Elmire must lure him not merely into the light but into a different setting, indeed, a different epoch: "The cinematic silhouette walks into the bedroom ... only to find itself confined by the frames of ... a pictorial space where bodily proximity and the distribution of light and shadow lead the black silhouette to be lost from sight."[24] Tartuffe's body – crude, loud, lascivious, and drunk – comes now to resemble those found in the bawdy and rambunctious tavern scenes depicted by seventeenth-century Dutch genre painters.[25] With Elmire's help, Murnau leads "the cinematographic shadow" out of the Romantic universe and into a more properly classical one, "where a genre corresponds to a subject and where characters have the physiognomy and language befitting their status."

Rancière thus pulls alongside Auerbach, for whom the decline of the Aristotelian "separation of styles" is matched by the increased importance of *milieu*. Literary regimes in which Aristotle's influence endured, French classicism in particular, trafficked in personages whose noble emotions were "freed of the turmoil of everyday life, cleansed of its odor and flavor," and who were thus impervious to history, history being for Auerbach the essential dimension of realism. The requisite unities of place, time, and plot foil this same dimension, "[reducing] the contacts of the action with its milieu to a minimum" (386). A significant step forward is found in Stendhal, whose characters are more deeply embedded in contemporary social and political life than had been seen in any of his predecessors. In treating as *tragic* the life of a commoner (the protagonist of *The Red and the Black*), he defies the fixed hierarchy of genres, which served to thwart the historical energy that could heave lives and careers upward or plunge them into the depths. Yet Stendhal's own revulsion at the reality his characters inhabit keeps him aloof from the social classes ushered in by rapidly changing conditions.

The vigour of Stendhal's realism is thus driven by a paradox. His knack for providing nuanced descriptions of any given milieu stems from his disdain for the bourgeois cult of making money and from his despair at the corresponding evaporation of *esprit*. Ivan Nagel, in a book on Mozart no less, has written that realism "does not emerge until knowledge of the real world becomes inseparable from disgust and anxiety at its relentless reification."[26] Whereas the denizens of the classical world are "cleansed of [life's] odor and flavor," a maturing realism presents figures who seem "sprung from the immanence of their historical, social, [and] physical ... situation." Madame Vauquer, the boarding house mistress of Balzac's *Old Goriot*, appears as little more than an evil excrescence of the oppressively malodorous domain over which she reigns. A presentiment of this is found in those tavern scenes mentioned by Rancière, with their excessive drinking, vulgar sensuality, rude humour, and remarkable degree of untidiness and filth. By contrast, the domestic scenes painted a generation later by Vermeer are truly "cleansed of [life's] odor and flavor." These paintings, which almost invariably portray subjects performing everyday tasks (reading or writing letters, pouring milk, weighing gold, studying maps and globes, taking music lessons), showcase the cardinal virtues of middle-class asceticism – something on which Moretti has expounded: "Vermeer's figures are clean, neatly dressed; they have washed their walls and their floors, their windows, their clothes ... They have learned to read, to write, to understand maps, to play the lute and the virginal. They have a lot of free time, yes, but they use it so soberly that it's as if they were always *working*."[27]

Moretti introduces these paintings as part of a thesis on the emergence of a modern narrative practice dominated not by grand or momentous actions but by mundane activities, extended gestures, episodes, daily rituals, things – unobtrusive features that conform to the structuralist term "filler," as opposed to "turning point." The term is especially appropriate given that these paintings depict milieux that are filled – furnished with the objects that provide the methodical conduct of daily life with its focus. The quiet discipline that is everywhere legible in these unexceptional scenes leaves them devoid of spontaneity. Similarly, the fillers that dominate modern narrative "are compatible with the new regularity of bourgeois life"; in "rationalizing the novelistic universe," they turn it "into a world of few surprises, fewer adventures, and no miracles at all."[28]

Miracles, then, are antithetical to routine, which, as the stock in trade of the modern novel, is the bequest of "rationality" in the Weberian sense – an instrumental efficiency that extends beyond the workplace and permeates the habits of the home, indeed, the soul. Such rationality forecloses the kind of abrupt change of which the miracle is the most pointed expression. The possibility of true transformation is smothered by the "fillers" that compose the primary freight of novels in which even the "turning points" are as typically unremarkable as a debt incurred or an engagement broken off. In this world, reversals of fortune have a place only insofar as "fortune" is understood in the modern sense of "acquired wealth." Case in point: Balzac's Goriot is an erstwhile millionaire who made his fortune during the Revolution while working as a journeyman for a manufacturer of vermicelli. When his patron fell prey to the *terreur*, ownership of the business passed to Goriot, whose defining mediocrity allowed him to get rich without attracting attention, for which reason he survived the bloodshed. Balzac's reader encounters him decades later, living in Madame Vauquer's decrepit boarding house. He has not squandered his immense wealth but has divided it equally between his two daughters in order that they might marry into the aristocracy. No sooner are they wed than Goriot is shunned by his disdainful sons-in-law and their families. He lives out his final years in poverty, content to meet with his daughters in secret or merely watch unseen as their carriages pass along the boulevards of Paris. When he dies, those same two carriages are dispatched to his funeral in lieu of the gentlewomen they normally convey.

The plot of Goriot's decline follows that of Shakespeare's King Lear, who divides his realm between two of his daughters, only to be barred from their households. Driven mad by his self-inflicted misfortune, the old man wanders the storm-swept wilderness, railing against his ungrateful offspring, struggling, in Auerbach's words, "to force heaven and earth to witness the extremes of his humiliation" (316). Lear dwells at the stylistic conduit along which the tragic mingles with the comic-grotesque. The eighty-year-old monarch is at times ridiculous in his senility and decrepitude, but his "brittle creaturality," as Auerbach puts it, is a foil against which his greatness is only magnified. In this way the "mixture of styles" is exemplifed in Shakespeare, whose tragedies exhibit the residual force of the religious tradition in which misery confers dignity upon the afflicted.

Auerbach locates the seminal occurance of this mixture of styles in Augustine's *Confessions*. Augustine's Latin exhibits many vestiges of Ciceronian rhetoric, which, given its particular ability to organize information into "strict hierarchies of priority," imposes, to cite Bryson, a "gubernatorial perspective on the information it purveys."[29] The classical style generally drew on a refined and specialized grammatical repertoire. The Roman style in particular, which "looks at and organizes things from above," is consistent with the political culture of ancient Rome, with its emphasis on vast organizational structures.

A decided parallel emerges between Auerbach's characterization of the classical style, with its "cool and rational procedure," and a style of the novel suffused with the instrumental rationality of modern society – a universe in which all spontaneity of action or expression is suffocated by order and routine. Ennui is the actual theme of *Madame Bovary*, which for Auerbach is the crowning example of the realist novel. His reading pivots on the following scene – a "random moment" in which, as he will claim, "nothing particular happens" (488). These few sentences come at the end of a passage the subject of which is Emma Bovary's "chronic discomfort" with her life in this provincial French setting:

> But it was above all at mealtimes that she could bear it no longer, in that little room on the ground floor, with the smoking stove, the creaking door, the oozing walls, the damp floor-tiles; all the bitterness of life seemed to be served to her on her plate, and, with the steam from the boiled beef, there rose from the depths of her soul other exhalations, as it were, of disgust. Charles was a slow eater; she would nibble a few hazel-nuts, or else, leaning on her elbow, would amuse herself making marks on the oilcloth with the point of her table-knife.
>
> (Flaubert, *Madame Bovary*, cited in Auerbach, 483)

Physical features of Dante's *Inferno* (smoking furnace, oozing walls) pass easily into the realistic (if concentrated) description of Emma's oppressive milieu. Auerbach focuses on something else, however, namely the fact that, in contrast to Balzac, neither Flaubert nor his narrator inflect the description with a personal bias.

Auerbach identifies in Flaubert, then, a certain "objective seriousness" that enables him to convey what is potentially convulsive behind the generalized ennui of the time. In concert with his larger argument that realism proper was made possible by an essentially Christian disruption of the classical style, Auerbach discerns a degree of mysticism in Flaubert's ability, as he describes it, "to penetrate to the depths of the passions and entanglements of human life" (490). In this definition, mimesis and empathy are one in the same. Rather than parading his own feelings, the writer "forgets himself, his heart no longer serves him save to feel the hearts of others" (487). Auerbach routes the genealogy of realism, and of what he calls "mystic-realistic insight," back to Augustine, for whom the syntactical complexity of Ciceronian rhetoric served as a frame for isolating something decidedly un-classical: "the dramatization of an inner event, an inner about-face" (71). This is a point at which to pause and recall Moretti's statement that the rationalized world of the modern novel brooks "few surprises, fewer adventures, and no miracles at all." The miracle that Augustine conveys is the miracle of conversion, which he represents over the course of a sentence that Auerbach describes as containing "a whole series of hypotactically introduced members," which lead to a "climax ... at once dramatic and paratactic: *aperuit oculos, et percussus est* ['he opened his eyes and was struck']" (70–1). This use of parataxis, whose character is more biblical than classical, enables Augustine to seed his Latin with something "urgently impulsive" (70).

This last phrase describes the action of Kafka's short narrative "The Sudden Walk." Included in the collection *Betrachtung* (1912), "The Sudden Walk" consists of a mere two sentences. The first of these, comprising almost three hundred words, is a veritable parody of the nested syntax for which German is notorious – the mechanism that displaces verbs to the end of stacked, dependent clauses. This syntactical trait was long thought to be the bequest of Latin, and while historical linguists now dispute this, it is hard to imagine that the Early Modern consolidation and refinement of this principle was not the work of scholastics and officials in whose minds the particular virtues of Latin had taken root. Auerbach characterizes Latin as an "almost excessively organizing language, in which the material and sensory side of the facts is ... viewed and ordered from above ... In Roman prose of the golden age there is a predominant tendency ... to put all the precision and vigor of expression into syntactical connections, with the result that the style acquires ... a strategic character, with extremely clear articulations" (89). In the early chapters of *Mimesis* Auerbach is concerned to show how certain writers like Ammianus, Augustine, and Gregory of Tours contended with the incongruity between the elevated style they had inherited and the often harsh, sensory immediacy of their subject matter. In Ammianus, this imbalance causes constructions to "writhe and twist" (57). Gregory's sentences become "grammatical monsters" (82). The distorting effects of Ammianus's "exaggeratedly sensory" style produce a "caricature of the normal human environment" (59). The "spectrally sadistic" aspect of Ovid, in whose *Metamorphoses* "desire is mixed with fear and horror," prompts Auerbach to invoke Kafka, "whose world of gruesome distortion suggests the consistency of insanity" (60).[30] Note that in almost six hundred pages Auerbach mentions Kafka once, and he does so in a chapter on works written in Latin no later than the fourth century. With Augustine, however, it is not a matter of distortion or manifest incongruousness, but rather an ability to exploit the tools of classical rhetoric to set the stage for something unclassically dramatic – the miracle of blinding insight ("He opened his eyes and was struck").

The first, long sentence of Kafka's "The Sudden Walk" – an extended "when-then" construction – likewise presents "a whole series of hypotactically introduced members" for the purpose of framing a miracle, where breaking free of one's domestic milieu is nothing short of miraculous. This conforms structurally to the Aristotelian notion of *peripeteia*, which denotes the change from one condition to its opposite, and which came to be appplied to experiences like Paul's sudden conversion on the road to Damascus. The conversion that Kafka narrates is far less profound. Roughly the first third of his opening sentence evokes, through a sequence of dependent clauses, the sedimented habits of a sedentary life – the aggregate of internalized arguments for staying put:

> When it looks as if you had made up your mind finally to stay at home for the evening, when you have put on your house jacket and sat down after supper with a light on the table to the piece of work or the game that usually precedes your going to bed, when the weather outside is unpleasant so that staying indoors seems natural, and when you have already been sitting quietly at the table for so long that your departure must occasion surprise to everyone, when, besides, the stairs are in darkness and the front door locked …

If the scene as described so far invites comparison to the passage from *Madame Bovary* cited earlier (the smoky kitchen with its creaking door and damp tiles), we observe that Kafka provides nothing in the way of real description – nothing to evoke a mood or atmosphere beyond a skeletal indication of indoor comfort and routine reinforced by "unpleasant" weather without. The word "besides," which interrupts and thus intensifies this last clause, cinches the reasoning whose grouped components are the basis of the subsequent "all that," which is part of the concessive phrase that now signals the reversal to be realized only in the main clause, which is still far off:

> … and [in spite of all that] you have started up in a sudden fit of restlessness, changed your jacket, abruptly dressed yourself for the street, explained that you must go out and with a few curt words of leave-taking actually gone out, banging the flat door more or less hastily according to the degree of displeasure you think you have left behind you, and when you find yourself once more in the street with limbs swinging extra freely in answer to the unexpected liberty you have procured for them …

The change, of both clothing and disposition, is "sudden," "abrupt," "hasty," "unexpected," even "free." This reversal, which is a true turning point, is thus far limited to actions. Now, however, this reversal acquires a more psychological dimension and comes to conform to what Auerbach, in a formulation already quoted, calls "the dramatization of an inner event, an inner about-face":

> when as a result of this decisive action you feel concentrated within yourself all the potentialities of decisive action, when you recognize with more than usual significance that your strength is greater than your need to accomplish effortlessly the swiftest of changes and to cope with it, when in this frame of mind you go striding down the long streets – then for that evening you have completely got away from your family, which fades into insubstantiality, while you yourself, a firm, boldly drawn black figure, slapping yourself on the thigh, grow to your true stature.[31]

Thus far, a single sentence – a syntactical *tour de force* consisting largely of a crescendo of dependent clauses that measure the escape velocity necessary to shake the immense gravity of the most mundane and innocuous routine. The long-awaited main clause comes not at the very end but immediately after the dash, introduced by the adverbial "then": " – then for that evening you have completely got away from your family." The "insubstantiality" into which the family now "fades" sets off a new-found selfhood, which is elaborated graphically: "while you yourself, *a firm, boldly drawn black figure*, slapping yourself on the thigh, *grow to your true stature*." The German original is especially significant in this instance: "während man selbst, *ganz fest, schwarz vor Umrissenheit*, hinten die Schenkel schlagend, *sich zu seiner wahren Gestalt erhebt*." (An alternative translation might substitute the phrase "boldly inked in black" so as to suggest the action of going over a lightly drawn outline repeatedly with a writing nib, so as to make the contour progressively darker.)[32] Slapping oneself on the hind flank as if one were one's own horse, one rises to one's true form (*sich zu seiner wahren Gestalt erhebt*). The "unexpected liberty" that, as the result of this "decisive action," the limbs have been granted suggests something of the physical completeness, not to mention the motor capacity, that the cramped existence of life at home had stifled. The metamorphosis constitutes the emancipation from the milieu inclined to shape the human frame and physiognomy in the form of stunted caricatures.

But what of the second, final sentence of Kafka's narrative? "All this is still heightened if at such a late hour in the evening you look up a friend to see how he is getting on." Is this second step in truth a fortification of the resolve already acted upon, or is it not instead a capitulation – a surrender to the gravity of the social routine? It seems so mundane, and so mundanely worded (*wie es ihm geht*). The discrepancy between these two stages in Kafka's story parallels the paradox identified by D.A. Miller regarding the conclusion of *Old Goriot*, in which a momentary exuberance yields to a resumption of the constraints whose suspension was the source of the euphoria.[33] Goriot has died. Balzac's protagonist, a young scion of an ancient but impoverished line of provincial aristocrats, has seen to the old man's burial, after which he contemplates the twilit cityscape and the conquest of the social world that has banished Goriot and left him destitute. These are the last lines of Balzac's novel:

> Thus left alone, Rastignac walked a few steps to the highest point of the cemetery, and saw Paris spread out below on both banks of the winding Seine. Lights were beginning to twinkle here and there. His gaze fixed almost avidly upon the space that lay between the column of the Place Vendôme and the dome of the Invalides; there lay the splendid world that he had wished to gain. He eyed that humming hive with a look that foretold its despoliation, as if he had already felt on his lips the sweetness of its honey, and said with superb defiance,
>
> "It's war between us now!"
>
> And by way of throwing down the gauntlet to Society, Rastignac went to dine with Madame de Nucingen.[34]

Like the scene in which Fitzgerald's Gatsby is observed trembling at water's edge before a distant green light, the above passage seems haunted by Romantic precedent.[35] But while Gatsby instinctively resists the disenchantment that attaining his coveted object would bring, Rastignac's fantasy of conquest is, in Miller's words, "ironized" by the disproportion between the grandiosity of his ambition and the modest scale of his *premier acte*.[36] The two sentences of Kafka's tale are extreme in their disproportion, the mundanity of the second action serving likewise to undercut the first. Rastignac plunges into compromise, though his dinner engagement with one of Goriot's daughters is consistent with the erotic fascination exercised by Paris itself. His disillusionment, which is the sum of his experiences thus far, "entitles" him, Miller asserts, to the possession he desires.

Disillusionment is the starting point of Karl Grune's *The Street* (1923), in which Paris affords a tableau of erotic possibility. The film opens with a shot of a man of middle age reclining on a couch in a dimly lit parlour, presumably at the end of a long day. His wife, who knows a thing or two about long days, is preparing dinner in the adjoining kitchen. Suddenly, a bright light from outside causes the ceiling to come alive with flickering shadows, which soon clarify into silhouettes that project the husband's fantasies of romance and flight. Rising from the couch, he steps to the window and gazes out onto the urban world – the source of the shadowy figures playing upon his ceiling. An ordinary street scene is soon absorbed by an alluring vision of metropolitan nightlife, conveyed through an intricate montage of high-contrast images in which excitement and foreboding commingle. First, shots of criss-crossing tram lines and speeding traffic are combined prismatically in the shape of a diamond (one of Mondrian's preferred formats around this time). This inaugurates a sequence of overlapping images: a clown, seen in close-up, tries out a variety of elastic expressions; an explosion of flame and smoke, possibly the work of a fire-eater, fills part of the screen and is constant within the evolving frame, which soon incorporates a roller-coaster ploughing through water and filling much of the shot with shimmering spray. Throughout, faces are superimposed over fireworks, dancers, acrobats, and amusement park attractions. Finally, separated from the foregoing by a dark screen, the ominous shot of a blind organ grinder fades in, then out (figures 37–42). The scene returns to the husband, now demonstrably disillusioned; his wife, curious as to what he has found so captivating, nudges him aside, only to behold a city street choked with traffic and exhaust. As she takes her place at the table and starts in on her soup, her husband grabs his hat and coat and dashes out the door. The next two shots, as if to emphasize precipitous moral decline, show him rushing down two flights of stairs before exiting the building. Finding himself on the threshold of the life he had fantasized about only minutes earlier, he now joins the procession of shadows to which his desires have given shape.

These first minutes of *The Street* are the most memorable. The remainder of the film is a high-production morality tale, the path of overnight misadventure leading the prodigal husband to the brink of suicide in a jail cell. Once released, he stumbles home through the pale dawn, straining to climb those same two flights of stairs before warily entering his apartment. Limp with shame, he watches as his wife, whose compromises are at least equal to his, places a tureen of still-warm soup on the table, where she has waited the night. She then steps toward the window to gaze out vacantly. Her husband, shuffling hesitantly behind her, lays his head submissively on her shoulder. With one hand she reaches back to comfort him, then turns and slowly lifts her eyes to meet his (figures 43–4).

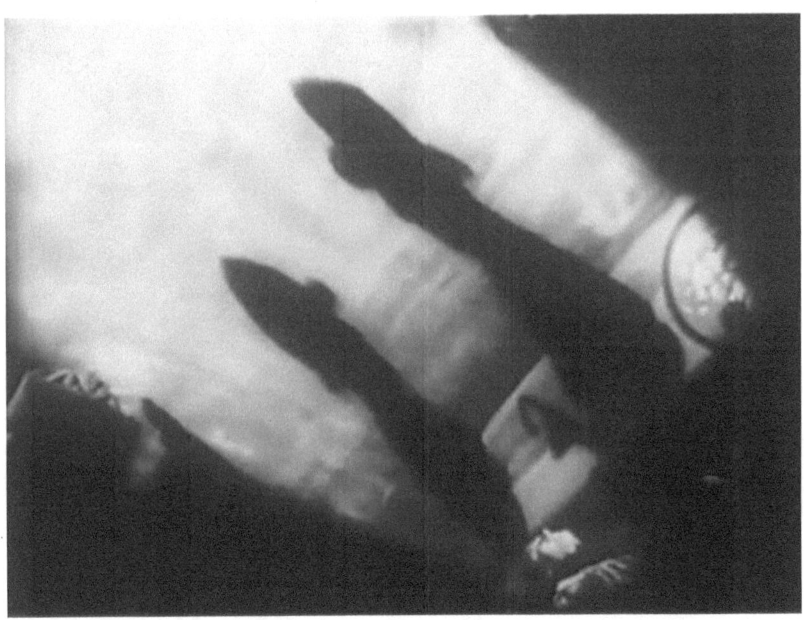

37–40. (this page and its verso) *The Street* (1923), dir. Karl Grune.

41–44. (this page and its verso) *The Street* (1923), dir. Karl Grune.

This closing pantomime of mutedly tender reconciliation reproduces a scene from some domestic drama. Realism prevails, not only as a stylistic approach to describing the world but also as an attitude of resignation – an acceptance that dreams simply don't come true. The wife, like Vermeer's milkmaid, is robust and comely. She is of a piece with her milieu, which, divided between kitchen and sitting room, is furnished with the assorted props of middle-class comfort: hearth, mantelpiece, china hutch, upholstered couch, decorative mirror, upright piano, hanging lamp. Blind to the vision that initially leads her husband astray, she moves about dutifully in a domain that is wholly realistic. Her summary gesture – of turning to face her husband and look into his eyes – is credibly and affectingly performed. By comparison, her husband reenters the home a caricature of defeat, his pained and crumpled posture true to Expressionist practices. Theirs, too, is a union of contraries. The wife's final gesture resolves a conflict of styles to realism's advantage. Her husband's unnaturally slumped and angular form, isolated within the interior over which she holds sway, may serve as a definitive foil to the subject of Kafka's "A Sudden Walk," which in breaking free of its domestic constraints "rises to its own true stature" (*sich zu seiner wahren Gestalt erhebt*). In suddenly standing and taking his leave, Kafka's figure not only occasions the surprise alien to bourgeois order but also revives the classicism defined by minimized contact between the action and those elements that constitute the subject *socially*.

Other Expressionist elements of *The Street* include the set designs by Ludwig Meidner,[37] as well as a number of unmistakable omens: the organ grinder, first seen at the close of the husband's reverie, reappears once the restless protagonist has actually stepped out into the night; a streetwalker, whose seductive smile momentarily dissolves into a death's head; and a large pair of bespectacled eyes, hanging above an optician's shop, which light up just as the husband is about to pass underneath.[38] There in fact seems to be "no place / that does not see you." Rilke's "Archaic Torso of Apollo" supposes a beholder admonished by a figure that has no eyes but, as a consequence of that very lack, is all-seeing. Misshapen by contrition, disfigured in the harsh glare of conscience, the errant husband returns, in the words of Rilke's poem, "distorted and short" (*entstellt und kurz*). He has been to the desert, as it were, his exile a condition of his being restored to his wife's "good graces." This restoration adheres to an untragic itinerary, which entails, as basic turning points, false incrimination and exculpation.

In his criticism of Grune's film, Kracauer identified a "militant realism," which rises to oppose the instinctual life projected by those "iridescent fluctuations" that first entice the husband from his couch.[39]

Fantasy is dispelled, and with it the cinema itself, the acme of which is realized both in that play of flickering shadows and in the dazzling, at times nightmarish montage that follows.[40] The opposition of styles in *The Street* parallels the contrast between the same oppressiveness at which Flaubert's Emma Bovary bridles ("it was above all at mealtimes that she could bear it no longer") and the new-felt freedom of Kafka's fugitive subject ("when in this frame of mind you go striding down the long streets"). Grune begins by summoning all the technical and aesthetic powers of filmmaking, yet he concludes with an appeal to the traditions of domestic theatre. The husband glimpses his own "true stature" in the mirror of his wife's forgiveness, cautious though it may be. In these last seconds of *The Street*, he sheds all vestments of style to merge fully with a realm whose prevailing seriousness – Auerbach's "mature expression" – is tantamount to an absence of style. By a certain reversal, then, the Expressionist contortions that mark the husband as socially (mis-)formed disappear from an interior that, while realistic, is cleansed of the vital spontaneity of the human psyche. In its allergy to surprises, adventures, and miracles, this milieu is a refuge from the "sudden shifts" that, again recalling Murch, the grammar of film shares with Beethoven's music. An entire aesthetic is sent into remission. The virtuoso montage-sequence described earlier, with its parade of physiognomies, gives way, over the long course of the film, to a simple scene of quietly dramatic, face-to-face recognition.

Davide Stimilli follows Gershom Scholem in venturing that the Greek *prosopolepsia* ("the respect of persons") derives from a Hebrew expression for the act of "lifting up the forehead of somebody kneeling in front of us."[41] This is precisely what the wife in *The Street* does. With a touch of her hand, she causes her supplicant-husband to straighten and return her gaze, which shimmers with the entreaty to "change your life." Rilke's sonnet propounds the classical ideal understood by Stimilli as "the pre-eminence of the figure over the face."[42] In the previous chapter of this study, it was observed how the creature of Mary Shelley's *Frankenstein* realizes his own "monstrosity" in contrast to the grace and beauty of the cottagers in whose proximity he has been sheltering; and how, in Whale's film adaptation, the absence of grace, which the classical world defined as an unreflected ease of movement, is rendered by means of the halting automatism of the creature, whose limbs have been harvested from stolen corpses and stitched crudely together. Stumbling stiffly toward his wife, the protagonist of *The Street* is similarly mechanical. Both creature and husband yearn for the grace in whose light their dismemberment would be undone. Recall the "grammatical monsters" that Auerbach found in Gregory of Tours, or the distortions that, in Ammianus, produce a "caricature of the normal human environment." Syntactically abrupt and descriptively indecorous, this highly unclassical mode achieves effects that are "very often like a bad dream" (59).

This may all seem quite far afield where a film from 1923 is concerned. But the closing moment of *The Street* – a domestic *tableau vivant* – may be read much in the way that Rancière reads the resolution of Murnau's *Tartuffe*, in which the classical separation of styles is reaffirmed, that is, "where a genre corresponds to a subject and where characters have the physiognomy and language befitting their status." The genre into which the husband is at last integrated exposes the *caricature* to which his character has been reduced. With downcast eyes he stands before his wife, his head and arms drooping like the appendages of a lifeless marionette. Emphasizing the dependence of the "social comedy" on imitation (52), Rancière argues that a stereotype-laden performance is not a matter of poor acting but instead "reflects the apparatus of visibility that sustains the character" (55). Listless in the extreme, the husband's bow is the posture of one brought low – an attitude in which the whole body bears the stamp of the social world. In 1903, Paul Klee produced an etching in which two human figures – unclothed and oddly proportioned – are shown bowing deeply before each other (figure 45). The artist provided the picture with the following caption: "Two men, each assuming the other to be of superior status, come face to face [*begegnen sich*]." Shaped by diffidence, the physiognomies of the two figures extend over their entire bodies, whose hard, uneven contours are themselves extensions of the bleak terrain. They have, in this maximum of courtly reverence, *sunk* to their own true stature. They possess something of the hunched malformation that Rilke's poem counterposes to the radiance of the statue, which, its truncation notwithstanding, is whole and self-sufficient. Standing before the sightless figure as before the averted countenance of God, the viewer, confronted with his own deficiencies, inverts the experience of "the *statue* in which," to adopt Lacan's precise wording, "man projects himself."[43] The image of the small child "leaning slightly forward" so as to examine its reflection, thereby gaining a degree of selfhood, contrasts emblematically with the two crouching figures in Klee's etching, who borrow from each other an excess of self-ingratiation.

A neoclassical/sculptural ideal echoes through Lacan's explanatory schema, following which the incipient subject overcomes its own motor incapacity via the fully exteriorized *Gestalt* beheld in the mirror. One implication of Kafka's story is that the subject's "true stature" (*wahre*

45. Paul Klee (1879–1940), *Two Men Meet, Each Believing the Other to Be of Higher Rank.*

Etching, 11.7 × 22.6 cm.
Museum of Modern Art, New York

Gestalt) is the perfect contrary of the cramped milieu to which the subject is bound to assimilate. Assimilation – the acquiescence to the pressures of one's social and cultural environment – is not unlike an organism's simulation of the colours, shapes, textures, even stillness, of its immediate surroundings. Mimicry in the natural world constitutes a diminished vitality akin to the social habits of asceticism. It also restores to mind the more original, biological sense of "milieu" as the "element in which an organism lives and upon which it depends for its sustenance."[44] Lacan drew upon the "facts" of mimicry and the morphological changes brought on by the mere sight of an Other, either similar or different in kind. As observed earlier, he followed Caillois in maintaining that natural mimicry was not an adaptive strategy for eluding predators. Rather, it signalled a susceptibility to the very "lure of space," space itself having the capacity to "devour."[45] Such figures of speech may suggest how a milieu is itself prone to the kind of figuration that Auerbach finds in Balzac, as exemplified by the boarding house mistress, whose "sexual repulsiveness" is in harmony with "the air of the room which she breathes without distaste," or whose petticoat "is appraised as a sort of a synthesis of the various rooms of the pension" (471).

For Auerbach, Balzac's milieux are manifestly demonic. A more benign account of middle-class habitat is found in the work of the Munich painter Carl Spitzweg. Born in 1808, nine years after Balzac, Spitzweg is known primarily for his genre paintings of German provincial life. *The Bookworm* (1850), easily the most widely circulated of his works, shows an elderly and fragile scholar standing atop a tall ladder in a library. He is holding one open book close to his face, while other large volumes are pressed between his knees or under an elbow. The precarious perch, and the *trompe-l'oeil* sky close overhead, identify this work as a pointedly ironic, Biedermeier domestication of a familiar Romantic motif. The conspicuous near-sightedness of the "Bookworm" contrasts with the expanse that opens up before Friedrich's wanderer, much as the imposing wall of books recalls Faust's sense of imprisonment as he rails against the narrow confines of his Gothic study. A new-found contentment with a world both small and immune to upheaval tallies with the literal myopia that Spitzweg frequently indicates in the form of thick eyeglasses rendered blank by reflected light. The interior depicted in *The Cactus Lover* (ca 1865) recasts what Faust derided as a house filled with the accumulated "junk" of one's forefathers (*Urväter-Hausrat*).[46] The irregular piles of string-bound manuscripts reflect the gradual sedimentation of a life defined by tempered desire – a scholastic existence reminiscent of that led by Dürer's St Jerome, as content as Faust is restless, his orderly workspace an aggregate of habits consistent with a serene and orderly soul. Likewise awash in morning sunlight, the cactus lover's unadorned domicile bespeaks cleanliness and temporal discipline (figure 46). Containment and equanimity coincide. The mantle and top hat hanging in the corner are almost beyond reach, as if seldom used. There is no hint of the Faustian impulse to flee an atmosphere that, in the Goethean setting, is thick with spectral possibility. The same hat and cloak, which lend the room a personality of its own, even give the impression of returning the figure's bow.

This bow is one of natural sympathy. In absent-minded absorption, the cactus collector *leans slightly forward*, mirroring the posture of the plant. Such empathic imitation, in which one being moulds itself to the form of another, is *mimesis* in the fullest sense, characterized by Hullot-Kentor in words that allude to the Adamic misstep to which all frail humanity is heir: "Mimesis ... is the affinity of subject and object as it is felt in one's knees on seeing someone else stumble on theirs."[47] This formulation, cited twice already and worth taking to heart, is itself empathetic

46. Carl Spitzweg (1808–1885), *The Cactus Lover* (after 1850).

Oil on canvas, 39.5 × 22 cm.
bpk Bildagentur / Museum Georg Schäfer, Schweinfurth, Germany
Art Resource, NY

in its capture of the internally felt continuum between our manner of understanding our experience of the external world through analogy to our bodily self-perception.[48] The gentle humour of Spitzweg's work restores the connection otherwise short-circuited by the rationality that had come to inform even the most private activities. In keeping with the conventions of the idyll, the details of everyday life are liberated from everyday life. True to that same tradition, Spitzweg's world is devoid of turning points, but also of the seriousness that, following Moretti, pervades the household scenes painted by Vermeer.[49]

Whatever their differences, the interior settings depicted by Vermeer and Spitzweg insulate against the world beyond those windows, which, shown obliquely, admit daylight while refusing the viewer a perspective onto the outside. In Murnau's *Nosferatu*, intramural space asserts itself with a vengeance when Count Orlok is lured out of the realm of shadows (the ambience that sustains him) and into a sunlit bourgeois domicile. The film is in many ways a contest between milieux – between, on the one hand, the Count's ancient castle in the Carpathians and, on the other, a middle-class home on the Baltic coast. The former is drafty and derelict, the latter comfortable and neatly appointed. In the end, the vampire simply evanesces before a window at daybreak. This outcome counteracts the consequences, about which the film initially warns, of pronouncing the word "Nosferatu": *Hüte dich es zu sagen, sonst verblassen die Bilder des Lebens zu Schatten* ("Beware of saying it, otherwise the images of life will dissolve into shadows"). A similar wariness vis-à-vis shadows is urged in a book about Nosferatu that Thomas Hutter, the hapless estate agent, is given en route to Orlok's castle: *Habet acht auf dass euch nicht sein Schatten als wie ein Alp mit graussigen Träumen beschwere* ("Take care lest his shadow weigh upon you like an incubus with frightful dreams"). Both advisories associate the power of the vampire with that of the cinema and of the proto-cinematic shadow-play that figures so frequently in German films of this period. *The Street* is a prominent example of this. *Nosferatu* thus verbalizes the bias that Rancière discerns in *Tartuffe*, in which the scheming imposter, in being drawn into the light, is dispossessed of a power that is cinematic. The effect of this dispossession is to lead the "cinematographic shadow" away from Romantic aesthetics (its native habitat) and into the "classical universe," in which, in keeping with the normative separation of styles, Tartuffe's "plebeian" body can be exposed as utterly out of place. Murnau's Count Orlok, as shadow personified, has no body. The device that neutralizes him is not dramatic but apotropaic – a protective magic by means of which the cinema effects its own undoing.

Chapter Seven

Music of the Third Kind: *Fantasia* and *Faustus*

Walt Disney's *Fantasia* (1940) opens on a dark screen, which presently divides to reveal a concert stage. Projected against a backdrop of deep cerulean blue are the giant, distended shadows of a harp and upright bass, which frame the image on either side. Shadows multiply and merge as musicians fill the scene and take their seats, tuning their instruments and rehearsing motifs that forecast the program to come. A master of ceremonies – composer and critic Deems Taylor – enters the stage from the rear to present a "new form of entertainment" consisting of "the designs and pictures and stories that music inspired in the minds and imaginations of a group of artists." The word "design" in this instance is most suited to the first musical selection, a symphonic setting of J.S. Bach's *Toccata and Fugue in D minor* for organ, which Taylor offers as an example of "music that exists simply for its own sake … what we call 'absolute music.'" "What you will see on the screen," he continues, "is a picture of the various abstract images that might pass through your mind if you sat in a concert hall listening to this music."[1] At the conclusion of his brief remarks Taylor introduces the conductor, Leopold Stokowski, who is seen from behind as he mounts the steps of the podium, in effect facing and eclipsing the announcer. The musicians and their instruments dissolve and disappear to leave Stokowski isolated against the blue background, a bold silhouette positioned squarely at the centre of the frame, his back to the audience (figure 47). The conductor opens his arms to his orchestra, rotating first to the right, then to the left to summon the first bright flourish from the violins. As the opening strains are heard, the maestro's face and hands are gilded by a spotlight, as if by the first rays of the sun. His arms outstretched, he is soon enveloped by a pale sphere of orange and magenta. However "abstract" this interpretation of "absolute music" was intended to

47. *Fantasia* (1940), Walt Disney.

be, the film casts Mr Stokowski as the author of the sunrise, which the swelling sound is made to simulate.

Stokowski's transcription for orchestra of Bach's solemn composition for organ recapitulates the rise of the symphony as the pre-eminent musical form during the late eighteenth and nineteenth centuries. This shift marked the emergence of musical practices for which the term "absolute music" was eventually coined (by Richard Wagner in 1846).[2] This coinage follows the advent of purely instrumental music, which, delivered of its subservience to liturgy or narrative program, was appreciated for its inherent, structural capacity for conveying mood, drama, and development. Symphonic structure and instrumentation form the foundation of Arthur Schopenhauer's understanding of music as such. Taking issue with Leibniz's alignment of music with numerical abstraction, Schopenhauer insisted that music, in its essence, was profoundly mimetic – the most immediate objectification of the will. Because unlike the other arts it transcended Platonic ideas, music did not imitate phenomena. Instead, its immense architecture of ascending pitch was analogous to creation itself: the deep tones of the bass corresponded to the inorganic mass of the earth, the intervals along the rising scale to the plant and animal species above its surface. Just as the plethora of living things had their inception in the earth, so too the great diversity of notes was derivative of the ground-bass. Melody, finally, moving above the harmonic mass, registering every impulse of the will, navigating between major and minor, spanning the long arc between beginning and end – between wish and gratification – disclosed in its protracted duration the deepest secrets of human desire and feeling. The inexhaustibility of possible melodies was commensurate with the boundless variety of individuals, physiognomies, and lived lives.[3]

In representing the world not by means of resemblance but by analogy, music readily incited human fantasy to flesh out these quintessential correspondences – to give shape to the invisible but vital spirit-world (*[jene] unsichtbare und doch so lebhaft bewegte Geisterwelt zu gestalten*).[4] Schopenhauer hereby accounted for the origin of song and eventually of the opera, though his wording is suggestive of cinematic animation and of *Fantasia* in particular, which, teeming with creatures of all kinds while presenting vast narratives of natural and planetary history, begins to look and sound like a popular, didactic excursus on the philosopher's claim of a fundamental concordance between music and the cosmos. A projection, in the announcer's words, "of the various abstract images that might pass through your mind if you sat in a concert hall listening to this music" – images that include "cloud forms or great landscapes" but also "vague shadows or geometrical objects floating in space" – Disney's film (and the cinema as such) would seem to realize to the fullest the phantasmatic experience of musical audition. Schopenhauer's own description of this experience already provides for an array of images passing in front of the mind's eye:

> In this intimate relation between music and the true essence of all things lies also the explanation for why ... he who submits entirely to the effect of a symphony will feel as if he were seeing all the possible processes of life and the world draw past him [*als sähe er alle möglichen Vorgänge des Lebens und der Welt an sich vorüberziehen*]. Yet if he thinks about it, he cannot point to any likeness between that play of sounds and the things that hovered before him. For music, as we have said, differs from all the other arts in that it is not a copy of the phenomenon ... but a copy of the will itself.[5]

Among the abstract forms that accompany the *Toccata and Fugue* are the opposed diagonals of crisscrossing violin bows, which corroborate the patterns of rain from which they are distilled. (A preliminary drawing for this sequence, even more than the sequence itself, attests to the film's modernist impulse, which the music seems bent on stifling.)[6] Moments later, much like a satellite in space, the fingerboard of a cello floats into view, rotating until the strings, merging with the axis of sight, form geometrical perspective lines that narrow sharply toward the vanishing point. Several times during the same "chapter" what appear to be waves of sound – parallel curves expanding outward, red against black – are recognized as ripples of water when they suddenly catch the first dancing rays of the rising sun. This last example may recall a famous episode from the history of music: In 1832 poet and critic Ludwig Rellstab wrote that he could not listen to the first movement of Beethoven's Piano Sonata No. 14 without picturing the moonrise over a Swiss lake. The popular piece thus came to be known by the sobriquet "Moonlight Sonata" instead of the composer's own appellation, whose echo can be discerned in the title of Disney's film: *quasi una fantasia*. Whether a deliberate allusion or not, the image is doubly significant in that it occurs during what is by far the least Romantic selection in a musical program that includes Beethoven's Symphony No. 6 ("Pastorale"), Schubert's "Ave Maria," Tchaikovsky's *Nutcracker*, Mussorgsky's *Night on Bald Mountain*, Paul Dukas's *The Sorcerer's Apprentice*, and Stravinsky's *Rite of Spring*. These various selections exemplify what Taylor characterizes as music that either "tells a definite story" or, in the absence of narrative, "paint[s] a series of more or less definite pictures." The *Toccata and Fugue*, by contrast, is unique in *Fantasia* as an example of a "third kind of music, music that exists simply for its own sake." Taylor's easy conflation of disparate musical epochs is consistent with the manner in which Disney's film assimilates Bach to the era of the symphony and to a mellifluousness not native to organ music of the German Baroque. Sharp, clarion figures meant for the organ, for example, are written for the harp as lilting arpeggios. The effect is to muffle the latent modernism of the original, much as the film blunts its own modernist potential through recourse to traditional mimeticism. The popular legacy of Rellstab's reception of Beethoven's piano sonata illustrates what Anton Webern derided as the general public's inability to come to terms with music's inherent abstraction: "How do people listen to music? ... Apparently they have to be able to cling to pictures and 'moods' of some kind. If they can't imagine a green field, a blue sky or something of the sort, then they are out of their depth."[7]

This dependence on images, which for Webern is altogether at odds with Bach's "staggering polyphonic thought,"[8] compatible with what Freud saw as the "formal regression" characteristic of dreams, which effect "the replacement of logical relations with pictorial equivalents ... and in general the return to concrete pictorial expression."[9] The regressiveness of

Fantasia is manifold and includes the puerile anthropomorphism wherein mammals, reptiles, fish – even mushrooms – exhibit the facial features and expressions of humans. The film, like the process of dreaming, instantiates the viewer as child, restoring the viewer to an archaic state in which perceptions are revived as hallucinations, and in which, correspondingly, wishes are unimpeded by the exigencies of the everyday. The title of Disney's film thus not only recalls the epithet that Beethoven assigned to his piano sonata, but is also synonymous with the *Phantasien* or "daydreams" from which, according to Freud, dreams proper borrow a certain coherence. Dreams dreamt during sleep often adapt to the structure of the waking reveries that precede them – fantasies of which, in contrast to actual dreams, the subject is the more or less conscious source. Correcting for the discontinuity and rupture otherwise typical of dreams, these daydreams, in which the subject is always the hero, project the grandiosity of, in Freud's words, "His Majesty the Ego."[10]

In *Fantasia,* this ego has a clear counterpart in the conductor, whose sovereign presence dominates the screen at the opening and conclusion of each musical selection.[11] Imperiously coaxing sights as well as sounds into existence ("As from the stroke of the enchanter's wand," to recall Byron's line),[12] Stokowski gives body to the "omnipotence of thoughts," the belief in which Freud identified as an attribute of narcissism. (Throughout, the film gives story-form to a mimeticism otherwise concentrated in the person of the conductor, who determines the energy and character of the performance by means of physical and facial expressions that suggest force, flow, urgency, menace, suspense, agitation, tranquility, or rest.) This tendency to exaggerate the power of one's own mental processes represented, according to Freud, an irrepressible residue of culturally superseded magical thinking, in which a wish and its fulfilment were essentially indistinct. This psychological overvaluation of the creative potential of human thought is akin to the epistemological concept of "intellectual intuition" (*intellektuelle Anschauung*) – the ability to create something in the mere act of thinking it – a capacity that Kant reserved for God alone.[13] The insistence on this cognitive limit is continuous with (if not equal to) the empiricism of John Locke and David Hume, who held that knowledge was derived, directly or indirectly, from sense-experience. Significantly, Freud quotes Hume in this matter, and one can discern in the philosopher's statement an implicit link between animism and the narcissistic inclination to find one's likeness everywhere and in all things: "There is a universal tendency among mankind to conceive all beings like themselves and to transfer to every object those qualities with which they are familiarly acquainted and of which they are intimately conscious."[14]

Fantasia, whose teeming menagerie displays countless variations on the human face, is a symptom of the tendency that Hume identifies – a rear-guard (albeit trite and benign) resistance to the wholesale disenchantment of which empiricism is a supreme example. *Dialectic of Enlightenment* is at hand, the opening salvo of which equates the advancement of thought with the functional "disenchantment of the world" (*Entzauberung der Welt*).[15] Modern scientific reason merely perfected the technique of primordial magic, which sought to banish like with like – to bind the power of local demons by showing them, by means of masks, their mirror-image. In *Fantasia*, the enchantment already intrinsic to cinema is embedded in the diegesis, most particularly in "The Sorcerer's Apprentice," which of all the musical compositions used in the film is the one that tells the most "definite story." Mickey Mouse, in the role of apprentice, is seen carrying heavy buckets of water while the sorcerer he serves, in a manner resembling the conductor himself, conjures a phantasmic shape from a column of smoke rising from a skull on the table before him. The figure, a ghoulish winged creature with glowing eyes, metamorphoses into a giant butterfly, which hovers briefly before dissipating. Once the sorcerer has left the chamber, the apprentice dons his master's hat and, with gestures that are again comparable to those of the conductor, brings a broom to life, which he then teaches to fetch water in his place. Having thus delegated his taxing chore, Mickey, reclining with his feet on a table, smugly directs the labour with quick, metronomic motions of his fingers before drifting off to sleep. Dreaming, he finds himself atop a rocky pinnacle, waves crashing at its base. The waves intensify as the apprentice, with sweeping movements of his arms, causes celestial bodies to wheel around him. When the sensation of rising water suddenly wakes him, the omnipotence of the dream yields to helplessness in the face of an actual deluge, which the tireless broom has caused. Mickey's frantic attempt to destroy the broom with an axe only produces an army of animated brooms – a labour force whose destructive power is realized as a cataclysmic flood.[16] When all seems lost, the sorcerer returns and, like Moses, parts the raging waters and restores calm. Because the action of this sequence is matched to the tempo and drama of the music, the manual gestures with which sorcerer and apprentice alike guide the action correspond closely to what one assumes are those of Stokowski himself.

Dispelled by the sudden sensation of dampness, Mickey's dream is proper to the pubescence of his fantasy. It corresponds to a number of episodes in Disney's film in which Stokowski's commanding position is reflected and redoubled.[17] In the visual narrative that accompanies Beethoven's 6th, a powerful thunderstorm is personified as the divine

Zeus hurling bolts of lightning from his rocky perch on Mount Olympus. In the episode set to *Night on Bald Mountain*, the demon-giant Chernobog summons the spirits of the dead to a midnight *dance macabre*, the excited gestures of his arms and hands accelerating with the music. The latter moment is a conspicuous tribute to a scene in Murnau's *Faust*, in which Mephistopheles appears towering above a village. While Chernobog casts an inky shadow that creeps in and out of the streets like a dark flood, Mephisto, played by Emil Jannings, discharges (as if from his bowels) a vile mist that spreads deathly plague among the unsuspecting townsfolk.[18]

Murnau's monumental adaptation of the Faust legend, along with other German films of the Weimar era, provided Disney's artistic directors and animators with a ready supply of images, a great many of which were in turn drawn from the Romantic repertoire.[19] *Faust* is itself a compendium of paintings by Friedrich, certain of whose canvases are cited in *Fantasia* as well as the earlier *Snow White and the Seven Dwarfs* (1937). A prominent example is his *Man and Woman Contemplating the Moon* (1824), which both *Faust* and *Snow White* incorporate. The final episode of *Fantasia* ("Ave Maria"), in which a sombre procession of torch bearers files past a Gothic ruin at dawn, is an extended composite of works by Friedrich, including his early drawing *Pilgrimage at Sunrise* (1805), which centres on a similar processional, as well as a great number of canvases depicting ruins, such as *Abbey in the Oak Forest* (1809–10).[20] The brief sequence from *Fantasia* described earlier, in which Stokowski calls forth the first, decisive measures of the *Toccata* from his musicians, opens and closes with pointed citations of two of Friedrich's signature works: *The Wanderer above the Sea of Mists*, discussed throughout this study, and *Woman before the Rising Sun* (ca 1818), in which the painter's wife, like the wanderer centred and facing away from the viewer, stands with her arms held out as if to absorb the golden radiance, the source of which her torso eclipses.[21] As Bach's composition resumes with a more tentative exploration of its theme, the viewer sees what Friedrich's wanderer sees, and from the same lofty height: mountains softened by clouds at daybreak.

Establishing these correspondences is not difficult, nor is doing so sufficient in itself. More challenging is the question as to why *Fantasia* should model its foundational gesture – a conductor bringing forth sounds and shapes from an apparent void – on a painting that, some 120 years earlier, cast the consolidation of the modern subject as Romantic adventure. Friedrich's works in oil, the first of which were painted in 1807, exhibit features that lend them a character both proto-cinematic and dream-like. These include a lucidity that verges on the surreal, a shimmer at the edges of figures and objects, a stereoscopic quality that, in suspending parallel planes in opposition, draws the background forward, and a confounding facility with layers of transparency and translucence.[22] Even more important, however, is a structural component conceivable in terms that film theory eventually devised for the understanding of cinematic spectatorship: a pronounced axis of identification that aligns the viewer with a subject position that is already a projection of the viewer's own.

Whatever opinion one might hold of the popular-commercial ambition driving Disney's project, *Fantasia* is an accurate measure of the historical dilation between the Romantic program of absolute music, which the film's announcer names, and the emergence, in the twentieth century, of the abstraction already latent in the Romantic landscape.[23] Writing on Beethoven, whose instrumental music embodied for him the essence of Romanticism, E.T.A. Hoffmann remarked that the compositions for voice were less successful, vocal music being limited to "emotions determined by words" (*durch Worte bestimmte Affekte*). Beethoven's instrumental works, by contrast, disclose "the realm of the vast and immeasurable" (*das Reich des Ungeheuern und Unermesslichen*), an empire of deepest night, pierced by glowing rays, in which gigantic shadows swell and recede like waves.[24] Hoffmann's imagery suggests a preliminary visual blueprint for *Fantasia* and particularly for the opening sequence, which is the most avowedly abstract ("the various abstract images that might pass through your mind if you sat in a concert hall listening to this music").

The abstraction in *Fantasia* was largely the contribution of émigré filmmaker Oskar Fischinger, who had distinguished himself in Germany in the 1920s and 1930s with short filmic experiments like *Circles* (1933) and *Composition in Blue* (1935) – films allied by their very titles with modernist painting.[25] Certain of these laid the groundwork for *Fantasia* in their synchronization of colour patterns and moving shapes with music (classical and some jazz). The later *Radio Dynamics* (1942), which includes a head credit reading "Please! No music! Experiment in Color Rhythm," displays certain similarities with Mondrian's *Broadway Boogie-Woogie* (1942–43). The beleaguered Fischinger was fired by Disney over creative differences, yet his influence over the film extended well beyond his brief tenure, as well as beyond the *Toccata and Fugue* sequence, which he conceived. His numerical motion-phase breakdown for "the Wave" in that same sequence (figure 48) brilliantly condenses the method that, under the flag of Imagism (contemporaneous with Einstein and consistent with his equation of mass and energy), had drawn images from the patterns that appear when matter is urged

48. Oskar Fischinger (1900–1967), numerical motion-phase breakdown for "The Wave" in *Fantasia*.

into motion.[26] Disney's animators proved adept at rendering these patterns – the undulation of water, the gentle entropy of rippling circles caused by falling drops, the distension of droplets on the verge of falling, the rotation of whirlpools (and galaxies), the flaring signatures of sonic pulses, ribbon-like arabesques of light draped over waves, and so on. When those orbiting cello strings cast their shadows upon the soft contours of sand dunes, their inflection makes for a study in the curvature of space (figure 49).

Fantasia effects the union of "absolute music" with the "absolute films" pioneered by Fischinger's close precursor Walther Ruttmann, best known for his *Berlin, Symphony of a City* (1927). As early as 1921, Ruttmann was making experimental shorts, the first two of which were paired with original scores by composer Max Butting. Ruttmann described his eleven-minute *Opus I* (1921), in which brightly coloured shapes swirl and swell against a dark background, as an "optical symphony."[27] A more rigid abstractionism informs his *Berlin*, a feature-length film in

49. *Fantasia* (1940), Walt Disney.

which the life of the modern metropolis is presented in documentary rather than narrative fashion and following "symphonic" movements, each with its own tempo and temperament and each corresponding to a time of day. The film opens with the camera moving low over the ruffled surface of a lake at first light. The image blurs before dissolving into an abstract field of wavering horizontals, over which, with increasing speed, geometrical shapes rotate up into frame and out again. These shapes give way in turn to a rapid montage of disconnected shots of the railway. Signal gates dip in quick succession; a locomotive barrels overhead; the tracks, shot from above, race beneath the viewer; wheels and pistons are framed at close range, while the flickering parade of passing windows replicates the effect of film itself. These shots repeat in accelerating alternation almost to the point of indecipherability. Gradually, however, the train begins to slow as it nears its destination. Trees, telegraph poles, and steel trusses continue to flutter past but are seen now from the more coherent position of a passenger aboard the train. This overture replays the history in which early rail travellers, unable to make visual sense of the landscape beyond their carriage windows,

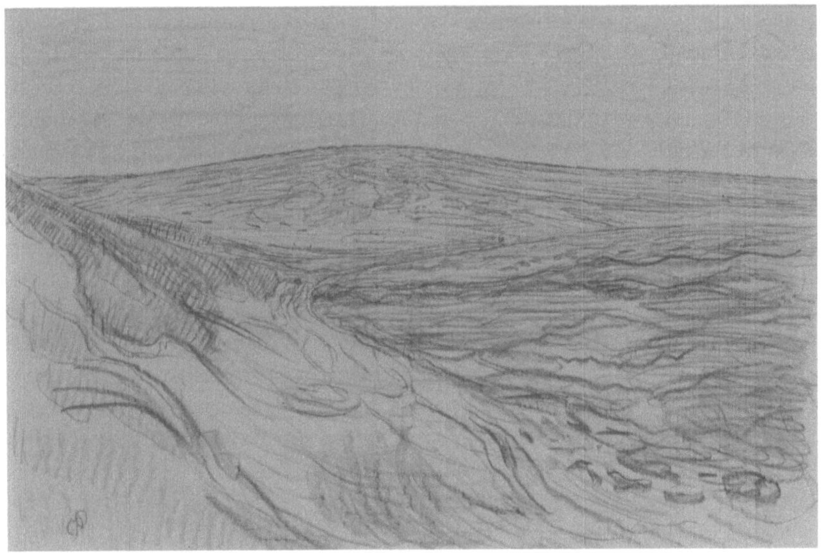

50. Piet Mondrain (1872–1944), *Dunes at Domburg*, ca. 1911.

Black chalk on light brown paper, 45.7 × 68.5 cm
Thaw Collection/The Morgan Library & Museum
© 2021 Mondrian/Holtzman Trust
Photo Credit: The Morgan Library & Museum, New York

struggled to adjust to the experience of industrial speed.[28] It likewise recalls the reaction of those allegedly traumatized Parisians reported to have mistaken the cinema for an oncoming locomotive (*L'Arriveé d'un train*). Ruttmann's placid shot of lapping water at daybreak may, on the one hand, serve to offset the anti-pastorale that is modern-day Berlin, the jarring tempo of which the film perforce enacts. On the other, it overlaps with the wave pattern in *Fantasia* and with Fischinger's precise engineering of that pattern. Fischinger's motion-phase schema in turn exposes the formal stringency of Mondrian's earlier studies of waves (of water and sand) (figure 50). These are themselves contemporaneous with the conception of space theorized by Einstein, to whom it also occurred to imagine an electric streetcar passing a clock tower at the speed of light.

The pre-eminence of energy over matter had already emerged a good century prior as both an aesthetic principle and a social one. It informs Eichendorff's "Mondnacht" (1837), introduced periodically in this study, which evokes waves of grain stirred by the faintest passage of air through moonlit fields (*Die Luft ging durch die Felder, / Die Ähren wogten sacht*).[29] In 1844, J.M.W. Turner, whose "impressionist" technique helped hasten European art in the direction of non-objectivity, produced a painting of an oncoming locomotive – the first of its kind – titled *Rain, Steam, and Speed*. Within four years, and regarding the sum of the effects of industrial modernization, Marx and Engels observed that everything permanent and rigid "melts into air" (*verdampft*). They went on to liken the new commercial class to a wizard (*Hexenmeister*) suddenly powerless to command the forces he had summoned from underground.[30] In so doing, they set the scene for Disney's vignette, which delegates said powerlessness to the bumbling apprentice while preserving the master's capacity to stem the tide of proletarian discontent – something achieved more literally in *Metropolis* after the workers, themselves a subterranean collective, unleash a deluge by destroying the machines they serve.

Cautionary tales both, "The Sorcerer's Apprentice" and *Metropolis* warn of the sinister consequences of the Faustian bargain. This is also the theme of Thomas Mann's *Doctor Faustus* (1947), a dense and extensive post-mortem of the aesthetic *pathos in distans* that the novel implicates in the vast human catastrophe of which *Fantasia*, in 1940, is still innocent. Mann's subject, the composer Adrian Leverkühn, is a musical autodidact who already as a youth proves himself a precocious master of abstract tonal relations. Indeed, he finds refuge in the arid calculus of these relations, his methodical evasion of musical key an effect of the detachment that defines his relationships with people. His one true mentor, the church organist Wendell Kretzschmar, has acquainted him with what he holds to be music's "inherent lack of sensuality," its "secret bias towards asceticism."[31] Adrian absorbs the idea that the strict procedures of Renaissance and Baroque polyphony amounted to a "prior penance" for the sensualism that would reach its apex with the Romantics. He advocates for an "ascetic chilling-off," which leads him to favour "inorganic instrumental sound" over the human voice, whose warmth he disparages as "bovine." His own compositional practice comports with the frigidity of his social life, as observed at the outset by his doting friend and biographer, the narrator Serenus Zeitblom: "All around him lay coldness" (8).

Adrian's haughty dispassion is on display in the third chapter of Mann's novel, which is taken up with a profile of Adrian's father, Jonathan. A plantsman whose spare time was devoted to the study of nature, Father Leverkühn sought to acquaint Adrian and his friend with those natural phenomena that, by Zeitblom's estimation, bordered on the occult. On many evenings the two boys crowded behind Jonathan's armchair as he paged through coloured illustrations of exotic moths and butterflies, or watched as he demonstrated how intricate figures appeared when, using a cello bow, he would stroke the rim of a glass disk strewn with sand. Together they examined the plant-like patterns of the hoarfrost that covered the windows in winter. These latter two examples represent, respectively, the music and the cold that would combine in Adrian, whose own early experiments with chord structure amount to exercises in apathy. In retrospect Zeitblom, a confirmed Humanist, characterizes Jonathan's natural-scientific pursuits as having an affinity with mysticism and sorcery, his fascination being for those phenomena whose *ambiguity* divided between beauty and poison, and ultimately, between the living and the non-living. Ambiguity is something that Adrian later ascribes to the intrinsic "uncertainty" of tonal relations – the fact that any one note could be "augmented from above or diminished from below" – a quality he would also refer to as "duplicity" (51). Leaving aside that augmentation from above is the very definition of *grace*, let it be emphasized that duplicity is a feature of those butterflies that dissemble by assuming the appearance of something else. With his many illustrated volumes Jonathan explained the "defensive mimicry" whereby the often exquisite markings of these winged insects – markings that sometimes reproduce even the impurities of the leaf they are simulating – enabled them to vanish utterly before the eyes of their predators. While some butterflies disappear, others float about insouciantly, their ostentatious decor a signal that they are vile to the taste. Yet another species, though perfectly edible, masquerades as its obnoxious cousin, sharing in the security the latter enjoys by virtue of its true indigestibility.

These discoveries provoked spasms of laughter on young Adrian's part, while his father, a reverent and brooding melancholic, appeared to empathize with these "sadly secure" creatures" (18). Nowhere was Jonathan's empathy more conspicuous than when he displayed the results of a certain chemical experiment: the sand at the bottom of an aquarium had been seeded with various crystals which, following the introduction of a solution of sodium silicate, had sprouted into a colourful muddle of "purely inorganic" forms resembling algae, mushrooms, tiny trees, even human limbs. Jonathan sought to instil feeling in the hearts of his two novices by demonstrating that these "woeful imitators of life" were heliotropic. When the aquarium was covered on all sides but one and placed in sunlight, this is what the boys beheld: "the whole dubious crew – mushrooms, phallic polyps, tiny trees, and algae meadows, plus those half-formed limbs – bent toward the pane of glass through which the light was falling, pressing forward with such longing for warmth and joy that they literally clung to the pane and stuck fast there" (23). The wretched and grotesque display of limbs straining for the light – a spectacle that inspired amusement in Adrian just as it moved his father to tears – is a veritable diorama of Dante's *Inferno*, parts of which Adrian will one day set to music. Zeitblom recoils at Dante's "penchant for cruelty and scenes of torture" (173), much as he bewails the horrors of modern German history, which the methodical torments of the *Inferno* seem to rehearse. Zeitblom invokes the theologically inflected schism of body and soul in opposition to the "bio-politics" of Hell, where the anguish of the spirit is figured as sheer animal suffering. Adrian's affinity for Dante's great and terrible poem is consistent with his propensity for self-denial. Insulation from human warmth is more than the condition of his deal with the devil – it is the *ideal* by which he lives. Hence the habit of losing himself in thoughts of the cold expanse of intergalactic space, which is so vast as to be available to the mind through numbers alone. The experience of the mathematical Sublime is itself commensurate with the "ascetic bias" of Adrian's music, flight from desire being sublimation's defining motive. Kant distinguished the subject of sublime experience from the superstitious individual quaking before thundering omnipotence, but the inadequacy of human cognition has its counterpart in what Zeitblom finds offensive in Dante: the nullity of human existence in the face of an inscrutable, unapproachable Good (172).[32] The Humanist credo with which Zeitblom redresses Adrian's surrender to the physical void is defined, in his words, "by proud awareness that [man] is not merely a biological creature, but rather that a decisive part of his nature belongs to a spiritual and intellectual world; by awareness … that [man] has been charged with the duty of approaching what is perfect" (288).[33]

Yet in the end Zeitblom is left meditating upon Michelangelo's *Last Judgment* ("that overpopulated wall swarming with bodies"), which, along with the *Inferno* and a cycle of woodcuts by Dürer, is part of the "visionary tradition" on which Adrian based a choral piece on the theme of the Apocalypse. There, in the lower right quadrant of the massive fresco, "one damned fleshy voluptuary, surrounded, carried, dragged by the grinning sons of the pit, takes his ghastly departure, a hand covering one eye, the other staring in horror at eternal damnation" (377) (figure 51). This forlorn soul in a state of spiritual free fall will for Zeitblom come to symbolize Germany in 1940 (the year of Adrian's death and the novel's close) – a nation that "in the embrace of demons ... plummets from despair to despair" (534). Doubled over, his one visible eye wide with terror, the falling figure is the measure of the failure to achieve the standard of spiritual and intellectual perfection championed by Zeitblom. It is a shortfall in which the Mannerist style of *The Last Judgment*, with its agitated movement, its writhing, straining, and overmuscled bodies, is made complicit. This same sensibility is exalted by Wackenroder's melancholic friar, who assays that Michelangelo, delving into the hidden workings of the "human machine," and risking the boldest and wildest attitudes and gestures, packed muscle on top of muscle while investing his figures' every nerve with his own "high poetic energy."[34]

In casting Michelangelo's efforts as a kind of probing of the tissues, Wackenroder's friar aligns the great artist with Joseph Berglinger's father, a physician who succumbed to an all-consuming and noxious obsession with the hidden secrets of the human body, its curiosities, its afflictions and infirmities. Berglinger's father in turn has a kinsman in Jonathan Leverkühn, the "speculator and brooder" whose "semi-mystical" pursuit of nature, in Zeitblom's view, amounted to a collaboration with the "Tempter" (20). Zeitblom characterizes Adrian's Apocalypse-themed chorale as a "sonorous painting" (377), thereby tracing its genesis back to Father Leverkühn's experiments in "visual acoustics" (21) and making father and son fellow travellers along the path to perdition. Berglinger too shares his father's heaviness of the soul, and the phrase "wondrous paroxysm," with which the friar seeks to convey the miracle of music born of hopelessness and heart-shredding pain,[35] recalls Eisner, who repeatedly invokes "paroxysm" with regard to the gestural and facial distortion typical of Expressionist screen performance. Her statement on actor Fritz Kortner – that he at times moved as if he were trying to shake free of his own appendages – is consistent with the traditional criticism of Mannerist painters, who were often faulted for depicting arms and legs that seemed to move not in concert with the body but independently of it. The figure in *The Last Judgment* gives a good idea as to why Mannerism endeared itself to many of the Expressionists.[36] He embodies the condition of being "convulsively swept up" (*krampfhaft emporgerissen*), to recall a phrase used by Worringer to describe the effect of Gothic architecture.[37] He personifies, in much the same manner, the fear on display in Peter Lorre's Beckert (in Lang's *M*) as he cowers and hunches before a tribunal of killers and thieves (figure 52).

The "half-formed limbs" chemically precipitated at the bottom of Jonathan Leverkühn's aquarium hint at a primordial element of style

51. Michelangelo Buonarroti (1475–1564), detail from *The Last Judgment* (1536–41).

Sistine Chapel, Vatican
Scala/Art Resource, NY

while grounding this style in something elemental. Lacan singles out Hieronymus Bosch for capturing in paint what in dreams often result from the "aggressive disintegration of the individual" – displaced limbs and bizarre anatomical excrescences.[38] This nightmare finds bodily form in the creature of Whale's *Frankenstein*, like his literary precursor an aggregate of ill-matched parts. Extending his long arms into the pale shaft of light his maker has let fall from an opening in the roof (figure 34), the creature demonstrates the heliotropism that Father Leverkühn noted in those grotesque chemical blooms. Wackenroder's friar likewise describes turning toward a favourite painting "like a sunflower to the sun," a tendency he documents in Berglinger himself, who is burdened with the *tristitia* that, for the cleric, is a matter of vocation.[39] The young Joseph even committed to heart, at first hearing, the *Stabat mater dolorosa*, a text of which Goethe's Gretchen pronounces her own vernacular variant (*Ach neige, / Du Schmerzensreiche ...*).

52. *M* (1931), dir. Fritz Lang.

Neoclassicism, from which Gretchen's plea signals a paradigmatic turn, entailed the disembodiment of sight and, more broadly, the uncoupling of "feeling," in the sense of external sensation, from "feeling," understood as an internally experienced state. The empathy to which Gretchen appeals erodes the heedless disinterest of classical form, restoring the agony of grief to the irreducible pain of physical suffering. The "farewell to Apollo," to recall Belting's term for this watershed moment, equates with a departure from post-Cartesian epistemology, which the aesthetics of neoclassicism reinforced. When for a moment Apollo re-emerges – in Rilke's sonnet of 1908 – it is as the vestige of a grace still traceable "in the gentle rotation / of the loins" (*im leisen Drehen / der Lenden*), an image that contrasts archetypally with, say, Michelangelo's *Bandini Pietà*, in which the arms and legs, manhandled from *without*, seem wrenched into incongruous planes. Modernist iterations of this convention – Mary grieving for her dead son – were drawn, modelled, and painted by, among others, Käthe Kollwitz, Ernst Barlach,

53. *The Hands of Orlac* (1924), dir. Robert Wiene.

Lovis Corinth, Oskar Kokoschka, Emil Nolde, and Otto Dix.[40] Bertolt Brecht's own interpretation of this tradition, in his *Mother Courage* (1939),[41] may well deviate from Expressionist practice, but his program of impregnating gestures with meaning recalls the theatricalized body of Baroque painting, in which limbs are isolated, by light, for expressive emphasis.[42] The mournful shot at the provisional close of Murnau's *The Last Laugh* – one in which the verb *neigen* has a pronounced resonance – has already been offered as an example of illuminated gesture. Another example is found in Wiene's *The Hands of Orlac* following the extended nighttime sequence in which rescue workers search the train wreckage for the injured and dead. This strikingly tenebrous scene is punctuated at the end by a lonely witness to universal woe – a man sitting motionless in the weary posture of the melancholic (figure 53).

Mann's *Doctor Faustus* and Auerbach's *Mimesis* were written at the same time, in American and Turkish exile respectively, and published within a year of each other. The former may be said to work out over its long course a principle later advanced by George Steiner, namely that "[each] new historical era mirrors itself in the picture and active mythology of its past."[43] In what amounts to a thumbnail sketch of an idea that informs Mann's narrative, Steiner places the ultimate historical catastrophe within a long tradition of European fantasizing: "For six hundred years the imagination dwelt on the flaying, the racking, the mockery of the damned, in a place of whips and hellhounds, of ovens and stinking air." As if to echo Zeitblom, Steiner alleges that the *Inferno* supplied the "literal guidebook" to the "millenary pornography of fear and vengeance" that preceded the horrors of 1942–5.[44] Auerbach (in his first book, from 1929) acknowledged the "dark pathos" behind this same "gruesome ingenuity," conceding that Dante "was indeed one of the creators of Romanticism" – that "his work was largely responsible for its fantastic Gothic dream-world and for its exaltation of the horrible and grotesque." He observes that it was Giambattista Vico who, "in a century hostile to Dante, gave expression for the first time to that form of admiration which culminated in Romantic aesthetics."[45]

The vividly sinister terrain of the *Inferno* was essential to this favourable reception, and Auerbach's evocation of this imagined world, in its vast and terrible scope, is suggestive of cinematic spectacle: "This Hell ... has landscapes, and its landscapes are peopled by infernal spirits; occurrences, events, and even transformations go on before our very eyes."[46] Dante has provided the souls of the damned with "phantom bodies," by means of which spiritual anguish is made palpable as physical agony, which in turn diffuses over the whole of the howling abyss. Bearing all the signs of zealous dismemberment, these bodies lend somatic form to a condition of the soul or psyche. Schiele, an Expressionist in whose "mannerist" paintings a monstrous self-image often extends over scenery that is arguably iconographic,[47] follows the same mechanism whereby Mann, in an act of grand retrospection, employs Michelangelo's despairing voluptuary as a vessel for the collective nightmare of modern German history. And much as the physical suffering of Dante's damned is "symptomatic" of their specific faults, so the "phantom bodies" that fill the Expressionist land- and cityscape produce a catalogue of legible affects (trembling in penitence, heaving with fear, wearing humiliation like a leaden mantle, etc.). The German Romantics, in superseding the aesthetics of neoclassicism, released for posterity an iconographic tradition in which elevation of the spirit was wedded, following Auerbach, to the experience of being "immeasurably forsaken."[48] The *pietà* is but one example from an image-repertoire of which writers, artists, and eventually Weimar filmmakers would avail themselves as a means of contending with the enormities of modern life. Like the *Mater Dolorosa*, it is native to the Early Modern pictorial traditions on which, where painting was concerned, Romantic writers trained their attention. Wackenroder is exemplary here, yet his focus on a musician at the end of his seminal *Outpourings* marks an impulse to abstraction that would not find its counterpart in the visual arts for another century. The longed-for autonomy achieved by instrumental music in the age of Beethoven forged a path toward modernism, in which abstraction, following Belting, asserted itself in agreement with Romantic criteria, namely *auf durchaus romantischen Denkwegen.*[49] Disney's *Fantasia* is remarkable for the way it places "absolute music" and visual abstraction – historically disparate but continuous moments – on a common plane, while recognizing the modern potential of the landscape as painted by Caspar David Friedrich in the earlier decades of the nineteenth century. But the fact that *Fantasia* was finished in 1940, the year of the fictional Leverkühn's death, underscores the film's obliviousness to the storm breaking over Europe and the world. Musically, it is anything but experimental. Its trajectory is conciliatory, and at the worst possible time. Devoid of discord, it is free of the anxiety that erupts on the face and jolts the limbs of the Weimar screen-performer, whose expressions are of a piece with that of Michelangelo's lost soul, aghast at the effects of his past spreading out before him as far as the eye can see.

54. *Metropolis* (1926), dir. Fritz Lang.

Filmography

10 Films. Dir. Oskar Fischinger [1921–43]. Center for Visual Music, 2006.

400 Blows, The (*Les quatre cents coups*). Dir. François Truffaut [1959]. Criterion, 2017. DVD.

A Kind of Murder. Dir. Andy Goddard. Magnolia. 2017.

Apocalypse Now Redux. Dir. Francis Ford Coppola [1979/2001]. Lionsgate, 2001. DVD.

Battleship Potemkin (*Bronenosets Potyomkin*). Dir. Sergei Eisenstein [1925]. Transit Film, 2007. DVD.

Berlin, Symphony of a Great City (*Berlin, die Symphonie der Grosstadt*). Dir. Walther Ruttmann [1927]. Image Entertainment, 1999. DVD.

Blue Angel, The (*Der blaue Engel*). Dir. Josef von Sternberg [1930]. Kino International, 2001. DVD.

Bram Stoker's Dracula. Dir. Francis Ford Coppola [1992]. Sony Pictures Home Entertainment, 2007.

Broken Jug, The (Der zerbrochene Krug). Dir. Gustav Ucicky [1937]. Sony, 2005. DVD.

Cabinet of Dr Caligari, The (*Das Kabinett des Doktor Caligari*). Dir. Robert Wiene [1919]. Kino Classics, 2014. DVD.

Death in Venice (*Morte a Venezia*). Dir. Luchino Visconti. Warner Brothers, 1971. DVD.

Double Indemnity. Dir. Billy Wilder. [1944] Universal Studios Home Entertainment. 2006. DVD

Fantasia. Dir. Joe Grant, Dick Huemer, Ben Sharpsteen, et al. [1940]. Walt Disney Studios, 2014. DVD.

Faust – A German Folk-Tale (*Faust – Eine deutsche Volkssage*). Dir. F.W. Murnau [1926]. Transit, 2012. DVD.

Frankenstein. Dir. James Whale [1931]. Universal Pictures Home Entertainment, 2014. DVD.

Goodbye, Dragon Inn. Dir. Ming-liang Tsai [2003]. Fox Lorber, 2005. DVD.

Grizzly Man. Dir. Werner Herzog [2005]. Lionsgate, 2005. DVD.

Golem, The (*Der Golem, wie er in die Welt kam*). Dir. Paul Wegener [1920]. Kino International, 2002. DVD.

Hands of Orlac, The (*Orlacs Hände*). Dir. Robert Wiene [1924]. Kino International, 2008. DVD.

Last Laugh, The (*Der letzte Mann*). Dir. F.W. Murnau [1924]. Eureka!, 2008. DVD.

Love of Jeanne Ney, The (*Die Liebe der Jeanne Ney*). Dir. G.E. Pabst [1927]. Kino Lorber, 2001. DVD.

M. Dir. Fritz Lang [1931]. Atlantic-Film, 1998. DVD.

Madame Dubarry. Dir. Ernst Lubitsch [1919]. Grapevine Video, 2012. DVD.

Marquise of O, The (*Die Marquise von O*). Dir. Eric Rohmer. [1976]. Continental Multimedia,

Metropolis. Dir. Fritz Lang [1927]. Kino International, 2010. DVD.

Nosferatu – A Symphony of Horror (*Nosferatu – Eine Symphonie des Grauens*). Dir. F. W. Murnau [1922]. Transit 2012. DVD.

Nosferatu the Vampyre (*Nosferatu – Phantom der Nacht*). Dir. Werner Herzog [1979]. Starz/Anchor Bay, 2002. DVD.

Siegfried. Dir. Fritz Lang [1924]. Kino International, 2002. DVD.

Snow White and the Seven Dwarfs [1937]. Dir. David Hand. Walt Disney Studios, 2013. DVD.

Street, The (*Die Strasse*). Dir. Karl Grune [1923]. Grapevine Video. DVD.

Student of Prague, The (*Der Student von Prag*). Dir. Stellan Rye [1913]. Alpha Video, 2004. DVD.

Suburbicon. Dir. George Clooney. Paramount, 2018. DVD

Talented Mr Ripley, The. Dir. Anthony Minghella [1999]. Paramount, 2017. DVD.

Tartuffe. Dir. F.W. Murnau [1926]. Kino Lorber, 2003. DVD.

Twister. Dir. Jan de Bont [1996]. Warner Brothers, 2008. DVD

Warning Shadows (*Schatten*). Dir. Arthur Robison [1923]. Kino International, 2006. DVD.

Waxworks (*Das Wachsfigurenkabinet*). Dir. Paul Leni [1924]. Kino Lorber, 2004. DVD.

Notes

Introduction

1 Freud, *The Standard Edition*, vol. 14, 247.
2 Koerner, *Caspar David Friedrich*, 221–2; Hofmann, *Caspar David Friedrich*, 56–60.
3 Bouvier and Leutrat, *Nosferatu*, 188–91.
4 Baudry, "The Apparatus," 183–4.
5 Ramdohr, "Über ein zum Altarblatte bestimmtes Landschaftsgemälde," 151.
6 Rancière, *Film Fables*, 6, 8. Friedrich's pronouncement on the aim of painting may serve as an example of the "dramaturgy of the painterly gesture" identified by Rancière: "A painting must stand as a painting, made by human hand; not seek to disguise itself as Nature" (*Ein Bild muss sich als Bild, als Menschenwerk gleich darstellen, nicht aber als Natur täuschen wollen*). In Hinz 115, cited in Grave, *Caspar David Friedrich*, 1.
7 Metz, *Impersonal Enunciation*, 10.
8 Freud, *The Standard Edition*, vol. 14, 247.
9 Maskarinec, *The Forces of Form in German Modernism*, 8–10. Maskarinec's excellent book has sweeping implications for the present study.
10 Worringer, *Abstraktion und Einfühlung*, 156. Except where otherwise indicated, translations from Worringer are my own.
11 Eisner, *The Haunted Screen*, 113; Heine, *Sämtliche Schriften*, vol. 3, 360.
12 Eisner 105.
13 Eisner 99.
14 Eisner 130.
15 Starobinski, *1789*, 173–80.
16 See, in addition to Starobinski, Hofmann, "Das Erwachen zum Tode."
17 I am alluding to psychoanalyst Otto Rank's small book *The Double* (1914), which begins with a treatment of Stellan Rye's film *The Student of Prague* (1913). Rank's book and its reception will be taken up in a later chapter.

18 Schönemann, *Fritz Lang*, 95; Frayling, *Nightmare*, 6–12.
19 Starobinski 180. Starobinski is referring specifically to the graphic work of William Hogarth.
20 Eisner 99.
21 Lee, *Beauty and Ugliness*, 53. Cited in Selz, *German Expressionist Painting*, 7.
22 See Beil and Dillmann, *Gesamtkunstwerk Expressionismus*, 121–3.
23 Hillmann, *Bildlichkeit der deutschen Romantik*, 95–130.
24 Rohmer, *The Taste for Beauty*, 49; Dalle Vacche, "Painting Thoughts." See also Dalle Vacche, *Cinema and Painting*.
25 Rohmer 51.
26 Rohmer 26. Emphasis added.
27 Koschorke, *Die Geschichte des Horizonts*, 169. See de Man, *The Rhetoric of Romanticism*, 1–17.
28 Alewyn, *Probleme und Gestalten*, 225.
29 Deleuze, *Cinema 1*, 23–5. Alewyn, who describes Eichendorff's landscape in terms of "spaced intervals" (*Abstände*) that fill out the space between near and far (225), invokes Henri Bergson (223), who also figures prominently in Deleuze's discussion. Eisner, by the way, Chief Curator at the Cinémathèque Française for forty years, is referenced multiple times by Deleuze in the notes to his sub-chapter on the "Pre-War French School" (32–40).
30 Lakoff and Johnson, *Philosophy in the Flesh*, 141–9. See also M. Johnson, *The Meaning of the Body*, 27–31. Maskarinec (60) argues that Lakoff and Johnson's proposal, namely that "we relate to the external world through schemas based on our corporeal experiences," has a precedent in the empathy aesthetics introduced by Theodor Lipps, whose broad line of argument is that "we make sense of and relate to the world of spatial bodies on the basis of our bipedal experience of force and counterforce."
31 "Auf dem Rhein," in Brentano, *Werke*, vol. 1, 98–101. I am indebted to Rembert Hüser for his help with this poem.
32 Deleuze 23, emphasis added.
33 Bryson, *Vision and Painting*, 88–9, 94.
34 See Emil Staiger's multifaceted discussion of Brentano's poem in *Die Zeit als Einbildungskraft des Dichters*, 23–103.
35 Rauth, "Nosferatu's Gesture."
36 Wellbery, *The Specular Moment*, 67, 12.
37 Wellbery 13.
38 Wellbery 12–13, emphasis added.
39 Silverman, *The Subject of Semiotics*, 195.
40 Elsaesser, *Weimar Cinema and After*, 235–9. Regarding Friedrich and the afterlife of Romanticism in Herzog, see L. Johnson, *Forgotten Dreams*, 12–20.

41 Jonas, *The Phenomenon of Life*, 20–1. Jonas figures prominently in the chapters that follow.
42 Elsaesser 238.
43 Jonas 20. In a short essay from 1878 titled "Natural Science and the Spirit World," Frederick Engels argued that the strict adherence to empiricism left its mostly Anglo-American disciples vulnerable to the superstition behind such practices as spirit rapping and ghost photography, which are part of the cinema's cultural if not its technical prehistory. Engels, *The Dialectics of Nature*. See Barnouw, *The Magician and the Cinema*.
44 Herzog: "But as a filmmaker, sometimes things fall into your lap which you couldn't expect, never even dream of. There is something like an inexplicable magic of cinema." See D. Johnson, "You Must Never Listen to This."
45 Lacan, *Écrits*, 2.
46 Lacoue-Lebarth and Nancy, *The Literary Absolute*, 4–5.
47 Dahlhaus, *The Idea of Absolute Music*, 1–17.
48 Belting, *Das unsichtbare Meisterwerk*, 29.
49 Rosenblum, *Modern Painting*, 192.
50 Coleridge, *Poetical Works*, vol. 1, 295–8.
51 Wackenroder and Tieck, *Herzensergiessungen*, 10.
52 Freud, *Studienausgabe*, vol. 6, 164, 167n1.
53 Goethe, *Faust*, trans. Arndt, 102.
54 Goethe, *Faust*, ed. Schöne, 156. Dora is subject to a "fantasy of defloration"; Gretchen is replenishing the flowers in a vase before a shrine to the Holy Virgin.
55 Belting 63–82. On the importance of Raphael's *Madonna* for Romantic painting and criticism, see Prager, *Aesthetic Vision*, 128–30.
56 Maskarinec (5) asserts that "the modernist avowal of uprightness as a corporeal and aesthetic ideal perpetuates a dominant classical aesthetic into the twentieth century."
57 M. Shelley, *Frankenstein*, 109.
58 Lacan, *The Four Fundamental Concepts*, 101, 109.
59 Lacan, *Écrits*, 4–5.
60 Eisner 141, 144, 149.
61 Leplanche and Pontalis, *The Language of Psycho-Analysis*, 194–5.
62 Eisner 9.
63 Eisner 13; Worringer 156.
64 Worringer (156): "How far [Nordic man] is from the harmonious Greek, who derives happiness from his absorption in the balanced, unecstatic repose of gentle organic life!" (*Wie fern steht [der nordische Mensch] dem harmonischen Griechen, dem alles Glück nur von der Versenkung in die ausgeglichene, aller Ekstase fremde Ruhe der sanften organischen Bewegung kommt*).

65 A comparable moment in Metropolis comes slightly earlier when Freder, clasping at his heart, watches aghast while stretcher-bearers – shadowy figures in the near foreground – file past robotically with the victims of an industrial explosion (a scene that must have resonated deeply with viewers still living in the shadow of the First World War). See Anton Kaes's evocative treatment of this scene in his *Shell Shock Cinema*, 179. Regarding his statement that "this is a world of machines in which there is no pause for mourning," see Brodnax, "Man a Machine," 76, 82–3.
66 Keats, *Complete Poems*, 282.
67 Kleist, *Sämtliche Werke und Briefe*, vol. 3, 543; Koschorke 167.
68 Metz, *Impersonal Enunciation*, 22. Compare Koschorke's statement, to be examined in a later chapter, that the Romantic landscape is no longer a view from the window "but a structured surface over which speech spreads out" (171).

1 The Turmoil of Forces

1 Rovelli, *Sette brevi lezioni di fisica*, 13–21.
2 Milner, *Mondrian*, 120. Mondrian drew and painted a number of variations of this theme, the most finished of which is his *Composition No. 10 (Pier and Ocean)*.
3 Worringer, *Abstraktion und Einfühlung*, 57. Unless otherwise indicated, all subsequent citations of Worringer are from this book.
4 Worringer 40, 48, 67.
5 Worringer (54) likened the impulse to represent phenomena abstractly to a longing for the "thing in itself" (*Ding an sich*).
6 Jonas, *The Phenomenon of Life*, 2, 36–7. Subsequent page references are given parenthetically.
7 Eichendorff, *Werke*, 271.
8 Marx, *Schriften*, vol. 2, 816.
9 Alewyn, *Probleme und Gestalten*, 207–9.
10 Wimsatt and Beardsley, "The Affective Fallacy."
11 Metz, *Impersonal Enunciation*, 3–4.
12 Balázs, *Der sichtbare Mensch*, 73. See Steimatsky, *The Face on Film*, esp. 28–35.
13 Worringer, *Abstraktion und Einfühlung*, 92.
14 "Story of a Lad Who Left Home to Learn the Meaning of Fear" (*Märchen von einem, der auszog, um das Fürchten [Gruseln] zu lernen*). *Brüder Grimm*, vol. 1, 41–51. A simpler version of this same tale – *Giovannin senza paura* – is the first selection in Italo Calvino's copious anthology of Italian folk tales. Calvino, *Fiabe italiane*, 3–4.
15 Balázs 74.

16 Worringer, *Abstraktion und Einfühlung*, 49.
17 *The Prophet* and *The Double Dream of Spring*, both painted by de Chirico in 1915, include panels, framed and placed on easels, in which the technique of linear perspective is precisely schematized – geometrical blueprints of the paintings that incorporate them.
18 Nietzsche, *On the Genealogy of Morals*, 26. I am referring to paintings that de Chirico painted between 1912 and 1916. These include *The Enigma of Arrival and the Afternoon* (1912) and *Mystery and Melancholy of a Street* (1914). V.S. Naipaul, who fashioned a book title out of the former, described the painting as follows: "A classical scene, Mediterranean, ancient-Roman – or so I saw it. A wharf; in the background, beyond walls and gateways (like cutouts), there is the top of the mast of an antique vessel; on an otherwise deserted street in the foreground there are two figures, both muffled, one perhaps the person who has arrived, the other perhaps a native of the port. The scene is of desolation and mystery; it speaks of the mystery of arrival. It spoke to me of that, as it had spoken to Apollinaire [who gave this and other of de Chirico's paintings their titles]." Naipaul, *The Enigma of Arrival*, 98. Concerning de Chirico and Nietzsche, see Merjian, *Giorgio de Chirico*, esp. 37.
19 Worringer, "Spätgotisches," 6.
20 Worringer, "Spätgotisches," 8.
21 Worringer, "Carlo Carrà's *Pinie am Meer*," 88. Haxthausen, "Modern Art," 127–30. I have adopted Haxthausen's translation of the passage cited.
22 Worringer, "Kritische Gedanken," 93.
23 "Heard melodies are sweet, but those unheard / Are sweeter." Keats, *Complete Poems*, 282.
24 The poem is "Ein Gleiches" (1780), a companion piece to Goethe's "Wandrers Nachtlied" (1776). Goethe, *Gedichte 1756–1799*, 388.
25 Worringer, *Abstraktion und Einfühlung*, 70.
26 Worringer, *Abstraktion und Einfühlung*, 71, 72.
27 Worringer, *Abstraktion und Einfühlung*, 155.
28 Goethe, *Ästhetische Schriften*, 107.
29 It is hard to imagine German poetry without the word "schweigen," an active verb indicating the seeming inaction of being (keeping) quiet. See Gerhard Kaiser's discussion of Eugen Gomringer's concrete poem "schweigen" in the context of a tradition that includes Goethe's "Wandrers Nachtlied," in *Augenblicke deutscher Lyrik*, 392–7. Compare David Rains Wallace who, in his luminous evocation of the wilderness straddling the border between Oregon and California, takes stock of the "intense quiet" offset only by the "faint sibilance in the pine needles" – a "reticence" that made him "reluctant to move" and left him wondering if "the most extraordinary things" might not be hidden within those twilit ridges. *The Klamath Knot*, 2.

30 Worringer, *Abstraktion und Einfühlung*, 71.

31 "Intellectual intuition" (*intellektuelle Anschauung*), for example, which Schelling defined as synonymous with the ego: "[an act of] producing in the process of becoming its own object" (*ein sich selbst zum Objekt werdendes Produzieren*). *Schellings Werke*, vol. 3, 370.

32 Novalis, *Schriften*, vol. 1, 209.

33 Schmidt, "Romantik und Gegenwart," 225. Cited in Selz, *German Expressionist Painting*, 21.

34 See Shen and Aisenman, "Heard melodies are sweet"; Johnson and Larson, "Something in the Way She Moves."

35 Waite, "Worringer's *Abstraction and Empathy*," 24.

36 Worringer, "Kritische Gedanken," 92.

37 Bollacher, "Nachwort," 202.

38 Wackenroder and Tieck, *Herzensergiessungen*, 99; idem, *Outpourings*, 105–6.

39 Ward, "Kracauer versus the Weimar Film City," 26–7.

40 Nietzsche, *Kritische Studienausgabe*, vol. 1, 50. See Calhoon, "*Sturmbild*."

41 Eichendorff 271.

42 Pfau, *Romantic Moods*, 302–5; Kaiser 179–80.

43 Concerning horizontal versus vertical iterations of metaphorical flight, see Hillmann, *Bildlichkeit der deutschen Romantik*, 234.

44 See the extensive editorial note to Bollacher's edition of the *Herzensergiessungen*, 158–60.

45 The term "patterned integrity" is borrowed from Kenner, *The Pound Era*, 145–62.

46 Emily Genauer for the New York *World-Telegram*, quoted in Culhane, *Walt Disney's Fantasia*, 43. Five years earlier, Benjamin wrote that the "reactionary attitude toward a Picasso painting changes into the progressive reaction toward a Chaplin movie. The progressive reaction is characterized by the direct, intimate fusion of visual and emotional enjoyment with the orientation of the expert." *Illuminations*, 234.

47 Allan, *Walt Disney and Europe*.

48 In a compact formulation that closely echoes the broad strains of the present argument, Hans Belting holds that the *symphony*, in which music attained a longed-for autonomy, found its counterpart in the visual arts only a century later, when abstraction asserted itself "along thoroughly Romantic paths of thought." *Das unsichtbare Meisterwerk*, 92.

49 Worringer, "Kritische Gedanken," 93.

50 Worringer, *Abstraktion und Einfühlung*, 69.

51 In his splendid book on German painter Albrecht Altdorfer, Christopher S. Wood provides a concise analysis of the relation between the physical frame and the compositional elements of landscape: "The concomitant of

the frame is the composition. A picture is 'composed' when its contents acknowledge, through their disposition, the edges of the surface they occupy. Such a picture will have trouble upholding the pretense of being a mere arbitrary excerpt from a plane of infinite extension. It becomes a visual 'field' unified by the presence of a fixed beholder. This is a picture that – true to Hegel's normative diagnosis of the 'accommodating' modern work of art – manifestly exists for its beholder, 'for us.' The literal frame – a drawn or painted border, a wooden brace – simply confirms a state of affairs that the surface data have already conceded." Wood, *Albrecht Altdorfer*, 118–19.

52 Anthologized in Uerlings, *Theorie der Romantik*, 282.
53 Busch, *Caspar David Friedrich*, 101–41.
54 Bouleau, *The Painter's Secret Geometry*, 249–51; Golding, *Paths to the Absolute*, 36; Milner 151.
55 Milner 176–9.
56 Worringer, *Abstraktion und Einfühlung*, 69ff. See also Worringer's discussion of the Egyptian "arabesque" and the woven ribbon patterns in Greek art (114–16).
57 Reprinted in Seuphor, *Piet Mondrian*, 301–52.
58 Seuphor 304.
59 Arnheim, *Art and Visual Perception*, 300–1. See M. Johnson, *The Meaning of the Body*, 231–3.
60 Standard translations of Kafka's collection render the title as "Meditation" or "Contemplation," though *Betrachtung* connotes, in addition to "examination" and "inspection," "viewing" and "consideration," as well as "meditation" and "contemplation."
61 Kafka, *Drucke zu Lebzeiten*, 24–5.
62 Schönemann, *Fritz Lang*, 64.
63 See Mary Ann Doane's discussion of *deixis* in Lang's film. "The Indexical," 138–41.
64 Kaes, *M*, 27–8. See James Baldwin: "Lang's concern, or obsession, was with the fact and the effect of human loneliness, and the ways in which we are all responsible for the creation, and the fate, of the isolated monster: whom we isolate because we recognize him as living within us. This is what his great German film, *M*, which launched Peter Lorre, is all about." *The Devil Finds Work*, 24.
65 Deleuze, *Cinema 1*, 17.
66 Milner 177.
67 Deleuze 16.
68 Milner 177.
69 Koerner, *Caspar David Friedrich*, 120.
70 Ramdohr 151–2.

71 Rousseau, *A Discourse on Inequality*, 99.

72 Novalis, *Schriften*, vol. 2, 545. Regarding this particular fragment of Novalis's, Peter Cochran has written: "A word ["Romanticism"] which means two opposing things has no useful meaning, and only serves to confuse." *"Romanticism,"* xiii. This opinion, in support of which Cochran cites a robust tradition of criticism, is glaringly at odds with a philological history that had its genesis in Romanticism and found a particular articulation in Freud – a history that turns on the insight that words, in fact, quite often "mean opposing things." Witness the Grimms' *Wörterbuch*, or Freud's own "The Antithetical Meaning of Primal Words."

73 Ramdohr 150.

74 Claudius, *Sämtliche Werke*, 218. Concerning the importance of this poem and of Claudius's poems generally for Eichendorff, see Kaiser 186–7.

75 Goethe, *Gedichte 1756–1799*, 303–4.

76 Freud, *Studienausgabe*, vol. 2, 275–6.

77 Goethe, *Aus meinem Leben*, 389–90.

78 Simmen, *Vertigo*, 112–14.

79 Simmen, "Elevation," 16–29.

80 See Cinematéque Française, ed., *Le cinéma expressionniste allemande*, esp. 142–5. This exhibition catalogue, presented as a tribute to Eisner, features drawings and set designs by Walter Röhrig, Emil Hasler, Hermann Warm, among others, most of which are paired with excerpts from Eisner's *The Haunted Screen*. Those by Robert Herlth (*Faust*), Erich Kettelhut (*Metropolis*), and Andrei Andrejew (Wiene's *Raskolnikoff*) are especially revealing in their manner of depriving viewers of any sense of equilibrium.

81 Rosenblum, "Horizons."

82 Goethe, *Faust*, ed. Schöne, 81.

83 Goethe, *Aus meinem Leben*, 408.

84 Schmitz, "Vertical Sequence." This brief discussion of the elevator in the cinema covers a range of examples, from René Clair's *La Tour* (1928), a documentary on the Eiffel Tower, to Louis Malle's *Elevator to the Gallows* (1957) and beyond. Schmitz refers to Lang's *Metropolis*, in which capacious elevator cars convey slow parades of listless workers between levels in their oppressive underground world, and in which the portal of a massive Gothic cathedral, from the roof of which the villain plummets to his death, frames the reconciliation between the workers and their masters. Schmitz makes no mention of *The Last Laugh*, however, which is surprising given his emphasis on the "lift" and the cinema as parallel moments in the "anthropological revolution in human perception in modern times" (79). It was in *The Last Laugh*, after all, that the elevator

provided the means of introducing the "unchained camera," pioneered by Murnau's cinematographer Karl Freund.

85 Gunning, "The Cinema of Attraction[s]."
86 Lacan, *Écrits*, 1–3.
87 Benjamin 236. Arnheim, *Film als Kunst*, 138. See Loew, "The Spirit of Technology." Also Loew, *Special Effects and German Silent Film.*
88 It is a veritable exorcism. The markedly racialized portrayal of Alberich is consistent with National Socialism's eventual embrace of neoclassical aesthetic ideals and the concomitant stigma of degeneracy assigned to Expressionism.
89 Balduin, the titular student of Prague, likewise runs his hand over the surface of the mirror from which his own reflection, which he has sold to a nefarious visitor, has emerged.
90 Novalis, *Schriften*, vol. 2, 650.
91 Novalis, *Schriften*, vol. 1, 196–8. See Burch, *Life to Those Shadows*, 162–85.
92 Girveau, "La nostalgie bâtisseuse," 220–1.
93 Einstein, *The Collected Papers*, vol. 7, 136.
94 Simmen, *Vertigo*, 24–45.
95 "Looking at pictures, even those most lacking in what is usually called the gaze, and which is constituted by a pair of eyes, pictures in which any representation of the human figure is absent, like a landscape by a Dutch or a Flemish painter, you will see in the end, as in filigree, something so specific to each of the painters that you will feel the presence of the gaze." Lacan, *The Four Fundamental Concepts*, 101.
96 Balázs 59–60.
97 Balázs 67.
98 Heine, *Sämtliche Schriften*, vol. 1, 187.
99 Calhoon, "Werner Herzog's View of Delft," 101–26.
100 "An Schwager Kronos" (1774/9) begins with a horse-drawn *post chaise* careening down a treacherous path, and the poem known as "Willkommen und Abschied" (1771) begins with the line "My heart pounded. Quickly, to horse!" The penultimate scene of *Faust I* is limited to a very brief and highly "expressionistic" exchange between Faust and Mephisto, shown "thundering past on black horses" (*auf schwarzen Pferden daherbrausend*). Goethe, *Faust*, 191. (Translation K.C.)
101 Gordon, "Marc and Friedrich Again."
102 Kafka 32–3. Thanks to Joyce Cheng for her insight concerning the parallel between Marc's painting and Kafka's "Wish to Become an Indian."
103 Marc, *Schriften*, 99. Discussed at length by Gordon and Simmons, both of whom bring Marc's work and thought into conjunction with Worringer.
104 Kafka 33.

105 Deleuze 22–3.
106 Simmons, "Abstraction and Empathy." The importance of Simmons's work and thought for my own far exceeds what this discrete citation would suggest.
107 Deleuze 25.

2 Under the Sign of Insomnia

1 Metz, *The Imaginary Signifier*, 48–9. See also Williams, *Figures of Desire*, 143–4.
2 Böhme, "Rückenfiguren," 54.
3 Bryson, *Vision and Painting*, 111.
4 Ricoeur, *Freud and Philosophy*, 160.
5 Regarding motionlessness as a component of fascination, see Weingart, "Contact at a Distance."
6 Metz 126.
7 Koschorke, *Die Geschichte des Horizonts*, 169.
8 Arendt, *Der "poetische Nihilismus,"* 145–6.
9 Novalis, *Schriften*, vol. 1, 205. See Koschorke 205.
10 Metz 49.
11 Koschorke 189.
12 Novalis 196–7.
13 Novalis 197.
14 Metz 126.
15 Eisner, *The Haunted Screen*, 113.
16 Kessler, "Öffentliche Lustbarkeiten"; Dobryden, "23 May 1920."
17 Viatte, "Un dessin de Caspar David Friedrich."
18 Verwiebe, "Transparentenmalerei und Romantik"; Hofmann, *Caspar David Friedrich*, 198, 208.
19 Plessen and Giersch, *Sehsucht*, 123.
20 Koerner, *Caspar David Friedrich*, 110–12.
21 P. Shelley, *Poetry and Prose*, 483–4. See especially Pyle, *Art's Undoing*, 59.
22 Faflak, "Dancing in the Dark with Shelley," 168.
23 Goethe, *Faust*, ed. Schöne, 56.
24 Translation K. C.
25 Koschorke 162.
26 Novalis 196.
27 Blumenberg, *Höhlenausgänge*, 55.
28 Goethe 65.
29 Starobinski, *1789*, 175–6.
30 Schneider, "Das Licht der Welt."
31 Goethe 68.

32 Barthes, *Camera Lucida*, 38–40.
33 Barthes: "Yes, indeed: the Photograph is *dangerous*" (28).
34 Marquard, "Über einige Beziehungen."
35 Ritter, *Subjektivität*, 141–63.
36 Alewyn, *Probleme und Gestalten*, 315–19.
37 Gaier, "'Schwankende Gestalten."
38 Gaudreault, "Theatralität, Narrativität, Trickästhetik."
39 See Frances Guerin's discussion of Alberich's cave in Fritz Lang's *Siegfried* (1924), a spectacle that reinforces Tom Gunning's now familiar conception of early cinema as an "attraction," its content (in Gunning's words) "absorbed by a cinematic gesture of presentation, and this technological means of representation that constituted the initial fascination of cinema." Gunning, "Now You See it, Now You Don't," 73; Guerin, *A Culture of Light*, 137–40.
40 Kracauer, *Das Ornament der Masse*, 314.
41 Marquard 96.
42 Freud, *Totem and Taboo*, 53; idem, *Studienausgabe*, vol. 9, 333.
43 Marquard 92.
44 Freud, *Studienausgabe*, vol. 4, 248–9. See Fenichel, *Uncanny Belonging*.
45 M. Shelley, *Frankenstein*, 93. The first example, which is cited in *Frankenstein*, is from Percy Shelley's "On Mutability," part of which is reproduced in the novel (93).
46 Clark, *Landscape into Art*, 167.
47 Eichendorff, *Werke*, 11. Guerin makes a brief reference to another poem by Eichendorff, "Tageslicht" ("Daylight"), in conjunction with the "haunting interstitial light of [Friedrich's] paintings" (91).
48 Metz 63.
49 Freud, *The Uncanny*, 135.
50 Schlegel, *Kritische Ausgabe*, vol. 2, 160. Chaouli, "Irony," 65.
51 Metz 73.
52 Kaes, *Kino-Debatte*, 27–9.
53 "It was that windless hour of dawn when madness wakes and strange plants open to the light and the moth flies forth silently." Joyce, *A Portrait of the Artist as a Young Man*, 217.
54 The concluding, climactic scene of Andy Goddard's *A Kind of Murder* (2016), adapted from Patricia Highsmith's novel *The Blunderer* (1954), is conspicuous as an homage to *Caligari*. Not only is a knife-wielding villain projected as a stylized shadow on a wall, but there are also, as in Wiene's film, abrupt shots of the victim's hands, shown in close-up, raised in self-defence. Goddard's film likewise quotes *Psycho*: this same scene is shot in an underground storage area filled with mannequins wrapped in heavy translucent plastic, closely resembling the knife-wielding Norman

Bates as seen through the shower curtain. In "The Sorcerer's Apprentice" – part of Disney's *Fantasia* (1940) – the hapless novice takes up an axe in an attempt to destroy the broom he has brought to life but can no longer control. An axe-murder as it were, the action is seen indirectly as a play of shadows on the wall of the subterranean chamber. In George Clooney's recent *Suburbicon* (2017), written by Joel and Ethan Coen, the camera pans away from a murder to the wall where, in a clear nod to *Caligari*, the lethal struggle is seen in silhouette.

55 Another man, arrested for a murder subsequent to Alan's, admits to committing this one crime in the belief that blame would fall upon the unknown perpetrator of the other murders, which had begun with Caligari's arrival in Holstenwall. Francis thus embeds a displaced confession within his own tale.

56 The "deepest sleep" is what Count Orlok, of Murnau's *Nosferatu* (1922), professes to relish while the sun is up.

57 Freud, *Studienausgabe*, vol. 3, 239.

58 Freud 292. See Calhoon, *Fatherland*, 82.

59 Freud, *Studienausgabe*, vol. 3, 184.

60 Schlüpmann, "The First German Art Film"; Peucker, *Incorporating Images*, 17–18; Hunt, "*The Student of Prague.*"

61 Burch, *Life to Those Shadows*, 165–7; Elsaesser, "Weimar Cinema," 48–9.

62 Elsaesser, *Weimar Cinema and After*, 250.

63 Bergstrom, "Sexuality at a Loss."

64 Eisner 113.

65 Fried in fact draws a sharp distinction between this new kind of beholder, for which Diderot advocated, and the brand of subjectivity presented by philosophers such as J.G. Fichte and "posited" in the paintings of Friedrich. *Absorption and Theatricality*, 104.

66 Benjamin, *Illuminations*, 239

67 Adorno, *Philosophy of New Music*, 31–4.

68 Elsaesser 252–3.

69 Adorno, *Notes to Literature*, 55–79.

70 Compare Barthes: "I imagine myself today something like the ancient Greek as Hegel describes him: he interrogated, Hegel says, passionately, uninterruptedly, the rustle of branches, of springs, of winds, in short, the shudder of Nature, in order to perceive in it the design of an intelligence. And I – it is the shudder of meaning I interrogate, listening to the rustle of language, that language which for me, modern man, is my Nature." *The Rustle of Language*, 79.

71 Eichendorff 33.

72 See especially Pfau, *Romantic Moods*, 255; also Brown, *The Tooth That Nibbles at the Soul*, 91–3.

73 Koschorke 171.

74 In a book that appears to take its title from Adorno's essay on Eichendorff, Carol Jacobs (writing on Percy Shelley's "On the Medusa of Leonardo da Vinci in the Florentine Gallery") observes a "grammatical failure" that makes a thought untraceable to its source and foils the distinction between beholder and beheld, making it impossible to "extricate our gaze from the scene." *Uncontainable Romanticism*, 8–9. In a similar vein, Koschorke (171) cites a grammatically convulsive exclamation from Tieck's *Blaubart* (1797): "Es ist alles wie ein fremdes *Mährchen*, wenn ich es aus der Ferne ansehe – und dann – dass ich im Mittelpunkte dieses entsetzlichen Gemäldes stehe!" See also Pyle's probing account of *The Triumph of Life*. While very different from Eichendorff's verse and that of the German Romantics generally, Shelley's poem supports a reading somewhat consistent with Koschorke's understanding: "If the cascading of Shelley's *terza rima*, a seemingly self-generating single sentence that unfolds over more than twenty wildly enjambed lines, makes it difficult to cite the instance of the shape's appearance, that seems precisely the point." Pyle, *Art's Undoing*, 62.

75 Böhme 72.

76 More recent examples of this *mise en abyme*, in which the history of the cinema is often embedded, are legion. Take *Twister* (1996), directed by Jan de Bont, in which a tornado bursts through the screen of a drive-in theatre during a night-time screening of Stanley Kubrick's *The Shining* (1980) at the very moment Jack Nicholson's deranged Jack Torrance, his menace reinforced by the whirlwind, smashes through a door with an axe. "Twister" is frequently also the name of amusement park thrill rides, and de Bont's film stages this particular episode in a way that recalls the visceral sensationalism of the "cinema of attractions," not to mention the legendary abuse of filmgoers fleeing the filmed approach of a locomotive in 1896. Far less sensational is the brilliant *Goodbye, Dragon Inn* (2003), by Taiwanese director Ming-liang Tsai. Consisting entirely of ponderous, mostly stationary shots, the film plays in real time in a decrepit and nearly deserted cinema on its last, rainy night of operation. The movie being shown is a martial arts blockbuster from 1967 (*Dragon Inn*), which the same theatre screened when it first opened, presumably that same year. Among the scattered attendees, like ghosts of their own past, are two elderly performers from the original film. As the film begins we are treated to a flashback of the original showing, to a full house. Framed by the lobby drapes, the screen is visible at a distance beyond the arrayed heads of the spectators, which are seen from behind.

77 Conley, "Landscape and Perception," 297.

78 Novalis 283.

79 Conley 297.
80 Metz, *Impersonal Enunciation*, 22; Conley 292.
81 Alewyn 217.

3 Nightwatching

1 *Das Glück im Winkel* is the title of a play from 1896 by Hermann Sudermann. Adorno employed the phrase to characterize the cozy provincialism of nineteenth-century Germany – something he finds absent from a particular poem by Eduard Mörike. *Noten zur Literatur*, vol. 1, 92–3. The same phrase is used commonly to convey contentedness on a small scale.
2 Wichmann, *Carl Spitzweg*, 378–9, 498–9.
3 Gillespie, "Introduction," xi. While the authorship of this text was long debated, it is now generally attributed to August Klingemann.
4 Bonaventura, *Nachtwachen*, 40–1.
5 Bonaventura 5.
6 Spitzweg's tiny *Serenade* (*Ständchen*, ca 1850), which can be seen in Dresden's Albertinum, is of particular interest with regard to *The Nightwatches*. A fiddler engaged to assist a would-be lover in his courtship is a common theme in Spitzweg. In this particular variation the tuxedo-clad musician, perched precariously atop a shed, raises his bow while peering in through a window. The interior behind the window is suffused with an infernal red. Through a side window, the viewer may behold the writhing lovers – a young woman and an apparent demon.
7 Compare this description, from Mary Shelley's *Frankenstein*, in which a flash of lightning suddenly reveals the "creature" lurking in the landscape: "As I said these words, I perceived in the gloom a figure which stole from behind a clump of trees near me; I stood fixed, gazing intently: I could not be mistaken. A flash of lightning illuminated the object, and discovered its shape plainly to me; its gigantic stature, and the deformity of its aspect, more hideous than belongs to humanity, instantly informed me that it was the wretch, the filthy daemon to whom I had given life." *Frankenstein*, 71.
8 Eisner, *The Haunted Screen*, 48.
9 Eisner 46.
10 Schivelbusch, *Lichtblicke*, 12–13; Ann Hollander observes that de La Tour only came to be regarded as great during "this movie-loving century" (the twentieth), a corroboration of his "prophetic pre-cinematic look." *Moving Pictures*, 114–18. See especially Judovitz, *Georges de La Tour*.
11 Elsaesser, *Weimar Cinema and After*, 251.
12 Deleuze, *Cinema 1*, 50–1. Italics in original.
13 Goetzmann, "Ludwig Meidner's Urban Iconography," 176.

14 Kafka, *Drucke zu Lebzeiten*, 34; idem, *The Penal Colony*, 40.
15 Deleuze 53, 225nn32 and 34.
16 Deleuze 53–5. Emphasis added.
17 See Burwick on Novalis's engagement with Goethe's *Theory of Colors* and his own plans for a "treatise on light." *The Damnation of Newton*, 102–38.
18 Kant, *Kritik der Urteilskraft*, 188.
19 Deleuze 92.
20 Freud, *Studienausgabe*, vol. 4, 256; Benjamin, *Gesammelte Schriften*, vol. 2/1, 210.
21 Calhoon, "Emil Jannings."
22 Fabe, *Closely Watched Films*, 43–4. Also Kreimeier, "Wie im Taumel," and in the same volume, Müller, "Lichtbildner" (35–62).
23 This scene is reprised at the beginning of Billy Wilder's *Double Indemnity* (1944), which begins with insurance salesman Walter Neff, wounded and slouching, being admitted to his office building by a kindly night porter.
24 Calhoon, "Silence Restored."
25 Schindler, "What Makes a Man a Man."
26 Deleuze 15–18.
27 "Das stolze Licht, das nun der Mutter Nacht / Den alten Rang, den Raum ihr streitig macht, / Und doch gelingt's ihm nicht, da es, so viel es strebt, / Verhaftet an den Körpern klebt / Von Körpern strömt's, die Körper macht es schön ...," Goethe, *Faust*, ed. Schöne, 65; "Proud light that now disputes with Mother Night / Her old status and space and never will / Prevail however hard it strives because / It clings to bodies, / Streams with bodies, makes them beautiful ...," Goethe, *Faust*, trans. Constantine, 47. See Deleuze: "It is an infinite opposition [of light and dark] as it appeared in Goethe and the Romantics: light would be nothing, or at least nothing manifest, without the opaque to which it is opposed and which makes it visible" (49).
28 Erlin, "Tradition as Intellectual Montage."
29 Elsaesser 251. Again Deleuze (citing Eisner): "It is the blended series of chiaroscuro, the continual transformation of all its degrees, forming a 'fluid range of gradations which constantly succeed one another,' Wegener and, above all, Murnau, were the masters of this formula" (50).
30 Starobinski, *1789*, 138.
31 Starobinski 138.
32 Starobinski 136–8.
33 Bouvier and Leutrat, *Nosferatu*, 190–2, 351. See also Emil Staiger's extended discussion of Kersting's painting *Lesender beim Lampenlicht* (1814), to which the shot from *Nosferatu* bears a strong, generic resemblance. Staiger, *Vor drei Bildern*, 9–33.
34 Eichendorff, *Werke*, 260.

35 Eichendorff 32.

36 Pfau, *Romantic Moods*, 305–6.

37 "Den Mond sah man schon in einiger Höhe, ein Postwagen fuhr in seinem Licht vorbei. Ein schwacher Wind erhob sich allgemein, auch im Graben fühlte man ihn, und in der Nähe fing der Wald zu rauschen an. Da lag einem nicht mehr soviel daran, allein zu sein." Kafka, *Drucke zu Lebzeiten*, 12; idem, *The Penal Colony* 23 (translation modified).

38 Novalis, *Schriften*, vol. 1, 252.

39 "Dem aufgehenden Vollmonde" (1828), in Goethe, *Gedichte 1800–1832*, 700.

40 Eichendorff 1158.

41 Hebel, *Sämtliche Schriften*, vols. 2–3, 410. At the end of the tale "Lange Kriegsfuhr," the narrator summarizes: "This is the story which an invisible friend [*ein unsichtbarer Freund*] bestowed upon the *Hausfreund* a year ago" (313).

42 Heidegger, *Hebel der Hausfreund*, 17.

43 Heidegger 12.

44 See Schneider, "Die sanfte Utopie."

45 Elsaesser 93.

46 Weber, "The Sideshow," 1133. Cited in Elsaesser 93.

47 Elsaesser 91.

48 Silverman, *The Subject of Semiotics*, 201ff.

49 Metz, *Impersonal Enunciation*, 3–4.

50 Metz 10. Compare the language that Peter Szondi used to characterize the irony in the comedies of Tieck: "In Tieck, the part (the theatrical part, the role) speaks about itself as role (reflexively)." *On Textual Understanding*, 71. Cited in de Man, *Aesthetic Ideology*, 182.

51 Metz 58.

52 Rank, *Der Doppelgänger*, 8–9.

53 Rank 29–31.

54 Metz 60–3.

55 Stoker, *Dracula*, 26.

56 Stewart, *Between Film and Screen*, 244.

57 Gombrich, *Shadows*, 30.

58 I have borrowed freely from my essay devoted to Herzog's homage to Murnau's film. Calhoon, "Werner Herzog's View of Delft."

59 See Metz's discussion of "secondary screens" and specifically his invocation of *The Golem* (57).

60 Kittler, *Literature, Media, Information Systems*, 90, 97.

61 Kittler 85, 87.

62 Dante Alighieri, *The Inferno*, 301.

63 Kittler 95.

64 Kafka, *The Penal Colony*, 25 (translation modified).
65 Novalis, *Schriften*, vol. 3, 377.
66 Metz 15.
67 Jonas, *The Phenomenon of Life*, 10.
68 Jonas 36.
69 Jonas 30–1.
70 Cahn, "Subversive Mimesis," 35.
71 Horkheimer and Adorno, *Dialectic of Enlightenment*, 45.
72 Hullot-Kentor, *Things beyond Resemblance*, 228. Around the time of this writing, the world of intercollegiate basketball supplied a dramatic illustration of mimesis as here defined: Kevin Ware, playing for the University of Louisville, landed badly after a jump and shattered his tibia. The sight of the grisly injury and of the young man's agony left his teammates on all fours, unable to stand for weeping.
73 Hamburger, *The Logic of Literature*, 139.
74 Hamburger 131.
75 Metz 157–8.
76 Hamburger 139.
77 Metz 157.
78 Hebel 134.
79 Hebel 208–11.
80 "I was not sleepy, as the long sleep yesterday had fortified me; but I could not help experiencing that chill which comes over one at the coming of the dawn, which is like, in its way, the turn of the tide. They say that people who are near death die generally at the change to the dawn or at the turn of the tide" (Stoker 25). See Calhoon, "The Moon," 132.
81 Jonas 31.
82 I am indebted to my graduate student Nadège Lejeune for her insights concerning the narratological status of Hebel's *Hausfreund*.
83 Jonas 153.
84 Bryson, *Vision and Painting*, 88–9, 94.
85 Herder, *Werke*, vol. 2, 414–16.
86 Jonas 154.
87 See Segeberg, ed., *Die Mobilisierung des Sehens*.
88 Burch, *Life to Those Shadows*, 34–41.
89 Hebel, *Kalendergeschichten*, 144.
90 Bloch, *Das Prinzip Hoffnung*, 1194. The quote is from *Faust*, line 6272.
91 Auerbach, *Mimesis*, 21.
92 Auerbach 18.
93 Nietzsche, *Will to Power*, 446.
94 Gordon, "Content by Contradiction."

95 Calhoon, "Silence Restored," 373–81.

96 See Maskarinec on the state of "fallenness" with respect to *uprightness* and *gravity*, to whose dynamic interplay form owes its genesis. *The Force of Form*, 3, 11.

4 A Pause in the Action

1 Ondaatje, *The Conversations*, 272–3.

2 Heintel, *Innehalten*, 10–11.

3 Auerbach, *Mimesis*, 71.

4 See Calhoon, *Affecting Grace*, 7.

5 For example, Murch says the following with respect to *The English Patient*, which was also directed by Minghella: "There was an amazing shot of [Hana's] back – her whole body expressing great loss." Ondaatje 134.

6 This "pause in the action" coincides with what Seymour Chatman, writing on Michelangelo Antonioni, refers to as "postdiegetic lingering" – a shot that "does not set the stage for another shot but ... is itself the scene." He continues: "Not that the simple place as stasis is turned into an event or action. It is rather that the camera's lingering makes the place pregnant with significance. We contemplate intently ... We are engaged ... in a scrutiny that we do not quite understand but that seems nonetheless urgent." Chatman underscores what he calls the *temps morts* in Antonioni's films, which, following Martin Lefebvre, are a means of removing a space (landscape) from the forward movement of the fiction, thereby making it "autonomous in the eyes of the spectator." Chatman, *Antonioni*, 126; Lefebvre, "Between Setting and Landscape, 39–40. In a similar vein, see Chatman's take on that final shot of Truffaut's *The 400 Blows*. Chatman, *Story and Discourse*, 133–4. See also J. Auerbach, "Chasing Film Narrative," 809.

7 Benjamin, *Illuminations*, 239.

8 Benjamin 222–3.

9 Benjamin 232, 239–40.

10 Fitzgerald, *The Great Gatsby*, 56. Cited henceforth in parentheses.

11 See chapter 6, note 35.

12 Hullot-Kentor states that the emergence of "a society of sports" (of which Gatsby's world may stand as a clear expression) is part of a general effort "to convert cultural objects into categories of physical performance." He adds: "The translation of novels into films would, for instance, be a variant of this." *Things beyond Resemblance*, 205.

13 Benjamin 235. Carraway himself seems alert to the newfound scientific-analytic capacity of film: "And so with the sunshine and the great bursts of leaves growing on the trees, just as things grow fast in movies, I had that familiar conviction that life was beginning over again" (Fitzgerald 4).

14 Moretti, *Atlas of the European Novel*, 44. An example that Moretti provides – from Walter Scott's *Waverley* (published 1814) – has a particular relevance for the episode from *Gatsby* discussed here. Approaching the Highlands at night, Waverley beholds a light over a lake, "a red glaring orb" that "seemed to rest on the surface of the very lake itself, and resembled the fiery vehicle in which the Evil Genius of an Oriental tale traverses land and sea." In time, the glowing sphere sheds its exotic unreality and is revealed to be nothing more mysterious than an encampment on the opposite bank, with torches made of pine and the red embers of a charcoal fire. "Near the border," Moretti extrapolates, "figurality goes up. Beyond the border, it subsides" (45).
15 Benjamin 231.
16 Eichendorff, *Werke*, 271.
17 Mann, *Death in Venice*, 55.
18 Novalis, *Schriften*, vol. 1, 234.
19 Novalis, *Schriften*, vol. 1, 320.
20 Mann 55.
21 Starobinski, *1789*, 38.
22 Rothko, *Writings on Art*, 125.
23 Freud, *Beyond the Pleasure Principle*, 43.
24 Freud, *Civilization and Its Discontents*, 11.
25 Novalis, *Schriften*, vol.1, 266–7.
26 Rosenblum, *Modern Painting*, 212.
27 Mann 30–1.
28 See Asendorf, *Ströme und Strahlen*.
29 An exhibit held in Munich in 1995 explored, through striking juxtaposition, the often explicit engagement on the part of modern German painters with the Romantics. Of particular relevance here is the manner in which the criss-crossing masts and yards of square-riggers pass over into the more purely abstract intersection of horizontal and vertical lines, as exemplified by the work of Blinky Palermo (Peter Schwarze). Vitaly, ed., *Ernste Spiele*, 290–3.
30 Mann 55.
31 Conrad, *Heart of Darkness*, 10. Subseqent page references appear parenthetically.
32 Mann 6.
33 Nietzsche, *The Birth of Tragedy*, 39; idem, *Kritische Studienausgabe*, vol. 1, 44.
34 Hullot-Kentor, "The Exact Sense."
35 See Brooks, *Reading for the Plot*, 256. Commenting on the sentence that summarizes the helmsman's sad and silent surcease, Garrett Stewart isolates a degree of Romantic morbidity within the resurgent materiality of Conrad's prose: "In this jungle world where death is so treacherously

slurred with life, where the landscape itself evinces a Coleridgean 'life-in-death,' the syllabic momentum of Conrad's studied euphony smoothes and blurs one noun into its stretched sibilant antonym, the stare of life into the blank of death: 'The lustre of inquiring *glance* faded swiftly into vacant *glassiness*.'" Stewart, "Lying as Dying," 362.

36 Freud, *Totem and Taboo*, 24. Freud emphasizes the ambivalence behind this "collocation" – *heilige Scheu* in the original. Freud, *Studienausgabe*, vol. 9, 311.

37 Coleridge, *Poetical Works*, vol. 1, 295–8.

38 Rothko 59. See Schjeldahl, "Inspired Lunacy."

39 López-Remiro, "Introduction," 182.

40 Mann 85, 107, 113, 115, 118. On a serendipitous note, the late British novelist John le Carré (David Cornwell), who taught German at Eton College and professed a lifelong passion for German literature, exhibited a predilection for such images. Here are two examples from an early novel: "Smiley stood for a moment on the pavement, an odd, lonely figure peering down the empty road"; "He remained there a long time after [the car] had gone, looking towards the end of the road, so that passers-by stared oddly at him, or tried to follow his gaze. But there was nothing to see. Only the half-lit street, and the shadows moving along it." *A Murder of Quality*, 94, 158.

41 Rancière, *The Emancipated Spectator*, 120.

42 Novalis 323.

43 See Ondaatje 77–80.

44 Richter, *The Daily Practice of Painting*, 100. See Nugent, "Gerhard Richter's 'Woodlands.'" For a contrary view of things, see Jae Emerling's bitingly critical review of this exhibit. "Selective Affinities."

45 Rosenblum 213. Compare Conrad: "In the offing the sea and the sky were welded together without a joint and in the luminous space the tanned sails of the barges drifting up with the tide seemed to stand still in red clusters of canvas, sharply peaked with gleams of varnished sprits. A haze rested on the low shores that ran out to sea in vanishing flatness" (7).

46 Eisenstein, *Film Form*, 31–2.

47 Rancière 123.

48 Eisenstein 40.

49 For example: "The long shadow of the forest had slipped downhill while we talked, had gone far beyond the ruined hovel, beyond the symbolic row of stakes. All this was in the gloom while we down there were yet in the sunshine, and the stretch of the river abreast of the clearing glittered in a still and dazzling splendor, with a murky and over-shadowed bend above and below. Not a living soul was seen on the shore. The bushes did not rustle" (58).

50 Caillois, "Mimicry and Legendary Psychasthenia."

51 Caillois, *The Mask of Medusa*, 96.
52 Brooks 238–9, 256. I am grateful to Joyce Cheng for her insight into the unique significance of owls in European modernism.
53 Calasso, *Tiepolo Pink*, 104–7. See, regarding the dependence of the image upon the frame, note 51 to chapter 1 of the present study.
54 Calasso 172.
55 Horkheimer and Adorno 22.
56 Moretti, *Atlas*, 47.
57 Caillois, "Mimicry and Legendary Psychasthenia," 30–1.
58 Alewyn, *Probleme und Gestalten*, 315–19.
59 Goethe, *Gedichte 1756–1799*, 128. See Wellbery, *The Specular Moment*, 35.
60 Freud, *Totem and Taboo*, 106.
61 Freud, *Totem and Taboo*, 27.

5 Facing the Image

1 Kracauer, *From Caligari to Hitler*, 69.
2 Hoch, *Caspar David Friedrich*, 30; Amstutz, "Caspar David Friedrich and the Anatomy of Nature."
3 Kracauer 69n11. Paintings by Feininger such as *On the Bridge* (1913) and *The Avenue of Trees* (1915) could easily be taken for set designs for *Caligari*.
4 Rosenblum, *Modern Painting*, 156.
5 I have borrowed a phrase from Hugh Kenner's account of Ezra Pound's superimposition of historically disparate vocabularies: "In transparent overlay, two times have become as one, and we are meant to be equally aware of both dictions (and yet they seem of the same diction). The words lie flat like the forms on a Cubist canvas." *The Pound Era*, 29. Regarding the Cubist ramifications of the sets of *Caligari*, see Kaes, *Shell Shock Cinema*, 84–6.
6 Likewise, the sharp diagonals that in Feininger's painting suggest shafts of light recall Friedrich's *Sea of Ice* (ca 1824), in which massive fragments of ice, flattened against one another while enfolding the splintered remains of a schooner, are thrust upward to form a jagged monolith. See Rautmann, *C. D. Friedrich, Das Eismeer*, 41–3. Rautmann's comparison of *The Sea of Ice* to monumental designs realized in metal by Walter Gropius reinforces the lineage linking Friedrich to Feininger, whom Gropius inducted into the Bauhaus in 1919.
7 P. Miller, "Anxiety and Abstraction," 207.
8 Böhme, "Rückenfiguren," 85–6.
9 Rosenblum 156; Haskell, "Redeeming the Sacred," 101.
10 Keitz, "Der Blick ins Imaginäre," 88, 99; Dalle Vacche, *Cinema and Painting*, 184; Calhoon, "*Horror vacui*," 158–61; Kaes: "Friedrich's gaze

is also Murnau's: ineffable, sublime nature produces in the viewer a shuddering pleasure tinged with anticipation and fear. On the beach Ellen is surrounded by crosses; they designate graves of sailors, but in this painterly setting they also connote the presence of death. Death is not visible but it is felt. A cut to the vessel that brings the undead vampire, first seen from a distance but then filling the frame, imbues the image with her intense death wish." *Shell Shock Cinema*, 116.

11 Rosenblum 192. In a similar vein, Belting writes that "the new abstraction seemed only now [in the twentieth century] to fulfill the true sense of the Romantic landscape." *Das unsichtbare Meisterwerk*, 29.

12 Friedrich's *Landscape with Grave, Coffin and Owl* (1836–7), discussed and reproduced in the previous chapter, is a good example.

13 P. Miller 207.

14 Milner, *Mondrian*, 120.

15 Amstutz, "Caspar David Friedrich and the Anatomy of Nature."

16 Golding, *Paths to the Absolute*, 26. I am greatly indebted to Sherwin Simmons for his insights, shared with me, into Mondrian's painting.

17 Golding 26; for the complete series see Bax, *Complete Mondrian*, 482–5.

18 Worringer, *Abstraktion und Einfühlung*, 155.

19 Deleuze, *Cinema 1*, 51. See, regarding the cinematic pseudo-Gothic, Schönemann, *Paul Wegener*, 82–90.

20 Milner 8–46.

21 This is especially true of Friedrich's *Ansicht eines Hafens* (1815/16). In his *Schiffe im Hafen von Greifswald* (1818/20), an anchored ship is centred within the frame, its horizontal spars reinforcing the divisions between the stratified colour fields of the sunset.

22 Koerner, *Caspar David Friedrich*, 10. Compare Johannes Grave: "By confronting the public with landscapes that openly declare their own pictoriality and artificiality even as they draw the viewer's gaze into incommensurable depth, [Friedrich] obliges the viewer to engage with an irreconcilable conflict." *Caspar David Friedrich*, 168.

23 Rosenblum 212.

24 Rosenblum 192.

25 Horkheimer and Adorno, *Dialectic of Enlightenment*, 18.

26 See Kuzniar, "The Vanishing Canvas."

27 Horkheimer and Adorno 16.

28 Lacan, *The Four Fundamental Concepts*, 92.

29 Caillois, "Mimicry and Legendary Psychasthenia," 16–32.

30 Freud, *Studienausgabe*, vol. 8, 149–50. I am indebted to Brigid Doherty for prodding me to introduce Freud's "Wolfman" into my discussion.

31 Cited in Hullot-Kentor, "The Exact Sense," 147.

32 Freud 153.

33 Bryson 106.
34 Lacan 115.
35 Lacan 101.
36 Eisenstein 40.
37 Magritte's *Key to the Fields* (1936) is one of many examples in which the two-dimensional picture plane is handled ironically. The painting depicts a tranquil landscape framed by a window draped on either side by curtains. The window has been shattered; jagged shards of glass are scattered along the sill and the baseboard below. Clearly visible on the broken pieces of glass are elements of the landscape – trees, sky, a grassy hillside, strips of reddish earth – as if the scene beyond had imprinted itself onto the very pane, as if upon a photographic plate.
38 Goethe, *Die Leiden des jungen Werthers*, 52-4.
39 Worringer 53. August Langen's classical study of "framed viewing" (*Rahmenschau*) in relation to eighteenth-century rationalism connects the preference for a limited, contained field of vision to a primordial human need (*Urbedürfnis des Menschen*) not dissimilar from that theorized by Worringer. Langen, *Anschauungesformen*, 5–7.
40 Worringer 49.
41 Andreas-Salomé, *The Freud Journal*, 100f.
42 Meyer Shapiro has described Cézanne's *The Suicide's House* (1872–3) in terms that highlight the same structural obstacles to vision and locomotion as are found in Friedrich's *Rocky Ravine*: "The symmetry of house and rock, with similar structure, the abruptness of their confrontation, the unstable ground with steep places and contending directions, the complicated, indirect entry into the depth of the landscape, and the view of the distance and horizon through the narrow opening between house and rock – these are highly evocative and create a space with a nuance of conflict and doubt." Shapiro, *Cézanne*, 58.
43 Kracauer 69.
44 To wit, from the conclusion of his account of *Caligari*: "Human destinies brought into sharp contrast with naked annihilation." Scheffauer, *The New Vision*, 53.
45 Scheffauer 42, 47–8.
46 Burch, *Life to Those Shadows*, 162–85.
47 Burch 183. Compare Eisner: "Through a reduction of gesture [Werner Krauss and Conrad Veidt] attain movements which are almost linear and which ... never go beyond the limits of the geometrical plane. The other actors, on the other hand, remain locked in a naturalistic style, though, owing to the old-fashioned ways in which they are dressed (cloaks, top-hats, morning-coats), their outlines do achieve an element of the fantastic." *The Haunted Screen*, 25.

48 Burch 162. The disdain for photography is shared by Scheffauer. See Baudry, "Ideological Effects."
49 This "profane appetite" was "disciplined" by Giotto, in whose work "volumes were inflated at low pressure to acknowledge the flatness of the wall, and the background was pushed no deeper than the backdrop of a stage." Greenberg, *The Collected Essays and Criticism*, vol. 1, 199.
50 Greenberg 201.
51 Greenberg 199.
52 Kracauer 69 (emphasis K.C.).
53 Burch 163.
54 Scheffauer 48.
55 Crary, *Techniques of the Observer*, 124.
56 Crary 125.
57 See Koerner's discussion (142–3) of Börsch-Supan's seminal analysis of Friedrich's manner of contrasting foreground and background by eliminating a "connective midground," evoking "an infinite expanse *between* the two pictorial zones" – something he achieved "by simultaneously deploying and rupturing the diagonals of conventional linear perspective."
58 Crary 126.
59 Brusati, *Artifice and Illusion*, 169.
60 Concerning the film's "affinity for the stage," see Kracauer 76n30.
61 This pattern, which Feininger's "bird cloud" seems to re-create, serves as a leitmotif throughout *Caligari* and even figures into the design of the title-cards.
62 In a matching scene, Francis is shown reading at his desk. Though his room is more biomorphically cavernous and more extreme in its distortions than Alan's, here too a chair – a plush chaise lounge – is positioned near the camera and to the right of centre.
63 Benjamin, *Illuminations*, 226.
64 For Kracauer, "the gigantic high back of the chair in Alan's attic testifies to the invisible presence of powers that have a grip on him" (72).
65 When during the assault we suddenly see a brief close-up of Alan's hands raised in self-defence, the point of view shifts abruptly to that of the killer. Given that the story is being told from Francis's own vantage point, this hints at the possibility that he himself is the assassin, or at least that the murder is something he has helped orchestrate.
66 Worringer 56–7.
67 Rosenblum 97–100. Rosenblum points out the structural as well as motivic similarity of Van Gogh's *Crows over Wheat Fields* to Friedrich's *Hill and Ploughed Field near Dresden* (ca 1824). In both, a flock of crows surges from beyond the horizon into the "constricting space of the spectator."

68 Bryson 106.
69 Koschorke, *Die Geschichte des Horizonts*, 174.
70 Koerner 124.
71 Ramdohr 151. See Prager's thorough discussion of Ramdohr's critique and especially the "anxiety" behind it. *Aesthetic Vision and German Romanticism*, 94–111.
72 See Grave 199; also Hofmann, *Caspar David Friedrich*, 236
73 Metz, *The Imaginary Signifier*, 50.
74 Metz 48–9.
75 Koerner 213. Koerner's claim that in Friedrich's art "a world suddenly becomes only visible through a transition within our own way of seeing" (218) squares with Joachim Ritter's more general conception of landscape, which is not the aggregate of natural phenomena but rather that which arises before a subject who, not bound to those phenomena by need or purpose, enters – in free contemplation – into the natural world. "With his venturing out nature changes its countenance" (*Mit seinem Hinausgehen verändert die Natur ihr Gesicht*). Ritter 151.
76 Hinz, *Caspar David Friedrich*, 92.
77 Kant, *Kritik der reinen Vernunft*, vol. 1, 93–5.
78 Freud, *Studienausgabe*, vol. 3, 43. On Kant's "empirical realism" in the psychoanalytic context, see Ricoeur, *Freud and Philosophy*, 432–3.
79 Metz 49.
80 Metz 64.
81 Koerner 195.
82 Emphasis added.
83 Panofsky, *Perspective as Symbolic Form*, 30.
84 See Gunning, "An Aesthetics of Astonishment."
85 Merleau-Ponty, "Celan's Doubt," in *The Merleau-Ponty Aesthetics Reader*, 64.
86 Bryson 106.
87 Gowing, "Cézanne," 182.
88 Greenberg 202.
89 Gowing 203.
90 Kracauer 99.
91 Lukács, *Fortschritt und Reaktion in der deutschen Literatur*.
92 Eisner 55. This is a point at which to recall Caillois's claim that the magic and mystery of the night, indeed the fear of the dark, derive from the self's permeability to darkness. Caillois, "Mimicry and Legendary Psychasthenia," 30–1.
93 Blumenberg, *Höhlenausgänge*, 55.
94 Blumenberg 59.
95 Blumenberg 27; Bayertz, *Der aufrechte Gang*; Maskarinec, *The Forces of Form*.

96 Baudry, "The Apparatus," 178.

97 Baudry 186.

98 Baudry 171.

99 Baudry 183–4.

100 Koerner 189.

101 Heidegger, *Holzwege*, ii.

102 Frost, *Collected Poems, Prose & Plays*, 103. In another poem from the same collection (*Mountain Interval*, 1916) – a collection that showcases a native intimacy with woodlands, brooks, snow, the use of an axe, or encounters with strangers on horseback – Frost evokes the pliant humility of birch trees, "dragged," "bowed," and "subdued" by ice in winter or boys swinging in summer. It is a wistful reflection framed as the contrast between empathetic leaning and the disciplined rectilinearity that was beginning to emerge in Mondrian at the same time: "When I see birches bend to left and right / Across the lines of straighter darker trees ..." Frost 117–18.

103 Byron, *Poetry and Prose*, 298. These very lines are alluded to in *Death in Venice* in the passage describing Aschenbach's arrival in Venice by boat. Translator Michael Henry Heim makes it clear that he is aware of the source: "He stood at the foremast, gazing into the distance, watching for land. He thought of the pensive yet ardent poet for whom the cupolas and bell towers of his dreams had once risen from these waves." Mann, *Death in Venice*, 32.

104 "Airy distance" recalls the *Luftdistanz* coined by Philipp Otto Runge as a close cognate of the "aerial perspective" by means of which painters enhance the illusion of distance by making far-off objects appear less vivid and distinct than those viewed at closer range. Kuzniar, "The Temporality of Landscape," 87.

105 Hamilton, *Music, Madness*, 147–8.

106 Wackenroder and Tieck, *Herzensergiessungen*, 99; idem, *Outpourings*, 105–6.

107 Burch 235.

108 Kracauer, *Das Ornament der Masse*, 311–12.

109 Goethe, *Faust*, ed. Schöne, 140 (emphasis added).

110 I can no longer locate the source of this translation, but I can safely say that the English rendering of the emphasized line is someone else's.

111 Böhme (71) introduces the phrase "diaphonous mediality" in a discussion of Friedrich's *Woman at Window* (1822), which depicts the artist's wife, seen from behind, gazing reflectively from the window of his studio in Dresden. It is a painting that exposes the mechanisms of the aesthetic tradition that equated paintings with windows. The slender crosspieces of the window above the woman's head make explicit the geometry

that underlies a painting notable for its multiple framings. The smaller, unshuttered opening, which must otherwise have served Friedrich as a viewfinder, is carefully centred within the painting and mirrors its format exactly. The narrow aperture, the darkening of the interior chamber, and the absence of a middle ground has a telescoping effect, pushing the trees, faintly visible in the background, farther into the distance while drawing the viewer into a shallow foreground. A contrastive dynamism resolves depth of field into a pronounced vertical alignment. The figure appears to be looking down at the boat, whose mast points toward the painting's upper edge, beyond which the viewer may feel compelled to complete mentally the rectangle of the upper window. The edges and vertical centrepiece of the window coordinate with the divisions between the floorboards, whose slight angle locates the viewer just to the left of the centric ray. A flat grid, the window introduces the picture plane into the visual field, accentuating the screen that otherwise disappears behind the illusion of recessional space. *Woman at Window* not only resembles the climactic scene in *Nosferatu* where Ellen throws open her bedroom window to expose herself to the vampire, who has been pitiably pining for her from the window opposite hers. And in a manner of more general application to Murnau's *mise en scène*, the painting reinforces a sense of spatial recession by placing frames within frames. At the same time, it heightens an awareness of the painting as a flat surface by drawing attention to its material limits. See Prager 109–12; Hevers, "Die *Kunst* der Wahrnehmung," esp. 132; Grave, 211–12; Calhoon, "F.W. Murnau, C.D. Friedrich, and the Conceit of the Absent Spectator," 637–9.

112 Blumenberg 13.

113 It is an attitude proclaimed by Faust, who – in the scene "Before the City Gate" – watches as the sun, speeding toward the horizon, defuses its rays into the deepening landscape: "Vor mir den Tag, und hinter mir die Nacht." Goethe, *Faust*, ed. Schöne, 56.

114 Blumenberg 20.

115 Proust, *In Search of Lost Time: Swann's Way*, vol. 1, 3.

116 M. Shelley, *Frankenstein*, 97.

117 Shelley 57.

118 "Of what a strange nature is knowledge! It clings to the mind, when it has once seized on it, like a lichen on the rock. I wished sometimes to shake off all thought and feeling; but I learned that there was but one means to overcome the sensation of pain, and that was death – a state which I feared yet did not understand" (Shelley 116).

119 Shelley 97–8.

120 Plato, *Collected Dialogues*, 748.

121 Resnik, "The Hands of Egon Schiele."

122 Shelley 109.
123 Wölfflin, *Bamberger Apokalypse*, 14. Cited by Selz, *German Expressionist Painting*, 15. Kirchner, writing under the pseudonym L. de Marsalle, said the following regarding his own prints: "The mysterious attraction that surrounded the invention of printing in the Middle Ages is felt again today by everyone who seriously occupies himself with printing and the details of craftsmanship ... The altering of individual forms goes hand in hand with the alteration of proportions ... Thus proportions order themselves according to the feeling engendered by the work, in order to represent this in the most powerful way ... Kirchner's deformations are not disturbing because they are correct for the picture." Long, *German Expressionism*, 145–6.
124 The cover of Willett's *Expressionism* features this very detail from Grünewald's altar. The animation of Frankenstein's creature constitutes a resurrection, a reversal of the *rigor mortis* that Grünewald's painting makes palpable. In the film, it is the hand, visible below the shroud covering the creature's body, that twitches to life, the effect of electricity culled from the heavens during a thunderstorm. The creature's supine placement on the laboratory table closely resembles that of Jesus in Holbein's *The Body of the Dead Christ in the Tomb* (1521–2), a long, horizontal panel that, in mirroring the dimensions of a shallow sarcophagus, evokes the extreme claustrophobia of entombment.
125 Lacan, *Écrits*, 3.
126 Gordon, *Expressionism*, 26–68.
127 Read, *Icon and Idea*, 45.
128 Koerner 255.
129 Lacan, *Écrits*, 2.

6 Necessary Advances

1 Ondaatje, *The Conversations*, 89–91.
2 Rancière, *Film Fables*, 6, 8.
3 Auerbach, *Mimesis*, 484. Subsequent page references appear parenthetcially.
4 Adorno, *Musikalische Schriften*, vol. 4, 17.
5 This may recall Rohmer's claim, mentioned in the introduction to this study, that the exaggeration of gesture and demeanour in Expressionism served to sever exterior from interior. Of Murnau's *Tartuffe*, to be discussed shortly, he writes: "What better homage to Molière than the hideous face of Jannings, sweating falsity from every pore ... But, one could argue, why refuse to penetrate man's heart? Doesn't a troubled face betray some interior emotion? Yes, it is a sign, but an arbitrary sign, as it denies the

powers of falsity and greatly shrinks the limits of the invisible world to which it proudly refers. To go from each of our gestures to its implied intention is the equivalent of reducing all of thought to a few always-identical operations. The novelist will rightfully smile when presented with the neophyte's ambition to give this elementary algebra the name *language*. To go from the exterior to interior, from behavior to the soul, such is the condition of our art. But how wonderful that, far from tarnishing what it shows us, this necessary detour enhances it, and thus liberated, appearance itself is our guide." *The Taste for Beauty*, 50–1.

6 Marquard, "Zur Bedeutung der Theorie," 388.

7 Rancière 9. Compare Chatman, who observes how the cinematic montage-sequence has been incorporated into verbal fiction, specifically in Vladimir Nabokov's *Lolita*. Chatman, *Story and Discourse*, 69–70. Chatman argues that the cinema has difficulty summarizing events, for which reason "directors often resort to gadgetry" (69). Somewhat to the contrary, Auerbach believes that "the concentration of space and time, such as can be achieved by film (for example the representation, within a few seconds and by means of a few pictures, of the situation of a widely dispersed group of people, of a great city, an army, a war, an entire country) can never be within the reach of the spoken or written word." Auerbach, *Mimesis*, 546.

8 Hegel, *Vorlesungen über die Ästhetik*, 62; idem, *Hegel's Aesthetics*, 833. See note 51 to chapter 2 of the present study.

9 Hegel, *Vorlesungen*, 60; idem, *Aesthetics*, 832.

10 Concerning Hegel's figurative usage of the terms "prose" and "prosaic," see Rokem, *Prosaic Conditions*, 3–19.

11 Rilke, *Werke*, 513.

12 Rilke, *Selected Poetry*, 61.

13 Hegel, *Vorlesungen*, 17; idem, *Aesthetics*, 797. See Belting 63–82.

14 Tobias, "Rilke, Phenomenology."

15 See Lysaker, *You Must Change Your Life*.

16 See Asendorf, *Ströme und Strahlen*.

17 Rancière 1.

18 Kenner, *The Pound Era*, 16.

19 Kenner 67–8.

20 Stimilli, *The Face of Immortality*, 19.

21 Freud, *The Interpretation of Dreams*, 328.

22 "The incapacity of dreams to express [logical relations] must lie in the nature of the psychical material out of which dreams are made. The plastic arts of painting and sculpture labour, indeed, under a similar limitation as compared with poetry, which can make use of speech; and here once again the reason for their incapacity lies in the nature of the material which these

two forms of art manipulate in their effort to express something. Before painting became acquainted with the laws of expression by which it is governed, it made attempts to get over this handicap. In ancient paintings small labels were hung from the mouths of the persons represented, containing in written characters the speeches which the artists despaired of representing pictorially." Freud, *The Interpretation of Dreams*, 328. I have pointed out elsewhere that Auerbach describes a scene from Genesis as if it were a Baroque painting. Calhoon, *Affecting Grace*, 14.

23 Rancière 36.

24 Rancière 42.

25 Murnau's Tartuffe is played by the famed German actor Emil Jannings, who frequently portayed figures who were arguably Falstaffian or Rabellaisian. See Calhoon, "Emil Jannings." Rancière cites Eisner on Karl Freund's camera work in *Tartuffe*: "He [Murnau] gets Karl Freund's camera to explore all the crevices, every wrinkle, every twitch, every blink, in order to reveal, along with the freckles and bad teeth, the dissimluated vices." Rancière, *Film Fables*, 36.

26 Nagel, *Autonomy and Mercy*, 105.

27 Moretti, "Serious Century," 380.

28 Moretti 381.

29 Bryson, *Vision and Painting*, 106.

30 Auerbach's account could well be applied to *Caligari*, in which the "gruesome distortion" of the sets reflects the skewed vision of Francis, the presumably insane source of the main narrative.

31 Kafka, *Drucke zu Lebzeiten* 17–18; idem, *The Penal Colony*, 27–8. Emphasis added.

32 I am grateful to Helmut Schneider for his suggestion here.

33 Miller, "Balzac's Illusions," 75.

34 Balzac, *Old Goriot*, 303.

35 Nick Carraway's empathic attunement (under a star-filled sky) to Gatsby's longing allies him with the grieving youth of Brentano's "Auf dem Rhein," who perceives in the ghostly vision of his bride a shivering, which in truth seems merely to project the bobbing of his tiny boat upon the waves. Fitzgerald's nocturnal scene is one of anticipatory mourning, as Nick will soon find himself "alone in the unquiet darkness."

36 Miller 76.

37 Eisner, *The Haunted Screen*, 252–4.

38 Kaes, "Urban Vision and Surveillance"; Dimendberg, "Down These Seen Streets," 128–32.

39 Kracauer, *From Caligari to Hitler*, 120–1.

40 The husband in *The Street* is seized by an excitement similar to what Alan of *Caligari* exhibits when, upon hearing the sounds from the nearby fair, he

rushes to the window, then grabs his coat and hat and hurriedly quits his attic apartment.

41 Stimilli 4.

42 Stimilli 1.

43 Lacan, *Écrits*, 2.

44 Spitzer, "Milieu and Ambience," 175.

45 Caillois, *The Edge of Surrealism*, 93–6.

46 Goethe, *Faust*, ed. Schöne, 34.

47 Hullot-Kentor, *Things beyond Resemblance*, 228. In this context, I cannot resist quoting these lines from Richard Wilbur's translation of a poem by Francis Jammes ("A Prayer to Go to Paradise with the Donkeys"): "Let me come with these donkeys, Lord, into your land, / These beasts who bow their heads so gently, and stand / With their small feet joined together in a fashion / Utterly gentle, asking your compassion." Wilbur, *New and Collected Poems*, 257.

48 Pinotti, "Body Building," 18.

49 Predictably, criticism has frequently dismissed Spitzweg for his escapism and idyllic harmlessness. See Hüppauf, "Spaces of the Vernacular," 222n31; and Schiff, "An Epoch of Longing," 20. By contrast, see the following two exhibition catalogues: Wichmann, *Carl Spitzweg*; Wipplinger, ed., *Carl Spitzweg, Erwin Wurm*.

7 Music of the Third Kind: *Fantasia* and *Faustus*

1 Here are Taylor's introductory remarks in their entirety: "How do you do? My name is Deems Taylor, and it's my very pleasant duty to welcome you here on behalf of Walt Disney, Leopold Stokowski, and all the other artists and musicians whose combined talents went into the creation of this new form of entertainment, "Fantasia." What you're going to see are the designs and pictures and stories that music inspired in the minds and imaginations of a group of artists. In other words, these are not going to be the interpretations of trained musicians, which I think is all to the good. Now there are three kinds of music on this "Fantasia" program. First, there's the kind that tells a definite story. Then there's the kind that while it has no specific plot, it does paint a series of more or less definite pictures. And then there's a third kind, music that exists simply for its own sake. Now, the number that opens our "Fantasia" program, the "Toccata and Fugue," is music of this third kind, what we call "absolute music." Even the title has no meaning beyond a description of the form of the music. What you will see on the screen is a picture of the various abstract images that might pass through your mind if you sat in a concert hall listening to this music. At first, you're more or less conscious of the orchestra.

So our picture opens with a series of impressions of the conductor and the players. Then the music begins to suggest other things to your imagination. They might be, oh, just masses of color, or they may be cloud forms or great landscapes or vague shadows or geometrical objects floating in space. So now we present the "Toccata and Fugue In D Minor" by Johann Sebastian Bach, interpreted in pictures by Walt Disney and his associates, and in music by the Philadelphia Orchestra and its conductor, Leopold Stokowski." *Fantasia*, dir. Joe Grant. Burbank, California: Walt Disney Entertainment, 1999, c. 1940. DVD.

2 Dahlhaus, *The Idea of Absolute Music*, 18.

3 Schopenhauer, *Die Welt als Wille und Vorstellung*, 357–61.

4 Schopenhauer 365.

5 Schopenhauer, *The World as Will and Representation*, 256. Translation altered; Schopenhauer, *Die Welt als Wille*, 366.

6 See Moritz, "Fischinger at Disney."

7 Webern, *The Path to the New Music*, 14.

8 Webern 34.

9 Ricoeur, *Freud and Philosophy*, 94–5. Freud, *The Interpretation of Dreams*, 587.

10 "Der Dichter und das Phantasieren," in Freud, *Studienausgabe*, vol. 10, 176.

11 However, Stokowski appears for the last time before *Night on Bald Mountain*, which transitions fluidly into the serenity of "Ave Maria."

12 Byron, *Poetry and Prose*, 298.

13 Kant, *Kritik der reinen Vernunft*, 93–5.

14 Freud, *Totem and Taboo*, 96–7.

15 Horkheimer and Adorno, *Dialektik der Aufklärung*, 19.

16 "The Sorcerer's Apprentice" not only figures upheaval as flood in a manner reminiscent of *Metropolis* but also cites the iconic scene from *Caligari* in which Alain's knife-wielding murderer appears only as an enlarged shadow on the wall above the victim's bed. When the apprentice (Mickey Mouse) uses an axe to destroy the broom that is causing the flood, he too appears only as a silhouette, while the flying splinters of wood re-create patterns that resemble the broken and jagged shapes that appear throughout Wiene's film. See Allan, "Les sources européenes de Disney," 126–9.

17 Concerning the Messianic self-conception that Stokowski and Disney apparently shared (as it pertains to the "connection between podiums and mountaintops that runs as a motif through the picture"), see Culhane, *Walt Disney's Fantasia*, 42.

18 Girveau, "Au-delá du mirior," 172–206. Also by Girveau, in the same richly illustrated volume "La nostalgie bâtisseuse" (208–36).

19 Ursula von Keitz, "Der Blick ins Imaginäre."

20 Allan, *Walt Disney and Europe*, 166–7.

21 Stokowski's positioning in *Fantasia* has a precursor in the priest-like figure credited in *Metropolis* with the conception of the Tower of Babel. Shown squarely from behind, arms spread and held aloft before his own shimmering vision of the tower, he is symmetrical with Maria, similarly positioned (though seen from the front) as she relates the legend of Babel to the rapt assembly of workers below ground.
22 Koerner, *Caspar David Friedrich*, 219.
23 Belting, *Das unsichtbare Meisterwerk*, 29, 91–2.
24 Hoffmann, *Werke*, 54.
25 See Keefer and Guldemond, eds., *Oskar Fischinger 1900–1967*.
26 "For the vortex is not the water but a patterned energy made visible by the water." Kenner, *The Pound Era*, 149. See William Moritz: "While the wave sequence is one of the more exciting, impressive moments in the Disney version, a comparison with Oskar's original sketches shows how much more powerful, subtle and imaginative the sequence might have been if Fischinger's intentions had been honoured. Oskar's original celadon 'waves' are part of a complex composition that includes concentric rhomboids in browns, Chinese reds, and graduated yellow-oranges, rising columns of circles, diagonal crescents, a graduated-shade oval, etc. The right/left waves are only a momentary manifestation of a radiating rounded triangle which fans through the frame." *Optical Poetry*, 87. I am greatful to Angelica Fischinger, of the Elfriede Fischinger Trust, for providing me with this drawing. A more finished version of the same design, of which I was unable to secure a usable image, is reproduced in Moritz, "Fischinger at Disney."
27 Daniels, "Absolute Sounding Images."
28 Schivelbusch, *Geschichte der Eisenbahnreise*, 61.
29 Eichendorff, *Werke*, 271.
30 Marx, *Schriften*, vol. 2, 821–4; Marx and Engels, *The Communist Manifesto*, 54, 57–8; Asendorf, *Ströme und Strahlen*, 63–4.
31 Mann, *Doctor Faustus*, 67. All subsequent citations in parentheses.
32 Kant, *Kritik der Urteilskraft*, 188–9.
33 Included in Zeitblom's reproach is Adrian's father, the object of whose curiosity, indeed empathy, is the rough natural-scientific equivalent of Adrian's own "inorganic sound." Jonathan is indeed like the God of Creation, his eyes tearing up at the sad sight of those chemical blooms – those images of organic life before the fact. In reaching for the light, the sprouting crystals seemed to attest to a yearning on the part of matter *to live*. In his summary of Jonathan's amateur endeavours, Zeitblom identifies a monism altogether at odds with the belief, espoused by Zeitblom himself, in the dual nature of man: "What concerned him was the unity of animate and so-called inanimate nature, the idea that we sin

against the latter if the boundary we draw between the two spheres is too rigid, when in reality it is porous, since there is no elementary capability that is reserved exclusively for living creatures or that the biologist could not likewise study on inanimate models" (Mann 21). Zeitblom here isolates a kernel of the critique that Jonas – advocate for an "empathic study of the many forms of life" – was to mount against the dualism of body and mind that would construe Jonathan's empathy as anthropomorphic. At the heart of this "existential interpretation of biological facts," as Jonas calls it, is the contention that mind is prefigured even in the lowest forms of organic life (xxiii). Contesting the view that "subjective phenomena" are but the chance products of a "mechanical permutation of indifferent elements," he asserts that the mere possibility of matter organizing itself for life must be seen as a "genuine potency" inherent in the very idea of physical substance. "[Even] the transition from inanimate to animate substance," Jonas ventures, "was actuated by a tendency in the depth of being toward the very modes of freedom to which this transition opened the gate." Jonas 1–2, 4.

34 Wackenroder and Tieck, *Herzensergiessungen*, 74.

35 Wackenroder and Tieck 114.

36 Käthe Kollwitz's bronze relief *Die Klage* (1938–41) consists of a face, with an expression of mourning or despair, a hand covering one eye.

37 Worringer, *Abstraktion und Einfühlung*, 156.

38 Lacan, *Écrits*, 4–5.

39 Wackenroder and Tieck 71, 107. It may not be an exaggeration to suggest that Van Gogh's attraction to sunflowers, and more generally the craving for warmth apparent in his many depictions of sun-drenched wheatfields, indicate a comparable heliotropism on the artist's part.

40 In an article on Kollwitz's use of the *pietà* to absorb and convey the visceral intensity of bereavement, Martina Kolb describes the artist's process in terms of "an ethically inclined empathic imagination." Kollwitz's *Woman with Dead Child* (1903) "communicates a strong sense of the haptic, as if an emaciated mourning woman's hand sought to touch one last time her dead boy's face." "Intimations of Mortality," 305, 309–10.

41 Roland Barthes addresses the "theatricality" of the *mater dolorosa* in his "Seven Photo Models of Mother Courage," 52. Kolb's probing account of the "mute scream," a gesture that Helene Weigel introduced to represent Mother Courage's shock at her son's death, along with her "refusal to affectively acknowledge or verbally express the violence of a war that is at the same time her livelihood," is of special relevance for a discussion of Expressionist performance. "Rather than provoking proximity or empathy," Kolb writes, "the image of the mute scream concentrates its

energies on distance and mimicry: it resembles a skull and imitates, remembers, and probably even mocks death." "Grave Action," 82.

42 Calhoon, *Affecting Grace*, 12.
43 Steiner, *In Bluebeard's Castle*, 3.
44 Steiner, 54–5.
45 Auerbach, *Dante*, 110–11.
46 Auerbach, *Mimesis*, 191.
47 Resnik, "The Hands of Egon Schiele."
48 Auerbach, *Mimesis*, 21.
49 Belting 92.

Works Cited

Adorno, Theodor W. *Noten zur Literatur*, vol. 1. Frankfurt am Main: Suhrkamp, 1958.

– *Musikalische Schriften*, vol. 4. Ed. Rolf Tiedemann. Frankfurt am Main: Suhrkamp, 1982.

– *Notes to Literature*, vol. 1. Trans. Shierry Weber Nicholsen. New York: Columbia UP, 1991.

– *Philosophy of New Music*. Ed. and trans. Robert Hullot-Kentor. Minneapolis: U of Minnesota P, 2006.

Alewyn, Richard. *Probleme und Gestalten: Essays*. Frankfurt am Main: Insel, 1974.

Alighieri, Dante. *The Inferno: Text and Commentary*. Trans. Charles Singleton. Princeton: Princeton UP, 1970.

Allan, Robin. *Walt Disney and Europe*. Bloomington: Indiana UP, 1999.

– *Les sources européenes de Disney*. In *Il Était une fois Walt Disney: Aux sources de l'art des Studios Disney*. Paris: Éditions de la Réunion des musées nationaux. 2006. 100–70.

Amstutz, Nina. "Caspar David Friedrich and the Anatomy of Nature." *Art History* 37 (2014): 454–81.

– *Caspar David Friedrich: Nature and the Self*. New Haven: Yale UP, 2019.

Andreas-Salomé, Lou. *The Freud Journal of Lou Andreas-Salomé*. Trans. Stanley Leavy. New York: Basic Books, 1964.

Arendt, Dieter. *Der "poetische Nihilismus" in der Romantik*. Tübingen: Niemeyer, 1972.

Arnheim, Rudolf. *Film als Kunst*. Berlin: Rowohlt, 1932.

– *Art and Visual Perception: A Psychology of the Creative Eye*. Berkeley: U of California P, 1974.

Asendorf, Christoph. *Ströme und Strahlen: Das langsame Verschwinden der Materie um 1900*. Giessen: Anabas, 1989.

Auerbach, Erich. *Mimesis: The Representation of Reality in Western Literature*. Trans. Willard Trask. Princeton: Princeton UP, 2003.

– *Dante: Poet of the Secular World*. Trans. Ralph Manheim. New York: NYRB, 2007.

Auerbach, Jonathan. "Chasing Film Narrative: Repetition, Recursion, and the Body in Early Cinema." *Critical Inquiry* 26 (2000): 798–820.

Balázs, Bela. *Der sichtbare Mensch*. Frankfurt am Main: Suhrkamp, 2001.

Baldwin, James. *The Devil Finds Work*. New York: Vintage, 2011.

Balzac, Honoré de. *Old Goriot*. Trans. Marion Ayton Crawford. New York: Penguin, 1951.

Barnouw, Eric. *The Magician and the Cinema*. Oxford: Oxford UP, 1981.

Barthes, Roland. "Seven Photo Models of Mother Courage." *Drama Review* 12 (1967): 44–55.

– *Camera Lucida: Reflections on Photography*. Trans. Richard Howard. New York: Hill and Wang, 1981.

– *The Rustle of Language*. Trans. Richard Howard. New York: Hill and Wang, 1986.

Baudry, Jean-Louis. "Ideological Effects of the Basic Cinematographic Apparatus." Trans. Alan Williams. *Film Quarterly* 28 (1974–75): 39–47.

– "The Apparatus: Metapsychological Approaches to the Impression of Reality in Cinema." In *Film Theory and Criticism*. Ed. Leo Braudy and Marshall Cohen. Oxford: Oxford UP, 2009.

Bax, Marty. *Complete Mondrian*. Burlington: Lund Humphries, 2001.

Bayertz, Kurt. *Der aufrechte Gang: Eine Geschichte des anthropologischen Denkens*. Munich: Beck, 2012.

Beil, Ralf, und Claudia Dillmann. *Gesamtkunstwerk Expressionismus: Kunst, Film, Literatur, Theater, Tanz und Architektur 1905–1925*. Berlin: Hatje Cantz, 2010.

Belting, Hans. *Das unsichtbare Meisterwerk: Die modernen Mythen der Kunst*. Munich: Beck, 1998.

Benjamin, Walter. *Illuminations*. Trans. Harry Zohn. New York: Schocken, 1969.

– *Gesammelte Schriften*. Ed. Rolf Tiedemann and Hermann Schweppenhäuser. Frankfurt am Main: Suhrkamp, 1991. 14 vols.

Bergstrom, Janet. "Sexuality at a Loss: The Films of F.W. Murnau." *Poetics Today* 6 (1985): 185–203.

Bloch, Ernst. *Das Prinzip Hoffnung*. Frankfurt am Main: Suhrkamp, 1959.

Blumenberg, Hans. *Höhlenausgänge*. Frankfurt am Main: Suhrkamp, 1999.

Böhme, Hartmut. "Rückenfiguren bei Caspar David Friedrich." In *Caspar David Friedrich: Deutungen im Dialog*. Ed. Gisela Greve. Tübingen: edition diskord, 2006.

Bollacher, Martin. "Nachwort." Wilhelm Heinrich Wackenroder and Ludwig Tieck. *Herzensergiessungen eines kunstliebenden Klosterbruders*. Stuttgart: Reclam, 2005. 179–204.

Bonaventura. *Nachtwachen*. Ed. Wolfgang Paulsen. Stuttgart: Reclam, 2014.
– *The Nightwatches of Bonaventura*. Ed. and trans. Gerald Gillespie. Chicago: U of Chicago P, 2014.
Bouleau, Charles. *The Painter's Secret Geometry: A Study of Composition in Art*. Mineola: Dover, 2014.
Bouvier, M., and J.- L. Leutrat. *Nosferatu*. Paris: Gallimard, 1981.
Brentano, Clemens. *Werke*. Ed. Wolfgang Frühwald, Bernhard Gajek, and Friedhelm Kemp. Munich: Hanser, 1968. 2 vols.
Brodnax, Mary. "Man a Machine: The Shift from Soul to Identity in Lang's *Metropolis* and Ruttmann's *Berlin*." In *Peripheral Visions: The Hidden Stages of Weimar Cinema*. Ed. Kenneth S. Calhoon. Detroit: Wayne State UP, 2001. 73–93.
Brooks, Peter. *Reading for the Plot: Design and Intention in Narrative*. New York: Vintage, 1985.
Brown, Marshall. *The Tooth That Nibbles at the Soul: Essays on Music and Poetry*. Seattle: U of Washington P, 2010.
Brusati, Celeste. *Artifice and Illusion: The Art and Writing of Samuel Van Hoogstraten*. Chicago: U of Chicago P, 1995.
Bryson, Norman. *Vision and Painting: The Logic of the Gaze*. New Haven: Yale UP, 1983.
Burch, Noël. *Life to Those Shadows*. Trans. Ben Brewster. Berkeley: U of California P, 1990.
Burwick, Frederick. *The Damnation of Newton: Goethe's Color Theory and Romantic Perception*. Berlin: De Gruyter, 1986.
Busch, Werner. *Caspar David Friedrich: Ästhetik und Religion*. Munich: Beck, 2008.
Byron, George Gordon Lord. *Poetry and Prose*. Ed. Alice Levine. New York: W.W. Norton, 2010.
Cahn, Michael. "Subversive Mimesis: Theodor W. Adorno and the Modern Impasse of Critique." In *Mimesis in Contemporary Theory*. Ed. Mihai Spiriosu. Philadelphia: John Benjamins, 1984. 27–64.
Caillois, Roger. *The Mask of Medusa*. Trans. George Ordish. New York: Potter, 1964.
– "Mimicry and Legendary Psychasthenia." Trans. John Shepley. *October* 31 (1984): 16–32.
– *The Edge of Surrealism: A Roger Caillois Reader*. Ed. Claudine Frank. Trans. Claudine Frank and Camille Nash. Durham: Duke UP, 2003.
Calasso, Roberto. *Tiepolo Pink*. Trans. Alistair McEwen. New York: A.A. Knopf, 2009.
Calhoon, Kenneth S. *Fatherland: Novalis, Freud, and the Discipline of Romance*. Detroit: Wayne State UP, 1992.
– "Emil Jannings, Falstaff, and the Spectacle of the Body Natural." *Modern Language Quarterly* 58 (1997): 83–109.

– *"Horror vacui."* In *Peripheral Visions: The Hidden Stages of Weimar Cinema*. Ed. Calhoon. Detroit: Wayne State UP, 2001.

–, ed. *Peripheral Visions: The Hidden Stages of Weimar Cinema*. Detroit: Wayne State UP, 2001.

– "The Moon, the Mail, and the Province of German Literature." In *1848 und das Versprechen der Moderne*. Ed. Jürgen Fohrmann and Helmut J. Schneider. Würzburg: Königshausen & Neumann, 2003.

– "F.W. Murnau, C.D. Friedrich, and the Conceit of the Absent Spectator." *Modern Language Notes* 120 (2005): 633–53.

– "Silence Restored: Three Re-Released Films by F.W. Murnau." *Modernism/modernity* 19 (2012): 373–81.

– "Werner Herzog's View of Delft; or, *Nosferatu* and the Still Life." In *A Companion to Werner Herzog*. Ed. Brad Prager. Malden: Blackwell, 2012. 101–26.

– *Affecting Grace: Theatre, Subject, and the Shakespearean Paradox in German Literature from Lessing to Kleist*. Toronto: U of Toronto P, 2013.

– "*Sturmbild*: Antinomies of Sound in Kleist's 'Die heilige Cäcilia oder die Gewalt der Musik.'" *Deutsche Vierteljahrsschrift für deutsche Literaturgeschichte und Geisteswissenschaft* 87 (2013): 549–65.

Calvino, Italo, ed. *Fiabe italiane*. Milan: Mondadori, 2002.

Chaouli, Michael. "Irony." In *German Aesthetics: Fundamental Concepts from Baumgarten to Adorno*. Ed. J.D. Mininger and Jason Michael Peck. New York: Bloomsbury, 2016. 60–7.

Chatman, Seymour. *Story and Discourse: Narrative Structure in Fiction and Film*. Ithaca: Cornell UP, 1978.

– *Antonioni or, The Surface of the World*. Berkeley: U of California P, 1985.

Cinematéque Française. *Le cinéma expressionniste allemand: Splendeurs d'une collection*. Paris: Éditions de La Martinière, 2006.

Clark, Kenneth. *Landscape into Art*. New York: Harper and Row, 1979.

Claudius, Matthias. Ed. Jost Perfahl. *Sämtliche Werke*. Munich: Winkler, 1984.

Cochran, Peter. *"Romanticism" – and Byron*. Cambridge: Cambridge Scholars, 2009.

Coleridge, Samuel Taylor. *Poetical Works*. Ed. E.H. Coleridge. London: Oxford UP, 1967. 2 vols.

Conley, Tom. "Landscape and Perception: On Anthony Mann." In *Landscape and Film*. Ed. Martin Lefebvre. New York: Routledge, 2006. 291–313.

Conrad, Joseph. *Heart of Darkness*. Ed. Robert Kimbrough, 3rd ed. New York: W.W. Norton, 1988.

Crary, Jonathan. *Techniques of the Observer: On Vision and Modernity in the Nineteenth Century*. Cambridge, MA: MIT Press, 1999.

Culhane, John. *Walt Disney's Fantasia*. New York: Abrams, 1983.

Dahlhaus, Carl. *The Idea of Absolute Music*. Trans. Roger Lustig. Chicago: U of Chicago P, 1989.
Dalle Vacche, Angela. "Painting Thoughts, Listening to Images: Eric Rohmer's *Die Marquise von O*." *Film Quarterly* 46 (1993): 2–15.
– *Cinema and Painting: How Art Is Used in Film*. Austin: U of Texas P, 1996.
Daniels, Dieter. "Absolute Sounding Images: Abstract Film and Radio Drama of the 1920s as Complementary Forms of a Media-Specific Art." In *The Music and Sound of Experimental Film*. Ed. Holly Rogers and Jeremy Barham. Oxford: Oxford UP, 2017. 30–2.
Deleuze, Gilles. *Cinema 1: The Movement Image*. Trans. Hugh Tomlinson and Barbara Habberjam. Minneapolis: U of Minnesota P, 1986.
de Man, Paul. *The Rhetoric of Romanticism*. New York: Columbia UP, 1984.
– *Aesthetic Ideology*. Minneapolis: U of Minnesota Press, 1996.
Dimendberg, Edward. "Down These Seen Streets a Man Must Go: Siegfried Kracauer, 'Hollywood's Terror Films,' and the Spatiality of Film Noir." *New German Critique* 89 (2003): 113–43.
Doane, Mary Ann. "The Indexical and the Concept of Medium Specificity." *differences: A Journal of Feminist Cultural Studies* 18 (2007): 128–52.
Dobryden, Paul. "23 May 1920. *Das Cabinet des Dr. Caligari* Brings Aesthetic Modernism to the Fairground." In *A New History of German Cinema*. Ed. Jennifer Kapczynski and Michael Richardson. Rochester: Camden House, 2012. 80–5.
Donahue, Neil H., ed. *Invisible Cathedrals: The Expressionist Art History of Wilhelm Worringer*. University Park: Pennsylvania State UP, 1995.
Éditions de la Réunion des musées nationaux. *Il Était une fois Walt Disney: Aux sources de l'art des Studios Disney*. Paris, 2006.
Eichendorff, Joseph von. *Werke*. Ed. Wolfdietrich Rasch. Munich: Hanser, 1971.
Einstein, Albert. *The Collected Papers*, vol. 7: *The Berlin Years 1918–1921*. Trans. Alfred Engel. Princeton: Princeton UP, 2002.
Eisenstein, Sergei. *Film Form*. Trans. Jay Leyda. New York: Harcourt Brace Jovanovich, 1969.
Eisner, Lotte. *The Haunted Screen: Expressionism in the German Cinema and the Influence of Max Reinhardt*. Trans. Roger Greaves. Berkeley: U of California P, 1969.
Elsaesser, Thomas. *Weimar Cinema and After: Germany's Historical Imaginary*. New York: Routledge, 2000.
– "Weimar Cinema, Mobile Selves, and Anxious Males: Kracauer and Eisner Revisited." In *Expressionist Film: New Perspectives*. Ed. Dietrich Scheunemann. Rochester: Camden House, 2003. 33–71.
Emerling, Jae. "Selective Affinities: On Friedrich – Richter." *Extra: Contemporary Art Quarterly* 9.3 (2007): 18–22.

Engels, Frederick. *The Dialectics of Nature*. Trans. Clemens Dutt. Moscow: Progress, 1954.

Erlin, Matt. "Tradition as Intellectual Montage: F.W. Murnau's *Faust*." In *Weimar Cinema: An Essential Guide to Classic Films of the Era*. Ed. Noah Isenberg. New York: Columbia UP, 2008. 155–72.

Fabe, Marilyn. *Closely Watched Films: An Introduction to the Art of Narrative Film Technique*. Berkeley: U of California P, 2014.

Faflak, Joel. "Dancing in the Dark with Shelley." In *Constellations of Contemporary Romanticism*. Ed. Jacques Khalip and Forest Pyle. New York: Fordham, 2016. 167–85.

Fenichel, Teresa. *Uncanny Belonging: Schelling, Freud, and the Vertigo of Freedom*. 2016. PhD diss., Boston College.

Fitzgerald, F. Scott. *The Great Gatsby*. New York: Scribner, 2004.

Frayling, Christopher. *Nightmare: The Birth of Horror*. London: BBC Books, 1996.

Freud, Sigmund. *Civilization and Its Discontents*. Trans. James Strachey. New York: W.W. Norton, 1962.

– *The Standard Edition of the Complete Psychological Works of Sigmund Freud*. London: Hogarth, 1966–74. 24 vols.

– *Studienausgabe*. Ed. Alexander Mitscherlich, Angela Richards, and James Strachey. Frankfurt am Main: Fischer, 1982. 13 vols.

– *Beyond the Pleasure Principle*. Trans. James Strachey. New York: W.W. Norton, 1989.

– *Totem and Taboo*. Trans. James Strachey. New York: W.W. Norton, 1989.

– *The Uncanny*. Trans. David McLintock. New York: Penguin, 2003.

– *The Interpretation of Dreams*. Trans. James Strachey. New York: Basic, 2010.

Fried, Michael. *Absorption and Theatricality: Painting and Beholder in the Age of Diderot*. Berkeley: U of California P, 1980.

Frost, Robert. *Collected Poems, Prose, and Plays*. Ed. Richard Poirier and Mark Richardson. New York: Library of America, 1995.

Gaier, Ulrich. "'Schwankende Gestalten': Virtuality in Goethe's *Faust*." In *Goethe's Faust: Theatre of Modernity*. Ed. Hans Schulte, John Noyes, and Pia Kleber. Cambridge: Cambridge UP, 2011. 54–68.

Gaudreault, André. "Theatralität, Narrativität, Trickästhetik: Neubewertung der Filme von Méliès." *Kintop: Jahrbuch zur Erforschung des frühen Films* 2 (1993): 31–44.

Gillespie, Gerald, ed. and trans. *The Nightwatches of Bonaventura*. Chicago: U of Chicago P, 2014.

Girveau, Bruno. "Au-delá du miroir: littérature et cinéma chez Walt Disney." In *Il Était une fois Walt Disney: Aux sources de l'art des Studios Disney*. Paris: Éditions de la Réunion des musées nationaux, 2006. 172–206.

– "La nostalgie bâtisseuse: Architecture et décor chez Disney." In *Il Était une fois Walt Disney: Aux sources de l'art des Studios Disney*. Paris: Éditions de la Réunion des musées nationaux, 2006. 208–36.

Goethe, Johann Wolfgang. *Aus meinem Leben: Dichtung und Wahrheit*. Ed. Klaus-Detlef Müller. Frankfurt am Main: Deutscher Klassiker Verlag, 1986.

– *Die Leiden des jungen Werthers*. Ed. Waltraud Wiethölter. Frankfurt am Main: Deutscher Klassiker Verlag, 1994.

– *Faust*. Ed. Albrecht Schöne. Frankfurt am Main: Deutscher Klassiker Verlag, 1994. 2 vols.

– *Ästhetische Schriften 1771–1804*. Ed. Friedmar Apel. Frankfurt am Main: Deutscher Klassiker Verlag, 1998.

– *Gedichte 1756–1799*. Ed. Karl Eibl. Frankfurt am Main: Deutscher Klassiker Verlag, 1998.

– *Gedichte 1800–1832*. Ed. Karl Eibl. Frankfurt am Main: Deutscher Klassiker Verlag, 1998.

– *Faust*. Trans. Walter Arndt, 2nd ed. New York: W.W. Norton, 2001.

– *Faust*. Trans. David Constantine. New York: Penguin, 2005.

Goetzmann, Sophie. "Ludwig Meidner's Urban Iconography: Optical Destruction and Visual Apocalypse." In *Wounded Cities: The Representation of Urban Disasters in European Art*. Ed. Marco Folin and Monica Preti. Leiden: Brill, 2015. 164–80.

Golding, John. *Paths to the Absolute*. Princeton: Princeton UP, 2000.

Gombrich, E.H. *Shadows: The Depiction of Cast Shadows in Western Art*. London: National Gallery, 1995.

Gordon, Donald E. "Marc and Friedrich Again: Expressionism as Departure from Romanticism." *Notes in the History of Art* 1 (1981): 29–32.

– *Expressionism: Art and Idea*. New Haven: Yale UP, 1987.

– "Content by Contradiction." *Art in America*, December 1992: 76–89.

Gowing, Lawrence. "Cézanne: The Logic of Organized Sensations." In *Conversations with Cézanne*. Ed. Michael Doran. Berkeley: U of California P, 2001. 180–212.

Grave, Johannes. *Caspar David Friedrich*. Trans. Fiona Elliot. Munich: Prestel, 2012.

Greenberg, Clement. *The Collected Essays and Criticism*, vol. 1: *Perceptions and Judgments, 1939–1944*. Ed. John O'Brian. Chicago: U of Chicago P, 1986.

Grimm, Jakob and Wilhelm. *Brüder Grimm: Kinder- und Hausmärchen*. Ed. Heinz Rölleke. Stuttgart: Reclam, 2001. 3 vols.

Guerin, Frances. *A Culture of Light: Cinema and Technology in 1920s Germany*. Minneapolis: U of Minnesota P, 2005.

Gunning, Tom. "The Cinema of Attraction[s]: Early Film, Its Spectator, and the Avant-Garde." *Wide Angle: A Film Quarterly of Theory, Criticism, and Practice* 8 (1986): 63–70.

– "'Now You See It, Now You Don't': The Temporality of the Cinema of Attractions." In *Silent Film*. Ed. Richard Abel. New Brunswick: Rutgers UP, 1996. 71–84.

– "An Aesthetics of Astonishment: Early Film and the (In)Credulous Spectator." In *Film Theory and Criticism*. Ed. Leo Braudy and Marshall Cohen. Oxford: Oxford UP, 2009. 736–50.

Hamburger, Käte. *The Logic of Literature*. Trans. Marilynn J. Rose, 2nd ed. Bloomington: Indiana UP, 1973.

Hamilton, John T. *Music, Madness, and the Unworking of Language*. New York: Columbia UP, 2008.

Haskell, Barbara. "Redeeming the Sacred: The Romantic Modernism of Lyonel Feininger." In *Lyonel Feininger: At the Edge of the World*. Ed. Haskell. New Haven: Yale UP, 2011. 1–197

Haxthausen, Charles W. "Modern Art after 'The End of Expressionism': Worringer in the 1920s." In *Invisible Cathedrals: The Expressionist Art History of Wilhelm Worringer*. Ed. Neil H. Donahue. University Park: Pennsylvania State UP, 1995. 119–34.

Hebel, Johann Peter. *Kalendergeschichten*. Ed. Ernst Bloch. Frankfurt am Main: Insel, 1973.

– *Sämtliche Schriften*. Ed. Adrian Braunbehrens, Gustav Adolf Benrath, and Peter Pfaff. Karlsruhe: C.F. Müller, 1990.

Hegel, G.W.F. *Vorlesungen über die Ästhetik*, vol. 3. Ed. Eva Moldenhauer and Karl Markus Michel. Frankfurt am Main: Suhrkamp, 1970.

– *Hegel's Aesthetics: Lectures on Fine Art*, vol. 2. Trans. T.M. Knox. Oxford: Clarendon, 1975.

Heidegger, Martin. *Hebel der Hausfreund*. Pfullingen: Neske, 1951.

– *Holzwege*. Darmstadt: Klostermann, 1994.

Heine, Heinrich. *Sämtliche Schriften*. Ed. Klaus Briegleb. Frankfurt am Main: Ullstein, 1981. 12 vols.

Heintel, Peter. *Innehalten: Gegen die Beschleunigung – für eine andere Zeitkultur*. Freiburg: Herder, 2007.

Herder, Johann Gottfried. *Werke*. Ed. Wolfgang Pross. Darmstadt: Wissenschaftliche Buchgesellschaft, 1987. 3 vols.

Hevers, Edda. "Die *Kunst* der Wahrnehmung: Zu Caspar David Friedrichs Fensterbildern." In *Caspar David Friedrich: Deutungen im Dialog*. Ed. Gisela Greve. Tübingen: edition diskord, 2006. 121–38.

Hillmann, Heinz. *Bildlichkeit der deutschen Romantik*. Frankfurt am Main: Athenäum, 1971.

Hinz, Sigrid, ed. *Caspar David Friedrich in Briefen und Bekenntnissen*. Berlin: Henschel, 1968.

Hoch, Karl-Ludwig. *Caspar David Friedrich in der Sächsischen Schweiz*. Dresden: Verlag der Kunst, 1995.

Hoffmann, E.T.A. *Werke*, vol. 14: *Fantasiestücke in Callot's Manier*. Ed. Hartmut Steinecke. Frankfurt am Main: Deutscher Klassiker Verlag, 2006.
Hofmann, Werner. "Das Erwachen zum Tode." Afterword to *Experiment Weltuntergang: Wien um 1900*. Munich: Prestel, 1981. 251–61.
– *Caspar David Friedrich: Naturwirklichkeit und Kunstwahrheit*. Munich: C.H. Beck, 2000.
Hollander, Ann. *Moving Pictures*. Cambridge, MA: Harvard UP, 1991.
Horkheimer, Max and Theodor Adorno. *Dialektik der Aufklärung: Philosophische Fragmente*. Frankfurt am Main: Suhrkamp, 1969.
– *Dialectic of Enlightenment: Philosophical Fragments*. Ed. Gunzelin Schmid Noerr. Trans. Edmund Jephcott. Stanford: Stanford UP, 2002.
Hullot-Kentor, Robert. *Things beyond Resemblance: Collected Essays on Theodor W. Adorno*. New York: Columbia UP, 2006.
– "The Exact Sense in Which the Culture Industry No Longer Exists," *Cultural Critique* 70 (2008): 137–57.
Hunt, Leon. "*The Student of Prague*." In *Early Cinema: Space, Frame, Narrative*. Ed. Thomas Elsaesser. London: British Film Institute, 1990. 389–401.
Hüppauf, Bernd. "Spaces of the Vernacular: Ernst Bloch's Philosophy of Hope and the German Hometown." In *Vernacular Modernism: Heimat, Globalization, and the Built Environment*. Ed. Hüppauf and Maiken Umbach. Stanford: Stanford UP, 2005. 84–113.
Jacobs, Carol. *Uncontainable Romanticism: Shelley, Brontë, Kleist*. Baltimore: Johns Hopkins UP, 1989.
Johnson, David. T. "'You Must Never Listen to This': Lessons on Sound, Cinema, and Mortality from Werner Herzog's *Grizzly Man*." In *Documenting the Documentary*. Ed. Barry Keith Grant and Jeannette Sloniowski. Detroit: Wayne State UP, 2014. 514–15.
Johnson, Laurie. *Forgotten Dreams: Revisiting Romanticism in the Films of Werner Herzog*. Rochester: Camden House, 2016.
Johnson, Mark. *The Meaning of the Body: Aesthetics of Human Understanding*. Chicago: U of Chicago P, 2007.
Johnson, Mark, and Steve Larson, "'Something in the Way She Moves': Metaphors of Musical Motion." *Metaphor and Symbol* 18 (2003): 63–84.
Jonas, Hans. *The Phenomenon of Life: Toward a Philosophical Biology*. Evanston: Northwestern UP, 2001.
Joyce, James. *A Portrait of the Artist as a Young Man*. New York: Penguin, 1976.
Judovitz, Dalia. *Georges de La Tour and the Enigma of the Visible*. New York: Fordham UP, 2018.
Kaes, Anton. *Kino-Debatte: Texte zum Verhältnis von Literatur und Film 1909–1929*. Tübingen: Niemeyer, 1978.
– *M*. London: British Film Institute, 2000.
– "Urban Vision and Surveillance: Notes on a Moment in Karl Grune's *Die Strasse*." *German Politics and Society* 23 (2005): 80–7.

– *Shell Shock Cinema: Weimar Culture and the Wounds of War*. Princeton: Princeton UP, 2009.

Kafka, Franz. *The Penal Colony: Stories and Short Pieces*. Trans. Willa and Edwin Muir. New York: Schocken, 1948.

– *Drucke zu Lebzeiten*. Ed. Wolf Kittler, Hans-Gerd Koch, and Gerhard Neumann. Frankfurt am Main: Fischer, 2002.

Kaiser, Gerhard. *Augenblicke deutscher Lyrik*. Frankfurt am Main: Insel, 1987.

Kant, Immanuel. *Kritik der reinen Vernunft*, vol. 1. Ed. Wilhelm Weischedel. Frankfurt am Main: Suhrkamp, 1976.

– *Kritik der Urteilskraft*. Ed. Wilhelm Weischedel. Frankfurt am Main: Suhrkamp, 1977.

Keats, John. *Complete Poems*. Ed. Jack Stillinger. Cambridge, MA: Harvard UP, 1982.

Keefer, Cindy, and Jaap Guldemond, eds. *Oskar Fischinger 1900–1967: Experiments in Cinematic Abstraction*. Amsterdam: EYE Filmmuseum, 2013.

Keitz, Ursula von. "Der Blick ins Imaginäre: Über 'Erzählen' und 'Sehen' bei Murnau." In *Die Metaphysik des Dekors: Raum, Architektur und Licht im klassischen deutschen Stummfilm*. Ed. Klaus Kreimeier. Marburg: Schüren, 1995. 80–99.

Kenner, Hugh. *The Pound Era*. Berkeley: U of California P, 1971.

Kessler, Frank. "Öffentliche Lustbarkeiten: Jahrmarkt, Varieté, Kino." *Kintop: Jahrbuch zur Erforschung des frühen Films* 2 (1993): 179–82.

Kittler, Friedrich. *Literature, Media, Information Systems*. Trans. Stefanie Harris. New York: Routledge, 2012.

Kleist, Heinrich von. *Sämtliche Werke und Briefe*, vol. 3. Ed. Klaus Müller-Salget. Frankfurt am Main: Deutscher Klassiker Verlag, 1990.

Koerner, Joseph Leo. *Caspar David Friedrich and the Subject of Landscape*, 2nd ed. London: Reaktion, 2009.

Kolb, Martina. "Grave Action: Last Rites in Brecht's *Mother Courage* and Beckett's *Endgame*." *Comparative Studies in Modernism* 5 (2014): 69–90.

– "Intimations of Mortality from Recollections of Atrocity: Käthe Kollwitz and the Art of Mourning." In *Women Writing War: From German Colonialism through World War I*. Ed. Katharina von Hammerstein, Barbara Kosta, and Julie Schoults. Berlin: De Gruyter, 2018. 305–27.

Koschorke, Albrecht. *Die Geschichte des Horizonts: Grenze und Grenzüberschreitung in literarischen Landschaftsbildern*. Frankfurt am Main: Suhrkamp, 1990.

Kracauer, Siegfried. *From Caligari to Hitler: A Psychological History of German Film*. Princeton: Princeton UP, 1974.

– *Das Ornament der Masse: Essays*. Frankfurt am Main: Suhrkamp, 1977.

Kreimeier, Klaus. "Wie im Taumel: Die Kamera im deutschen Film der frühen zwanziger Jahre." In *Gleissende Schatten: Kamerapioniere der zwianziger Jahre*. Ed. Michael Esser. Berlin: Henschel, 1994. 9–34.

Kuzniar, Alice. "The Vanishing Canvas: Notes on German Romantic Landscape Aesthetics." *German Studies Review* 11 (1988): 359–76.

– "The Temporality of Landscape: Romantic Allegory and C.D. Friedrich." *Studies in Romanticism* 28 (1989): 87.

Lacan, Jacques. *Écrits: A Selection*. Trans. Alan Sheridan. New York: W.W. Norton, 1977.

– *The Four Fundamental Concepts of Psychoanalysis*. Ed. Jacques-Alain Miller. Trans. Alan Sheridan. New York: W.W. Norton, 1998.

Lacoue-Lebarth, Philippe, and Jean-Luc Nancy. *The Literary Absolute: The Theory of Literature in German Romanticism*. Trans. Philip Barnard and Cheryl Lester. Albany: SUNY P, 1988.

Lakoff, George, and Mark Johnson. *Philosophy in the Flesh: The Embodied Mind and its Challenge to Western Thought*. New York: Basic, 1999.

Langen, August. *Anschauungsformen in der deutschen Dichtung des 18. Jahrhunderts: Rahmenschau und Rationalismus*. Darmstadt. Wissenschaftliche Buchgesellschaft, 1965.

le Carré, John. *A Murder of Quality*. New York: Penguin, 2012.

Lee, Vernon. *Beauty and Ugliness*. London: John Lane, 1912.

Lefebvre, Martin. "Between Setting and Landscape in the Cinema." *Landscape and Film*. Ed. Martin Lefebvre. New York: Routledge, 2006: 19–59.

Leplanche, J., and J.-B. Pontalis. *The Language of Psycho-Analysis*. Trans. Donald Nicholson-Smith. New York: W.W. Norton, 1973.

Loew, Katharina. "The Spirit of Technology: Early German Thinking about Film." *New German Critique* 41 (2014): 125–44.

– *Special Effects and German Silent Film: Techno-Romantic Cinema*. Amsterdam: Amsterdam UP, 2021.

Long, Rose-Carol Washton, ed. *German Expressionism: Documents from the End of the Wilhelmine Empire to the Rise of National Socialism*. New York: G.K. Hall, 1993.

López-Remiro, Miguel. "Introduction to Mark Rothko's 'The Romantics Were Prompted …'" In *The Abstraction of Landscape: From Northern Romanticism to Abstract Expressionism*. Madrid: Fundación Juan March, 2007. 181–3.

Lukács, Georg. *Fortschritt und Reaktion in der deutschen Literatur*. Berlin: Aufbau, 1950.

Lysaker, John T. *You Must Change Your Life: Poetry, Philosophy, and the Birth of Sense*. University Park: Pennsylvania State UP, 2002.

Mann, Thomas. *Doctor Faustus: The Life of the German Composer Adrian Leverkühn as Told by a Friend*. Trans. John E. Woods. New York: Vintage, 1999.

– *Death in Venice*. Trans. Michael Henry Heim. New York: ecco, 2004.

Marc, Franz. *Schriften*. Ed. Klaus Lankheit. Cologne: DuMont, 1978.

Marquard, Odo. "Über einige Beziehungen zwischen Ästhetik und Therapeutik in der Philosophie des neunzehnten Jahrunderts." In *Literatur und Gesellschaft*. Ed. H.J. Schrimpf. Bonn: Bouvier, 1963. 22–55.

– "Zur Bedeutung der Theorie des Unbewussten für eine Theorie der nicht mehr schönen Künste." In *Die nicht mehr schönen Künste: Grenzphänomene des Ästhetischen*. Ed. Hans-Robert Jauss. Munich: Fink, 1968. 375–92.

Marx, Karl. *Schriften*. Ed. Hans-Joachim Lieber and Peter Furth. Darmstadt: Wissenschaftliche Buchgesellschaft, 1975. 6 vols.

Marx, Karl, and Frederick Engels. *The Communist Manifesto*. Trans. Gareth Stedman Jones. New York: Penguin, 2002.

Maskarinec, Malika. *The Forces of Form in German Modernism*. Evanston: Northwestern UP, 2018.

Merjian, Ara H. *Giorgio de Chirico and the Metaphysical City: Nietzsche, Modernism, Paris*. New Haven: Yale UP, 2014.

Merleau-Ponty, Maurice. *The Merleau-Ponty Aesthetics Reader*. Ed. Galen A. Johnson. Trans. Michael B. Smith. Evanston: Northwestern UP, 1993.

Metz, Christian. *The Imaginary Signifier: Psychoanalysis and the Cinema*. Trans. Celia Britton, Anwyl Williams, Ben Brewster, and Alfred Guzzetti. Bloomington: Indiana UP, 1982.

– *Impersonal Enunciation, or The Place of Film*. Trans. Cormac Deane. New York: Columbia UP, 2016.

Miller, D.A. "Balzac's Illusions Lost and Found." In *Honoré de Balzac*. Ed. Harold Bloom. Philadephia: Chelsea House, 2003.

Miller, Philip B. "Anxiety and Abstraction: Kleist and Brentano on Caspar David Friedrich." *Art Journal* 33 (1974): 205–10.

Milner, John. *Mondrian*. London: Phaidon, 1992.

Mondrian, Piet. "Natural Reality and Abstract Reality." Reprinted in Michel Seuphor. *Piet Mondrian: Life and Work*, 301–52. New York: Abrams, 1956.

Moretti, Franco. *Atlas of the European Novel, 1800–1900*. London: Verso, 1999.

– "Serious Century." In *The Novel*, vol. 1. Ed. Moretti. Princeton: Princeton UP, 2006.

Moritz, William. "Fischinger at Disney or, Oskar in the Mousetrap." *Millimeter* 5 (1977): 25–8, 65–7. http://www.michaelspornanimation.com/splog/?p=2409

– *Optical Poetry: The Life and Work of Oskar Fischinger*. Eastleigh: John Libbey, 2004.

Müller, Robert. "Lichtbildner: Zur Arbeit des Kameramannes." In *Gleissende Schatten: Kamerapioniere der zwanziger Jahre*. Ed. Michael Esser. Berlin: Henschel, 1994. 35–62.

Nagel, Ivan. *Autonomy and Mercy: Reflections on Mozart's Operas*. Trans. Marion Faber and Ivan Nagel. Cambridge: Harvard UP, 1991.

Naipaul, V.S. *The Enigma of Arrival*. New York: A.A. Knopf, 1987.

Nietzsche, Friedrich. *Will to Power*. Trans. Walter Kaufmann and R.J. Hillingsdale. New York: Vintage, 1968.

– *Kritische Studienausgabe*. Ed. Giorgio Colli and Mazzino Montinari. Berlin: de Gruyter, 1988. 15 vols.

– *On the Genealogy of Morals*. Trans. Walter Kaufmann and R.J. Hollingdale. New York: Vintage, 1989.

– *The Birth of Tragedy and the Genealogy of Morals*. Trans. Francis Golffing. New York: Random House, 1990.

Novalis. *Schriften: Die Werke Friedrich von Hardenbergs*. Ed. Richard Samuel. Stuttgart: Kohlhammer, 1977–88. 5 vols.

Nugent, Jeanne Anne. "Gerhard Richter's 'Woodlands' and Other Things of the Past." In *From Caspar David Friedrich to Gerhard Richter: German Paintings from Dresden*. Ed. Jon L. Syed and Anna Greve. Los Angeles: Getty, 2006. 95–8.

Ondaatje, Michael. *The Conversations: Walter Murch and the Art of Editing Film*. New York: A.A. Knopf, 2002.

Panofsky, Erwin. *Perspective as Symbolic Form*. Trans. Christopher S. Wood. New York: Zone Books, 1997.

Peucker, Brigitte. *Incorporating Images: Film and the Rival Arts*. Princeton: Princeton UP, 1995.

Pfau, Thomas. *Romantic Moods: Paranoia, Trauma, and Melancholy, 1790–1840*. Baltimore: Johns Hopkins UP, 2005.

Pinotti, Andrea. "Body Building: August Schmarsov's *Kunstwissenschaft* between Psychophysiology and Phenomenology." In *German Art History and Scientific Thought: Beyond Formalism*. Ed. Mitchell Frank. New York: Routledge, 2016. 13–31.

Plato. *The Collected Dialogues*. Ed. Edith Hamilton and Huntington Cairns. Trans. Paul Shorey. Princeton: Princeton UP, 2009.

Plessen, Marie-Louise von, and Ulrich Giersch, eds. *Sehsucht: Das Panorama als Massenunterhaltung des 19. Jahrhunderts*. Frankurt/Basel: Stroemfeld/Roter Stern, 1993.

Prager, Brad. *Aesthetic Vision and German Romanticism: Writing Images*. Rochester: Camden House, 2007.

Proust, Marcel. *In Search of Lost Time: Swann's Way* (vol. 1). Trans. C.K. Scott Moncrieff. New York: Modern Library, 2003.

Pyle, Forest. *Art's Undoing: In the Wake of a Radical Aestheticism*. New York: Fordham UP, 2014.

Ramdohr, F.W.B. von. "Über ein zum Altarblatte bestimmtes Landschaftsgemälde von Herrn Friedrich in Dresden." In *Caspar David Friedrich in Briefen und Bekenntnissen*. Ed. Sigrid Hinz. Berlin: Henschel, 1968.

Rancière, Jacques. *The Emancipated Spectator*. Trans. Gregory Elliott. London: Verso, 2011.

– *Film Fables*. Trans. Emiliano Battista. London: Bloomsbury, 2016.

Rank, Otto. *Der Doppelgänger: Eine psychoanalytische Studie*. Leipzig: Internationaler Psychoanalytischer Verlag, 1925.

Rauth, Eric. "Nosferatu's Gesture: Ciné-kinesis in the Silent Era, East and West." *Mise en geste: Studies of Gesture in Cinema and Art*. Ed. Ana Hedberg Olenina and Irina Schulzki. Special issue of *Apparatus. Film, Media, and Digital Cultures in Central and Eastern Europe* 5 (2017).

Rautmann, Peter. *C.D. Friedrich, Das Eismeer: Durch Tod zu neuem Leben*. Frankfurt am Main: Fischer, 1991.

Read, Herbert. *Icon and Idea: The Function of Art in the Development of Human Consciousness*. New York: Schocken, 1965.

Resnik, Salomon. "The Hands of Egon Schiele." *International Forum of Psychoanalysis* 9 (2000): 113–23.

Richter, Gerhard. *The Daily Practice of Painting: Writings and Interviews, 1962–1993*. Cambridge, MA: MIT P, 1995.

Ricoeur, Paul. *Freud and Philosophy: An Essay on Interpretation*. Trans. Dennis Savage. New Haven: Yale UP, 1970.

Rilke, Rainer Maria. *The Selected Poetry of Rainer Maria Rilke*. Trans. Stephen J. Mitchell. New York: Random House, 1982.

– *Werke*, vol. 1: *Gedichte 1895–1910*. Ed. Manfred Engel and Ulrich Fülleborn. Frankfurt am Main: Insel, 1996.

Ritter, Joachim. *Subjektivität: Sechs Aufsätze*. Frankfurt am Main: Suhrkamp, 1974.

Rohmer, Eric. *The Taste for Beauty*. Trans. Carol Volk. Cambridge: Cambridge UP, 1989.

Rokem, Na'ama. *Prosaic Conditions: Heinrich Heine and the Spaces of Zionist Literature*. Evanston: Northwestern UP, 2013.

Rosenblum, Robert. *Modern Painting and the Northern Romantic Tradition: Friedrich to Rothko*. New York: Harper and Row, 1975.

– "Horizons." In *The Perception of the Horizontal*. Ed. Andreas Hapkemeyer. Cologne: Walter König, 2005. 22–3.

Rothko, Mark. *Writings on Art*. Ed. Miguel López-Remiro. New Haven: Yale UP, 2006.

Rousseau, Jean-Jacques. *A Discourse on Inequality*. Trans. Maurice Cranston. New York: Penguin, 1984.

Rovelli, Carlo. *Sette brevi lezioni di fisica*. Milan: Adelphi, 2014.

Scheffauer, Herman George. *The New Vision in the German Arts*. New York: Huebsch, 1924.

Schelling, Friedrich Wilhelm Joseph. *Schellings Werke*. Ed. Manfred Schröter. Munich: Beck, 1965. 6 vols.

Schiff, Gert. "An Epoch of Longing: An Introduction to German Painting of the Nineteenth Century." In *German Masters of the Nineteenth Century: Paintings and Drawings from the Federal Republic of Germany*. Ed. John P. O'Neill. New York: Metropolitan Museum of Art, 1981. 9–39.

Schindler, Stephan. "What Makes a Man a Man: The Construction of Masculinity in F.W. Murnau's *The Last Laugh*." *Screen* 37 (1996): 30–40.

Schivelbusch, Wolfgang. *Lichtblicke: Zur Geschichte der künstlichen Helligkeit im 19. Jahrhundert*. Frankfurt am Main: Fischer, 1986.

– *Geschichte der Eisenbahnreise: Zur Industrialisierung von Raum und Zeit im 19. Jahrhundert*. Frankfurt am Main: Fischer, 1989.

Schjeldahl, Peter. "Inspired Lunacy: A Closer View of Caspar David Friedrich." *The New Yorker*, 1 October 2001, 116.

Schlegel, Friedrich. *Kritische Ausgabe*, vol. 2. Ed. Ernst Behler. Paderborn: Schöningh, 1967.

Schlüpmann, Heide. "The First German Art Film: Stellan Rye's *The Student of Prague*." In *German Film and Literature*. Ed. Eric Rentschler. New York: Routledge, 1986.

Schmidt, Paul F. "Romantik und Gegenwart." *Feuer* 3 (1922): 219–26.

Schmitz, Norbert M. "Vertical Sequence: The Lift in Film." In *Vertical: Lift Escalator Paternoster*. Ed. Jeannot Simmen and Joseph Imorde. Berlin: Ernst & Sohn, 1994. 78–89.

Schneider, Helmut J. "Die sanfte Utopie: Zu einer bürgerlichen Tradition literarischer Glücksbilder." In *Idyllen der Deutschen*. Ed. Schneider. Frankfurt am Main: Insel, 1981. 353–418.

– "Das Licht der Welt: Geburt und Bild in Goethes Faustdichtung." *Deutsche Vierteljahrsschrift für Literaturwissenschaft und Geistesgeschichte* 75 (2001): 107–22.

Schönemann, Heide. *Fritz Lang: Filmbilder, Vorbilder*. Berlin: Hentrich, 1992.

– *Paul Wegener: Frühe Moderne im Film*. Stuttgart: Axel Menges, 2003.

Schopenhauer, Arthur. *Die Welt als Wille und Vorstellung*, vol. 1. Ed. Wolfgang Frhr. von Löhneysen. Frankfurt am Main: Suhrkamp, 1986.

– *The World as Will and Representation*. Trans. E.F.J. Payne. New York: Dover, 1966.

Segeberg, Harro, ed. *Die Mobilisierung des Sehens: Zur Vor- und Frühgeschichte des Films in Literatur und Kunst*. Munich: Fink, 1996.

Selz, Peter, *German Expressionist Painting*. Berkeley: U of California P, 1957.

Seuphor, Michel. *Piet Mondrian: Life and Work*. New York: Abrams, 1956.

Shapiro, Meyer. *Cézanne*. New York: Abrams, 2004.

Shelley, Mary Wollstonecraft. *Frankenstein, or The Modern Prometheus: The 1818 Text*. Ed. James Rieger. Chicago: U of Chicago P, 1982.

Shelley, Percy Bysshe. *Poetry and Prose*. Ed. Donald H. Reiman and Neil Fraistat. New York: W.W. Norton, 2002.

Shen, Yeshayahu, and Ravid Aisenman. "'Heard melodies are sweet, but those unheard are sweeter': Synaesthesia and Cognition." *Language and Literature* 17 (2008): 101–21.

Silverman, Kaja. *The Subject of Semiotics*. Oxford: Oxford UP, 1983.

Simmen, Jeannot. *Vertigo: Schwindel der modernen Kunst*. Munich: Klinkhardt und Biermann, 1990.

– "Elevation: Eine Kulturgeschichte von Aufzug und Lift." In *Access for All: Zugänge zur gebauten Umwelt*. Ed. Wolfgang Christ. Basel: Birkhäuser, 2009. 16–29.

Simmons, William S. "Abstraction and Empathy on the Eve of World War I." *Konturen* 5 (2014): 15–18. http://journals.oregondigital.org/index.php/konturen/article/view/3246

Spitzer, Leo. "Milieu and Ambience: An Essay in Historical Semantics." *Philosophy and Phenomenological Research* 3.2 (1942): 169–218.

Staiger, Emil. *Die Zeit als Einbildungskraft des Dichters*. Zurich: Atlantis, 1963.

– *Vor drei Bildern*. Zurich: Artemis, 1983.

Starobinski, Jean. *1789: The Emblems of Reason*. Trans. Barbara Bray. Charlottesville: U of Virginia P, 1982.

Steimatsky, Noa. *The Face on Film*. New York: Oxford UP, 2017.

Steiner, George. *In Bluebeard's Castle: Some Notes towards the Redefinition of Culture*. New Haven: Yale UP, 1971.

Stewart, Garrett. "Lying as Dying in *Heart of Darkness*." In *Heart of Darkness: Norton Critical Edition*. Ed. Robert Kimbrough, 3rd ed. New York: W.W. Norton, 1988.

– *Between Film and Screen: Modernism's Photo Synthesis*. Chicago: U of Chicago P, 1999.

Stimilli, Davide. *The Face of Immortality: Physiognomy and Criticism*. Albany: SUNY P, 2005.

Stoker, Bram. *Dracula*. New York: Signet, 2007.

Szondi, Peter. *On Textual Understanding and Other Essays*. Minneapolis: U of Minnesota P, 1986.

Tobias, Rochelle. "Rilke, Phenomenology, and the Sensuality of Thought." *Konturen* 8 (2015). http://journals.oregondigital.org/index.php/konturen/article/view/3700/3517

Uerlings, Herbert. *Theorie der Romantik*. Stuttgart: Reclam, 2013.

Verwiebe, Birgit. "Transparentenmalerei und Romantik." In *Ernste Spiele: Der Geist der Romantik in der deutschen Kunst 1790–1990*. Ed. Christoph Vitali. Stuttgart: Oktagon, 1995. 532–3.

Viatte, Françoise. "Un dessin de Caspar David Friedrich (1774–1840) au musée du Louvre: Allégorie de la musique profane." *Revue du Louvre* 3 (1999): 13–15.

Vitaly, Christoph, ed. *Ernste Spiele: Der Geist der Romantik in der deutschen Kunst 1790–1990*. Munich: Haus der Kunst, 1995.

Wackenroder, Wilhelm Heinrich, and Ludwig Tieck. *Outpourings of an Art-Loving Friar*. Trans. Edward Mornin. New York: Ungar, 1975.

– *Herzensergiessungen eines kunstliebenden Klosterbruders*. Ed. Martin Bollacher. Stuttgart: Reclam, 2005.

Waite, Geoffrey O.C. "Worringer's *Abstraction and Empathy*: Remarks on Its Reception and on the Rhetoric of Criticism." In *Invisible Cathedrals:*

The Expressionist Art History of Wilhelm Worringer. Ed. Neil H. Donahue. University Park: Pennsylvania State UP, 1995. 13–40.

Wallace, David Rains. *The Klamath Knot: Explorations of Myth and Evolution*. Berkeley: U of California P, 2003.

Ward, Janet. "Kracauer versus the Weimar Film City." In *Peripheral Visions: The Hidden Stages of Weimar Cinema*. Ed. Kenneth S. Calhoon. Detroit: Wayne State UP, 2001. 21–37.

Weber, Samuel. "The Sideshow: or Remarks on a Canny Moment." *Modern Language Notes* 88 (1973): 1102–33.

Webern, Anton. *The Path to the New Music*. Trans. Leo Black. London: Universal, 1975.

Weingart, Brigitte. "Contact at a Distance: The Topology of Fascination." In *Rethinking Emotion: Interiority and Exteriority in Premodern, Modern, and Contemporary Thought*. Ed. Rüdiger Campe and Julia Weber. Berlin: de Gruyter, 2014. 72–100.

Wellbery, David. *The Specular Moment: Goethe's Early Lyric and the Beginnings of Romanticism*. Stanford: Stanford UP, 1996.

Wichmann, Siegfried. *Carl Spitzweg und die französischen Zeichner Daumier, Grandville, Gavarni, Doré*. Weyarn: Seehamer, 1996.

Wilbur, Richard. *New and Collected Poems*. New York: Harcourt Brace, 1988.

Willett, John. *Expressionism*. New York: McGraw-Hill, 1978.

Williams, Linda. *Figures of Desire: A Theory and Analysis of Surrealist Film*. Berkeley: U of California P, 1981.

Wimsatt, W.K., Jr, and M.C. Beardsley. "The Affective Fallacy." *The Sewanee Review* 57 (1949): 31–55.

Wipplinger, Hans-Peter, ed. *Carl Spitzweg, Erwin Wurm: Köstlich! Köstlich?* Cologne: Walther König, 2017.

Wölfflin, Heinrich. *Bamberger Apokalypse*. Munich: Curt Wolff, 1920.

Wood, Christopher S. *Albrecht Altdorfer and the Origins of Landscape*, 2nd ed. London: Reaktion, 2014.

Worringer, Wilhlem."Spätgotisches und expressionistisches Formsystem." *Wallraf-Richartz Jahrbuch* 2 (1925): 1–8.

– "Kritische Gedanken zur neuen Kunst." In *Fragen und Gegenfragen: Schriften zum Kunstproblem*. Munich: Piper, 1956. 86–105.

– *Abstraktion und Einfühlung*. Munich: Piper, 1976.

– "Carlo Carrà's *Pinie am Meer*." Reprinted in *Realismus: Zwischen Revolution und Reaktion, 1919–1939*. Munich: Prestel, 1981.

Index

GERMAN AND EUROPEAN STUDIES

General Editor: Jennifer L. Jenkins

1 Emanuel Adler, Beverly Crawford, Federica Bicchi, and Rafaella Del Sarto, *The Convergence of Civilizations: Constructing a Mediterranean Region*
2 James Retallack, *The German Right, 1860–1920: Political Limits of the Authoritarian Imagination*
3 Silvija Jestrovic, *Theatre of Estrangement: Theory, Practice, Ideology*
4 Susan Gross Solomon, ed., *Doing Medicine Together: Germany and Russia between the Wars*
5 Laurence McFalls, ed., *Max Weber's 'Objectivity' Revisited*
6 Robin Ostow, ed., *(Re)Visualizing National History: Museums and National Identities in Europe in the New Millennium*
7 David Blackbourn and James Retallack, eds., *Localism, Landscape, and the Ambiguities of Place: German-Speaking Central Europe, 1860–1930*
8 John Zilcosky, ed., *Writing Travel: The Poetics and Politics of the Modern Journey*
9 Angelica Fenner, *Race under Reconstruction in German Cinema: Robert Stemmle's Toxi*
10 Martina Kessel and Patrick Merziger, eds., *The Politics of Humour: Laughter, Inclusion, and Exclusion in the Twentieth Century*
11 Jeffrey K. Wilson, *The German Forest: Nature, Identity, and the Contestation of a National Symbol, 1871–1914*
12 David G. John, *Bennewitz, Goethe,* Faust: *German and Intercultural Stagings*
13 Jennifer Ruth Hosek, *Sun, Sex, and Socialism: Cuba in the German Imaginary*
14 Steven M. Schroeder, *To Forget It All and Begin Again: Reconciliation in Occupied Germany, 1944–1954*
15 Kenneth S. Calhoon, *Affecting Grace: Theatre, Subject, and the Shakespearean Paradox in German Literature from Lessing to Kleist*
16 Martina Kolb, *Nietzsche, Freud, Benn, and the Azure Spell of Liguria*
17 Hoi-eun Kim, *Doctors of Empire: Medical and Cultural Encounters between Imperial Germany and Meiji Japan*
18 J. Laurence Hare, *Excavating Nations: Archeology, Museums, and the German-Danish Borderlands*
19 Jacques Kornberg, *The Pope's Dilemma: Pius XII Faces Atrocities and Genocide in the Second World War*
20 Patrick O'Neill, *Transforming Kafka: Translation Effects*

21 John K. Noyes, *Herder: Aesthetics against Imperialism*
22 James Retallack, *Germany's Second Reich: Portraits and Pathways*
23 Laurie Marhoefer, *Sex and the Weimar Republic: German Homosexual Emancipation and the Rise of the Nazis*
24 Bettina Brandt and Daniel L. Purdy, eds., *China in the German Enlightenment*
25 Michael Hau, *Performance Anxiety: Sport and Work in Germany from the Empire to Nazism*
26 Celia Applegate, *The Necessity of Music: Variations on a German Theme*
27 Richard J. Golsan and Sarah M. Misemer, eds., *The Trial That Never Ends: Hannah Arendt's* Eichmann in Jerusalem *in Retrospect*
28 Lynne Taylor, *In the Children's Best Interests: Unaccompanied Children in American-Occupied Germany, 1945–1952*
29 Jennifer A. Miller, *Turkish Guest Workers in Germany: Hidden Lives and Contested Borders, 1960s to 1980s*
30 Amy Carney, *Marriage and Fatherhood in the Nazi SS*
31 Michael E. O'Sullivan, *Disruptive Power: Catholic Women, Miracles, and Politics in Modern Germany, 1918–1965*
32 Gabriel N. Finder and Alexander V. Prusin, *Justice behind the Iron Curtain: Nazis on Trial in Communist Poland*
33 Parker Daly Everett, *Urban Transformations: From Liberalism to Corporatism in Greater Berlin, 1871–1933*
34 Melissa Kravetz, *Women Doctors in Weimar and Nazi Germany: Maternalism, Eugenics, and Professional Identity*
35 Javier Samper Vendrell, *The Seduction of Youth: Print Culture and Homosexual Rights in the Weimar Republic*
36 Sebastian Voigt, ed., *Since the Boom: Continuity and Change in the Western Industrialized World after 1970*
37 Olivia Landry, *Theatre of Anger: Radical Transnational Performance in Contemporary Berlin*
38 Jeremy Best, *Heavenly Fatherland: German Missionary Culture and Globalization in the Age of Empire*
39 Svenja Bethke, *Dance on the Razor's Edge: Crime and Punishment in the Nazi Ghettos*
40 Kenneth S. Calhoon, *The Long Century's Long Shadow: Weimar Cinema and the Romantic Modern*

www.ingramcontent.com/pod-product-compliance
Lightning Source LLC
LaVergne TN
LVHW090154080826
844660LV00013B/801/J

* 9 7 8 1 4 8 7 5 2 6 9 5 5 *